Microsoft SharePoint 2003 For Dummies®

KU-330-799

Page Flow

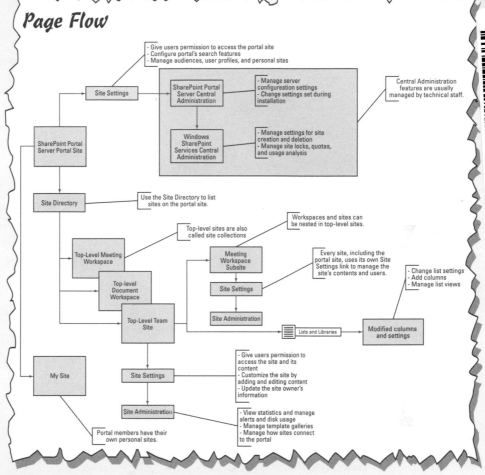

- Give users permission to access the portal site
- Configure portal's search features
- Manage audiences, user profiles, and personal sites

Site Settings

SharePoint Portal Server Central Administration
- Manage server configuration settings
- Change settings set during installation

Central Administration features are usually managed by technical staff.

Windows SharePoint Services Central Administration
- Manage settings for site creation and deletion
- Manage site locks, quotas, and usage analysis

SharePoint Portal Server Portal Site

Site Directory
Use the Site Directory to list sites on the portal site.

Top-level sites are also called site collections

Workspaces and sites can be nested in top-level sites.

Top-Level Meeting Workspace

Top-level Document Workspace

Top-Level Team Site

Meeting Workspace Subsite

Site Settings

Every site, including the portal site, uses its own Site Settings link to manage the site's contents and users.

- Change list settings
- Add columns
- Manage list views

Site Administration

Lists and Libraries

Modified columns and settings

My Site

Site Settings
- Give users permission to access the site and its content
- Customize the site by adding and editing content
- Update the site owner's information

Site Administration
- View statistics and manage alerts and disk usage
- Manage template galleries
- Manage how sites connect to the portal

Portal members have their own personal sites.

Portal site groups

- Guest: Can only access a very limited portion
- Reader: View only access to the site
- Member: Add listing, upload documents, configure alerts, add a site to the site directory, have a personal site
- Contributor: Manage content, edit page, and create sites
- Content Manager: Change settings, Manage portal site
- Web Designer: Modify page layout, site settings
- Administration: everything

SharePoint Site groups

- Guest: assigned per list permissions
- Reader: view only
- Contributor: add to existing lists
- Web Designer: add new lists and change page layouts
- Administrator: full control

Microsoft SharePoint 2003 For Dummies®

Cheat Sheet

Templates

Team Site
- Announcements
- Events
- Links
- Contacts
- Discussion
- Document Library

Meeting Workspace
- Objectives
- Agendas
- Attendees
- Document Library

Document Workspace
- Document Library
- Tasks
- Members
- Links
- Events
- Discussion

WSS Site Templates

- ✔ Team: Announcements, Events, Links, Contacts, Tasks, Discussion, Document Library
- ✔ Meeting: Objectives, Agendas, Attendees, Doc library
- ✔ Document: Announcements, Doc library, Tasks, Members web part, Links, events, discussion

Content templates

Built-in SharePoint lists

- ✔ Announcements: Share information; includes expiration date field
- ✔ Links: Store hyperlinks; links can be reordered
- ✔ Contacts: Can link to Outlook, import/export contacts
- ✔ Events: Link to Outlook, export events as appointments
- ✔ Tasks: Provides assigned to field with priority and status
- ✔ Issues: Provides assigned to field with email notification; track progress, relate issues together; view a summary report of issues
- ✔ Custom lists: can import and link to spreadsheets

Other built-in content

- ✔ Surveys: A series of questions and answers; view summary and responses
- ✔ Discussion Boards: threaded discussions and replies
- ✔ Web pages and web parts pages

Built-in libraries

- ✔ Documents: Store any kind of file
- ✔ Forms: Store xml-based data entry forms
- ✔ Picture: Store images; view thumbnails, download images, and send images to the programs

For Dummies: Bestselling Book Series for Beginners

Microsoft® SharePoint® 2003

FOR

DUMMIES®

by Vanessa L. Williams

WILEY

Wiley Publishing, Inc.

Microsoft® SharePoint® 2003 For Dummies

Published by
Wiley Publishing, Inc.
111 River Street
Hoboken, NJ 07030-5774

www.wiley.com

Copyright © 2006 by Wiley Publishing, Inc., Indianapolis, Indiana

Published by Wiley Publishing, Inc., Indianapolis, Indiana

Published simultaneously in Canada

WILEY

About the Author

Vanessa Williams is a developer and systems analyst whose work experience spans several industries — including transportation, petroleum marketing, manufacturing, retail, and (most recently) motor-sports entertainment. She spent last year implementing SharePoint Portal Server 2003 for a local sports entertainment venue. She has ten years of experience in systems administration, implementation, and software development. In previous lives she was a shipping clerk, a payroll clerk, a forklift driver, and a candlestick maker (just kidding).

Vanessa grew up in Indianapolis, where she graduated from the Kelley School of Business at Indiana University with a Bachelor of Science degree in Business Management and Computer Information Systems.

In addition to writing and consulting, Vanessa maintains the sharepointgrrl.com Web site where she aggregates SharePoint content. She is feverishly at work on her next title, *Visual Studio 2005 All-in-One Desk Reference For Dummies*.

Vanessa welcomes comments and suggestions about this book. Send your comments to books@sharepointgrrl.com.

Dedication

Look Ma, I wrote a *For Dummies* book!

Author's Acknowledgments

Never write a book over the summer. No swimming, no biking, no Lake Michigan. I'm ten pounds heavier, and I can't decide who I've missed more: Buffy or Spike.

Nevertheless, it has been a very rewarding experience. Yes, my brother is very grateful that I used my advance to buy his first car. (I didn't really *need* that new furnace.) I'm more intimate with SharePoint than I could have ever imagined possible (and much less so with my partner). And I picked up the invaluable skill of squeezing 1,000 pages of content into 400 pages of bullet points and numbered lists. Thankfully, that's a transferable skill.

Oh, and I almost forgot! I also spawned the alter ego *sharepointgrrl*. She lives at `sharepointgrrl.com`. (That's two *R*s as in *Grr, Argh.* That's just what I needed — a Web site to maintain.)

I think I'm supposed to be thanking someone. Isn't that the point of an acknowledgment? Let's see. There's the obligatory thanks to the editorial staff. Thank you for telling me in a very gentle way that I'm not funny. Thanks for seeing a *For Dummies* book in my public-school grammar and business-school fluff. Mostly, thanks for seeing me as more than just text on paper. Nothing says love like strikeouts and insertions.

Thanks also to Katie Feltman for throwing me a bone with this book. I'm not sure who owes whom.

Finally, I thank my former employer (you know who you are) for being so stubborn about not embracing SharePoint. I've written a better book because of it. As Bill Gates once said, "SharePoint is one of the most underutilized assets in the Office system." Ain't it the truth, Bill?

Publisher's Acknowledgments

We're proud of this book; please send us your comments through our online registration form located at www.dummies.com/register/.

Some of the people who helped bring this book to market include the following:

Acquisitions, Editorial, and Media Development

Project Editor: Pat O'Brien

Acquisitions Editor: Katie Feltman

Copy Editors: Barry Childs-Helton, Laura Miller

Technical Editor: Scott Hofmann

Editorial Manager: Kevin Kirschner

Media Development Manager: Laura VanWinkle

Media Development Supervisor: Richard Graves

Editorial Assistant: Amanda Foxworth

Cartoons: Rich Tennant (www.the5thwave.com)

Composition Services

Project Coordinator: Maridee Ennis

Layout and Graphics: Carl Byers, Barbara Moore, Julie Trippetti

Proofreaders: Leeann Harney, Jessica Kramer, TECHBOOKS Production Services

Indexer: TECHBOOKS Production Services

Special Help: Heidi Unger

Publishing and Editorial for Technology Dummies

 Richard Swadley, Vice President and Executive Group Publisher

 Andy Cummings, Vice President and Publisher

 Mary Bednarek, Executive Acquisitions Director

 Mary C. Corder, Editorial Director

Publishing for Consumer Dummies

 Diane Graves Steele, Vice President and Publisher

 Joyce Pepple, Acquisitions Director

Composition Services

 Gerry Fahey, Vice President of Production Services

 Debbie Stailey, Director of Composition Services

Table of Contents

Introduction

S harePoint is one of those technologies that few people really *get*. If you're one of the lucky people who get SharePoint, a whole new world of possibilities is opened to you. If you're like the rest of us, then you're probably still trying to figure out why something as indefinable and immeasurable as *collaboration and information-sharing* is so hot. Yeah, those things add value in some touchy-feely parallel universe where everyone has a pension and health insurance. But that ain't here.

Nevertheless, that hasn't stopped SharePoint — and the products like it that promise increased information-worker productivity — from becoming the hottest technologies around.

So, what is SharePoint, and why is it so hot? It's all about buzzwords.

The Buzz about SharePoint

In our sound-bite-and-bullet-point society, everything gets reduced to buzzwords. The latest buzz in the business community is about *knowledge management, business intelligence, information sharing,* and *collaboration.* Whatever you call it, it's all about getting information into the minds of people who need it in order to run a business. (Well, that's the benevolent view of what it's about, anyway.)

Anytime businesses start buzzing about something, technologists are never far behind with some new technology that can solve the problem they're buzzing about. Before long, the technology and the buzz get so intertwined that it becomes impossible to separate the two. SharePoint is a product of all this buzz.

With SharePoint, a company can build Web sites where teams can collaborate online on documents, policies, projects — whatever teams need to collaborate on. SharePoint also provides a *portal site* that connects all these team sites together. The SharePoint portal allows companies to categorize and search content stored in lots of places — on team Web sites, file shares, public folders, and public Web sites. SharePoint allows you to conduct a search that spans across your entire enterprise and even outside its boundaries.

Imagine your company has an initiative to bring a new product to market called The Next Big Thing. Your company can use SharePoint to

- ✔ Create a team site for the new product team
- ✔ Set up a site on the team site for all the new product meetings that stores the names of everyone who attended, what was discussed, and a list of action items
- ✔ Manage brochures and presentations in a single repository with a version history
- ✔ Send notifications every time an action item on the to-do list is updated
- ✔ Store links to competitors' sites and distribution opportunities
- ✔ Update a list of vendor contacts
- ✔ Create marketing forecasts in Excel and display them on the team site
- ✔ Survey team members' advice about product features

SharePoint lets you keep all this in one Web site where team members can access it — and add to it. For example, they can use Microsoft Office 2003 to access documents and to-do lists from the site — and create meeting notices that update the site.

Before you can bring The Next Big Thing to market, however, your company needs to know about it. You can use the portal feature of SharePoint to get the word out in various ways:

- ✔ Post news about the product's release
- ✔ Share a promotions schedule
- ✔ Build an entire Web page that displays the team's brochures, presentations, and other marketing materials

Using the search features in SharePoint, you can search your portal for The Next Big Thing and pull up every document, meeting, person, and link related to that product.

Sound too good to be true? Meet my good friend the buzzkill.

While you *can* use SharePoint to build portals and encourage collaboration among your employees, in reality it's a daunting task. Just ask the folks at Yahoo! or Google, who make a business out of categorizing and searching Web sites. If it were all that easy, everyone would be doing it.

At its heart, SharePoint is a tool for building Web sites. SharePoint Web sites have a consistent look and feel, tons of reusable functionality, and work wonderfully with Office 2003 — all without making anybody write a single line of code.

And — at its heart — that's what this book is about: Showing you how to use SharePoint to build internal team Web sites that your company can actually use. How you decide to use those Web sites is up to you.

Yeah, this book shows you how to use SharePoint as a portal. And, yes, it shows you how you can use SharePoint to collaborate with others. The bottom line, however, is that this is a book about using SharePoint in a way that *adds value to your business*. You get to decide what that means.

Making the Business Case

When technologists start describing *your* knowledge of how you do *your* job as a software feature, you know you're in trouble. This is not the book to debate the many definitions of information and knowledge. And this is certainly not the book to ponder whether something as nebulous as knowledge can even be managed (or, more important, whether there *is* value in managing it).

Regardless of the latest buzzwords, you should not implement a technology without having a clear business case for doing so. This book offers you plenty of advice on making your SharePoint business case. Most important, however, it shows you how to deliver.

Get Productive Right Out of the Box

I believe that SharePoint finally fulfills a promise that technology vendors made a long time ago. With SharePoint, you really *can* be productive right out of the box. That's true not only for the people who build the solutions, but also for the users whose work gives the solutions a trial by fire — and SharePoint can make it happen rapidly.

All examples in this book show you how to use SharePoint as it is, right out of the box. Although there are plenty of ways to extend SharePoint — using .Net, Front Page 2003, and other Microsoft server technologies — they're outside the scope of this book. I focus instead on getting you up and running with minimal tech know-how. I do show you a few tricks, but they don't alter the standard SharePoint product. Strong basics are the goal.

Solving Real-World Problems

This book shows you how to use SharePoint to solve some typical real-world business problems. I do not expect these scenarios to match perfectly with your environment. They are intended to provide a starting point for building solutions. My hope is that you can find some keys to your organization's problems in the scenarios I present. If you can see how a scenario relates to your problem, then you'll find the solution too.

Who Should Read This Book

SharePoint is one of those technologies where it's hard to draw the line between where the technical role stops and the nontechnical role begins. That's because SharePoint is a tool for building solutions — whether the user is an IT pro or a department power user.

Joe User

Because you can use SharePoint to build rich, highly functional Web sites with no code, this is a book for any end user with administrative access to SharePoint. For those of you unfortunate enough to work for a company where your IT staff is afraid to give you access to SharePoint, never fear. Microsoft provides access to a trial site where you can access a fully functional SharePoint site for 30 days. That should be plenty of time for you to work through the examples in this book (and hone your business case for why your business community needs access to SharePoint).

To start your free 30-day trial of a SharePoint site, visit www. sharepointtrial.com.

I also expect that some of you are reading this book because you've been appointed administrator or content manager for your department. Hang in there. You will definitely benefit from reading this book.

For the techies

I know that many of you techies would *never* let your coworkers see you reading a *For Dummies* book about a technical topic. Sure, you might read *Wine For Dummies* or *Sex For Dummies*, but that's okay because wine and sex aren't in your technical domain. (So to speak.)

It's all right. Take a deep breath. Count to ten. You can do it. You can overcome your addiction to overpriced, densely worded technical books. Say it with me, "My name is [*insert your name here*], and I buy overpriced technical books."

Let me dispel a myth that persists among many technical professionals: Dummies books are not for "dummies." Surprise! They are for people who need an overview of a technology and want to get up to snuff pronto without a bunch of technical overhead. (Sound familiar?) While your comrades are struggling with their 1,000-page tomes on SharePoint, you'll be wowing your business users with real solutions that work. Who's the dummy now?

I'm not saying this book is for every technical user. But you should read this book if you see yourself in any of these scenarios:

- ✔ Has your company evaluated all the software in the portal space and chosen SharePoint because it has the best features and the right value for your organization?

- ✔ Are you a Microsoft shop, in which case you haven't bothered to evaluate anything else because your company does everything Microsoft?

- ✔ Are you hearing so much buzz about portals in general (and SharePoint specifically) that you figure you'd better get up to speed before your boss tells you to?

- ✔ Have you seen SharePoint in magazines, on the Web, or at conferences — and still have no clue what the heck it's used for?

Welcome to the club.

How to Use This Book

Although you can get maximum value from this book by working through all the steps (yeah, right), it's set up so you can find what you need to know quickly, without having to read it from cover to cover. It's a resource for technical and nontechnical readers who need to find out more about SharePoint fast. You'll be speaking SharePoint in no time!

Even if your company is undecided about SharePoint, this book is useful if you are

- ✔ **Conducting a feasibility analysis:** Use this book to help you evaluate SharePoint before you commit.

- ✔ **Planning an upgrade:** While this book does not explicitly address how to upgrade from SharePoint 2001, you can use it to get up to speed on all the new features. And make a strong argument for upgrading!

- ✔ **Just starting your project planning:** Build a better project plan with the tips in this book.

- ✔ **Already implemented:** Get more out of your existing implementation with the examples in this book.

Foolish Assumptions

The examples in this book use Microsoft SharePoint Portal Server 2003 and Windows SharePoint Services, which is part of Windows Server 2003. While some of the examples in this book could be applied to previous versions of SharePoint, they aren't intended to. While I can't predict the future, most of these examples should be compatible with future versions of SharePoint as well.

No matter how SharePoint has come into your life, I've made some assumptions about the environment you live in:

- **You already have SharePoint installed in some fashion**. It's up and running, whether it's an evaluation version or a full-blown production-level server farm. (You did know that servers grow on farms, right?)

- **You have administrative access to SharePoint.** While you can perform many of these examples with Web-designer and contributor access, other examples require administrative access.

- **You are using SharePoint Portal Server 2003 with Windows SharePoint Services.** If you are unsure, check with whoever built your machine. You can do many of the examples in the scenario chapters without the portal product.

I recommend *against* using your production server to work the examples in this book. While none of the examples are likely to break your production server, it's just not good practice.

How This Book Is Organized

Most technology books are organized by feature. If a technology has features a, b, and c, then you can expect to find three corresponding chapters, one covering each feature. I wanted this book to be different. I wanted it to be organized around how you might actually *use* SharePoint.

So, instead of finding chapters that cover features per se, you find chapters that offer usage examples to illustrate SharePoint's features. If you already know what features you want to use, then I suggest you look 'em up in the index; if you're looking for ideas on how to use SharePoint in your business, use the Table of Contents to find a scenario that sounds similar to your needs.

Also, you don't have to read the book from cover to cover to find it useful. The chapters are intended to be self-contained so you can skip around to the examples that are most applicable to your situation. Where necessary, content is cross-referenced so you can easily find more information.

For example, if you work in human resources, Chapter 10 demonstrates some of the SharePoint features you can use to implement solutions that work for a human resources department.

Also, there are a few code examples in this book — not many, because remember, this is an out-of-the-box solution. For those few code examples that you do find, you can get all the code on my Web site at `www.sharepointgrrl.com`. (And find lots of other great SharePoint resources, too!)

The book is divided into eight convenient, engrossing parts . . .

Part 1: Getting the Lay of the Land

In the first part, I'm your SharePoint tour guide. If you've never seen SharePoint, this part shows you what it looks like after it's installed. As part of your tour, you get the hang of getting around a SharePoint portal and site.

Part 11: Central Portal Administration

Part II shows you how to modify a default SharePoint installation. You get some practical pointers, starting with how to remove all the content that Microsoft installs but which has no meaning to your business. As part of that process, you also get a feel for how to add new content.

You also get a handle on the different ways you can access SharePoint. I show you how to give your people access to the portal and sites, advise you on how to manage user permissions, and show you how to import user information from your network.

Part 111: Portal Design

Part III is where I really challenge you to start thinking about SharePoint's role in your business. I help you build your project team and start your implementation plan. Don't be surprised if you end up scouring your company for ways you can use SharePoint to add value — and finding a slew of 'em.

I discuss what constitutes good content and point out how to drive your employees to your portal (as well as how to make it worth the trip). For example, I show you how to display content on your portal and keep it fresh.

Later in the part, I show you how to change the look and feel of SharePoint to make it consistent with your company's branding.

Part IV: Build It, and Hope They Come

In this part, I show you how to use SharePoint to encourage collaboration. You get to create workspaces for managing meetings and documents. You also get the word on how to use SharePoint with other Office applications (such as Excel) and save Office documents as Web pages that you can display in SharePoint.

Then I show how you can store all your company's templates for fax cover letters and memos in a single repository. You see how to manage a library for images such as logos and branding graphics.

Part V: Power to the People: Engaging Employees with SharePoint

This part really starts to get into the meat and potatoes of using SharePoint. It shows you how to create a self-service human resources site for sharing news, posting jobs, and displaying the organization chart.

I show you how a marketing department can use SharePoint — both to keep themselves organized and educate others about the company's products and promotions.

Part VI: Throw Away the Spreadsheets

The rubber hits the road in Part VI: I show you how to use SharePoint to replace manual forms and improve business processes. You get the skinny on using InfoPath and SharePoint to automate an expense-forms reimbursement process. Later in the part, I show you how to create a self-service help desk, using native SharePoint features.

Part VII: Maintenance

No SharePoint book would be complete without some advice on maintenance. In this part, I show you how to monitor the health of your SharePoint installation and offer pointers on creating a backup-and-restore strategy.

Part VIII: The Part of Tens

Just in case you missed it elsewhere, this part drives home the value of making your SharePoint business case. I give you ten ways that SharePoint can add value to your business. And because SharePoint is a complex beast, I share with you a word to the wise: ten ways to royally screw up your SharePoint implementation (with my full confidence that you won't).

Part I
Getting the Lay of the Land

The 5th Wave   By Rich Tennant

"So, someone's using your credit card info to buy stylish clothes, opera tickets and exercise equipment. In what way would this qualify as 'identity theft'?"

In this part . . .

You'll spot the differences between Microsoft SharePoint Portal Server 2003 and Windows SharePoint Services. More importantly, you'll see how the two products work together to create a central place for navigating a company's information assets.

After completing this part you'll be able to get around hassle-free in any portal and sites created with SharePoint.

Chapter 1

Getting to Know SharePoint

There's SharePoint, and then there's SharePoint. Microsoft has two products with the same name:

✔ Windows SharePoint Services (WSS)

✔ SharePoint Portal Server 2003 (SPS)

With me so far?

You can have Windows SharePoint Services (WSS) without having SharePoint Portal Server 2003 (SPS). But you *can't* have SPS without WSS. Clear as mud? I thought so. Wait, it gets better:

✔ **WSS is part of Windows Server 2003.** When you install Windows Server 2003, WSS is included by default.

✔ **SPS is part of Office 2003.** But when you install Office 2003, you don't automatically get SPS. You have to buy it separately.

Keeping It Simple with WSS

Windows SharePoint Services (WSS) is part of the core technologies of Windows Server 2003. WSS is the engine behind SharePoint sites; without WSS, there is no SharePoint site. Which reminds me . . .

SharePoint sites are internal Web sites intended for team collaboration. But a SharePoint site isn't just any old Web site. It has features that would require many programming hours to create if you built it on your own. WSS is so valuable on its own — you can create an entire Web site for any number of people to use, complete with these features:

- Built-in security and e-mail notification to new users
- Administrative tools to back up and restore
- A database for storing Web site content
- Reusable templates for adding content

You get all these features with just the click of a few buttons. WSS provides templates that let you specify which kind of site you want to create. WSS provides templates for

- Team sites
- Meeting workspaces
- Document workspaces

Each of these site templates creates a Web site that has all the administrative features mentioned in the bulleted list earlier in this section. The sites also let you add content by using reusable templates. Here are some handy examples of what you can add with reusable templates.

- Libraries for
    - Managing documents by using version control and check-in/ check-out
    - Entering data into data-entry forms
- Lists for entering data into forms or grids such as spreadsheets
- Reusable pieces of content (called *Web parts*) that can display any library or list on the site — and other content as well, such as the weather
- Threaded discussions and surveys, similar to what you'd find in a newsgroup or online forum
- Additional pages for displaying all this content and more

Figure 1-1 shows an example of a team site created with WSS. On the team site's home page, you can see

- Announcements
- Events
- Links

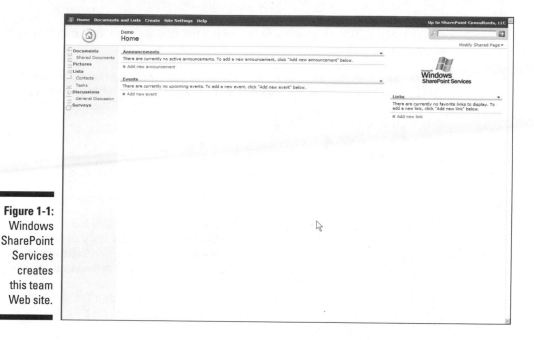

Figure 1-1:
Windows
SharePoint
Services
creates
this team
Web site.

You can customize everything you see on the team Web site shown in Figure 1-1; you can add, modify, and remove everything. Plus you have a lot more options to play with that you can't see from just this screen. (For more about customizing team sites, get a look at Chapter 3.) Best of all, you can do all this customizing from your Web browser — you don't have to know HTML, CSS, or any programming languages. If you can point and click, then you can build a usable team Web site with Windows SharePoint Services.

Kicking It Up a Notch with SPS

You can create hundreds, even thousands, of Web sites by using the site and content templates of Windows SharePoint Services. But having hundreds of individual team Web sites creates a new set of problems.

Say a company is trucking along, using Windows SharePoint Services to create sites whenever the need arises. Before long, this company has sites for

✔ Filling out benefits forms

✔ Submitting ideas to the new product development team

✔ Surveying employees for ideas for Christmas decorations

✔ Storing and organizing the warehouse manager's music collection

Okay, you have all these sites — but no real way to connect them. You have no central jumping-off place where the people in your company can go to find what they're looking for.

The problem is classic: A technology that solves a problem often creates new needs. So how do you solve this dilemma? Use a new technology, of course!

You need a centralized administration tool that lets you

- ✔ Search across all your WSS sites
- ✔ Bring in content from WSS sites to a central site
- ✔ Connect with people on other WSS sites

Back in the early days of the Internet, you could have a really hard time finding other people's Web sites. People soon discovered that they needed a directory. Enterprising entrepreneurs invented Web sites like Yahoo and Google to connect all the sites that had just been floating around on the Web.

At Yahoo, you find Web sites grouped into categories. Such sites (which categorize other sites) are called *portals.* Yahoo is a central place that many people go to look for something on the Web.

Google, on the other hand, provides a tool for searching other Web sites: a *search engine.* (Yahoo also has a search engine, in addition to its portal.) A search engine is a valuable way to find information without using structured categories. Portals often use search engines in addition to their categorizing of Web sites.

As more people use highly connected sites such as Yahoo and Google, suddenly the world is a little smaller. It's like the game the Six Degrees of Kevin Bacon. In this game, you try to figure how to connect an actor or actress to Kevin Bacon through common costars, using the fewest links possible. Amazingly, you can connect most actors and actresses to Kevin Bacon within three links. (Don't believe me? You can play an online version of Six Degrees of Kevin Bacon at the University of Virginia's Web site at www.cs. virginia.edu/oracle.)

Kevin Bacon is highly connected in the same way that a portal like Yahoo is highly connected: Easy to find, and easy to use to find others.

To solve the problem of having hundreds of unconnected Windows SharePoint Services sites, Microsoft created Microsoft SharePoint Portal Server 2003 (SPS). The SPS portal is as highly connected as Yahoo (or, for that matter, Kevin Bacon). As with any portal, you can use SPS to

   ✔ Categorize WSS sites

   ✔ Provide links to WSS sites or sites on the Web

   ✔ Search WSS sites for content and people

   ✔ Display content from WSS sites

SPS creates a small world of connected WSS sites so you can perform central-ized administration tasks such as site backups and WSS site creation. It gives your users a single place to go when they're looking for information in your enterprise. (In this case, even the capitalist inside Bill Gates can attest that centralization is better.)

You can see the SharePoint Portal Server home page in Figure 1-2.

The SPS home page may look familiar because SharePoint Portal Server 2003 is a kind of Windows SharePoint Services site; SPS and WSS use the same underlying technology. SPS just expands on the already-wonderful WSS fea-tures. Think of SPS as a WSS site on steroids, where you can create

   ✔ Lists

   ✔ Libraries

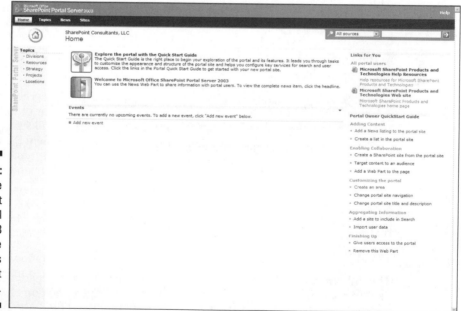

Figure 1-2:
The
SharePoint
Portal
Server 2003
home page
connects
SharePoint
sites.

- New pages
- Everything else you can create on a WSS site

Many WSS features take on different names in SPS. For example, you call a Web page an *area*, and links (as in hyperlinks) become *listings*.

In addition to the standard WSS features, SPS also has the following features:

- **Area pages:** These display links to WSS sites and other content stored on the SPS site.
- **Tools:** Among these are Topics and Keyword Best Bets for directing people to content.
- **Site directory:** This feature categorizes and browses all WSS sites connected to the SPS site.
- **Search engine:** This searches the content in the WSS sites connected to the site directory — as well as the content on the portal itself.

SharePoint Portal Server is both a portal *and* a site, so you may sometimes hear it called the *portal site*. SPS can do everything a WSS site can do, plus it has features you would expect of a highly connected portal such as Yahoo.

Splitting Hairs

At the end of the day, you can call it WSS, SPS, or SharePoint. Heck, I just call it *the portal*. Here's why:

- If your company uses only WSS, you call it SharePoint.
- If your company uses WSS *with* SPS, you still call it SharePoint.
- If your company starts out using WSS, and then adds SPS later . . . yep, you call it SharePoint in this case, too.

Here's where it gets, um, interesting: The products do have different setup approaches. WSS can be installed as part of Windows Server 2003, but SharePoint Portal Server requires a separate server or two (at minimum). Even if you use only WSS, at some point you probably want to evaluate SPS. Either way, you still use SharePoint.

The only time this distinction really matters is when you're reading a book like this one or getting help on the Web. You may buy a book on SharePoint without understanding whether the book covers WSS or SPS. And people on the Web can be brutal if you ask a question about SPS on a site that discusses

WSS. (They assume you already know the difference and treat the two as separate. Picky, picky.)

From the perspective of someone using SharePoint, I argue that you may not even want to use the name SharePoint to describe your portal. You can give your portal a functional name like *corporate portal* or *company intranet.* SharePoint is the underlying technology, not the solution itself. (You don't gab with your average end user about the fine points of .NET, CSS, Java, and iterative development, right?)

In this book, I usually refer to SPS as *SharePoint, the portal,* or *the portal site.* If I talk about a WSS site, I call it a *SharePoint site.* Outside of this chapter, I don't differentiate between SPS and WSS again. It's all SharePoint to me.

Equal-Opportunity Content

This book takes a marble-cake approach to the two SharePoint products. Some chapters may be more about SPS than WSS and vice versa, but there is often a little bit of both sprinkled throughout.

Any time you add content to SharePoint, you face the question of which SharePoint to use. You have several options:

- ✔ Store the content on the portal (meaning SPS) and display it on the portal
- ✔ Store the content on a site (meaning WSS) and display it on the portal
- ✔ Store the content on a site, and display it on a site *and* on the portal
- ✔ Store and display the content on a site, but don't display it on the portal
- ✔ Store the content outside SharePoint altogether (in a file share, for example) and display it on a site, the portal, or both

Because you have so many choices, you need to understand the role of each SharePoint product. Also, some limitations can influence this decision. You need to understand your available options and the advantages and limitations of choosing the portal site or a regular site. This book shows you how to decide whether to store content on the portal, a site, or both.

I recommend that you store as much as possible on sites — then you can use the portal to search and categorize. The only content I like to store on the portal itself is all the listings and links to site and external content.

I think this approach works well because it makes administration and maintenance easier. You can group like content together on a site and assign an administrator to the site. You can assign an administrator for the whole portal or divide the portal for many administrators. You can have one administrator for one area of the portal and a different administrator for another area. The site administrators can then submit content to the portal administrators, or the portal administrators can solicit content from the site administrators. You don't have to give a ton of people administrative access to your enterprise portal.

This approach allows people to specialize because you can have enterprise folks who are really good at navigation or Web design. You can put additional talent on figuring out ways to drive employees to use the portal.

Deciding Whether to Invest

This book assumes that your company uses SharePoint Portal Server 2003, even if it's only installed in a test environment right now. If you aren't already using WSS, SPS installs WSS for you.

You have to take SharePoint as a serious investment. Implementing SharePoint takes significant resources:

✔ **Software:** An SPS installation requires this software:

- Windows Server 2003

- Internet Information Server 6.0

- SQL Server 2000

- Windows SharePoint Services

You get the best bang for your buck if you use SharePoint with Microsoft Office 2003, even though Office 2003 isn't required.

It's technically possible to host everything on one server, but SharePoint flourishes with two different servers for

- Hosting the front-end Web pages that users see

- Running all the jobs and storing data on the back-end server

✔ **Hardware:** Each server needs

- At least two CPUs

- One to two gigabytes of memory

✔ **Hard-drive space**

- **Less than 50 gigabytes (GB):** Use this small amount if you're just playing around

- **250GB:** Now you're getting serious

- **One terabyte:** Thank goodness storage is cheap

The nice thing about SharePoint is that you can start with one or two servers and expand as your needs grow.

For more about the hardware requirements for SharePoint, you can find a useful Microsoft article on capacity planning at this location:

```
www.microsoft.com/technet/prodtechnol/office/sps2003/plan/cappisps.mspx
```

If you aren't quite sure that you want to make the commitment to SharePoint just yet, you can test-drive a Windows SharePoint Services site free for 30 days at `www.sharepointtrial.com`. Thirty days gives you enough time to work the examples in this book and decide whether SharePoint is right for your business.

If you don't have the extra hardware for building a test server, you can use Microsoft Virtual PC instead. You use Virtual PC to host all the software you need to run SharePoint on an existing piece of hardware. I installed Virtual PC on my computer running Windows XP and then hosted Windows 2003 Server and SharePoint on the Virtual PC. My test environment worked great after I bumped the machine up to 1GB of memory.

No matter what your installation environment looks like, many technologies play a part in setting up SharePoint. Having access to the folks with the right skills to support these technologies makes a huge difference.

Chapter 2

Starting with the Basics

SharePoint uses a consistent layout throughout all its pages. This chapter walks you through the basic SharePoint layout, showing you similarities and differences among the portal and site pages.

Playing the Shell Game

SharePoint looks and feels like a Web page. Heck, it *is* a Web page. But, it's a Web page that doesn't have any real content or do anything meaningful. SharePoint is a big faker!

SharePoint is really just a shell of a portal. It's waiting on someone like you to give it some meat.

Although it may be a shell, it's a powerful portal-building tool. Anything powerful has to have a lot of confusing terminology to go with it, which is certainly the case with SharePoint! Before you can appreciate the power of SharePoint, you need to know some of the basics of how the portal shell is laid out. Oh, and you get to add some confusing terminology to your memory bank along the way.

What does a portal look like?

The start page for any Web site is usually called its *home page;* the first page you see when you browse to your portal is the *portal home page.* It looks like the screen in Figure 2-1.

To browse to your portal home page, enter the address (in the form of `http://server_name`) in your browser. Get the server name from your systems administrator and use that address to browse to your SharePoint portal.

All good Web sites use a consistent layout so users know what to expect from page to page. You also find this consistency in SharePoint. The portal home page layout has several elements, which you can read more about in the following bulleted list and see illustrated in Figure 2-2.

The layout of a Web page is often called a *template*. Each of the SharePoint portal pages uses a template.

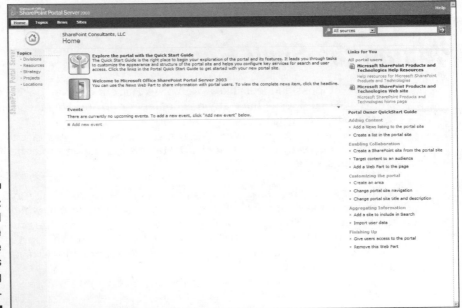

Figure 2-1:
The portal home page is the portal's starting place.

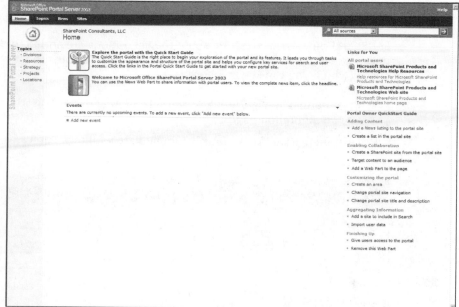

Figure 2-2:
The portal
page layout
uses
consistent
elements
across
pages.

✔ **Page banner:** This is the top banner that goes completely across the page.

✔ **Page-banner navigation:** Use this special set of links to access help, administrative tasks, or a special personal Web site called My Site at the far right of the page banner.

✔ **Primary navigation:** It's the horizontal navigation bar directly below the page banner.

✔ **Left navigation:** This is a list of topics — another kind of navigation that links you to the Topics pages that organize portal content.

✔ **Page title:** The portal name and the name of the current page show here.

✔ **Search box:** This is where the user can search the portal for content.

✔ **Page content:** Content specific to the current page shows up here.

As you browse the portal, most of these elements remain consistent, although the page content changes. This consistency gives users a sense of place.

Looking at things like an administrator

For SharePoint administrators, some special options are added to the page, but the basic layout remains intact. The following list notes the major differences (which you can see in Figure 2-3):

✔ **Page-banner navigation:** Site Settings allows administrators to access site configuration pages.

✔ **Left navigation:** An Actions list immediately follows Topics.

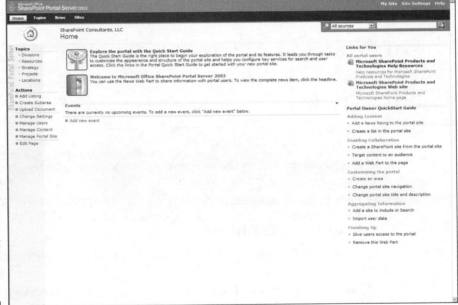

Figure 2-3:
The portal administrative layout adds a few more features.

Oh, the Pages You'll See

The SharePoint portal installs four default pages:

✔ **Home:** The portal home page

✔ **Topics:** A navigational aid that directs users to content

✔ **News:** A page for consolidating news information

✔ **Sites:** A directory for finding sites accessible from the portal

These pages are called *areas* in SharePoint.

Each of the SharePoint portal pages uses a template that suits the layout for that particular page's use. (For more information on content templates, see the "Page content templates" sidebar.)

Page content templates can be applied to new portal pages to give them a consistent look right away.

Starting out at the home page

The home page uses a unique contents template because it is unlike any other page in the portal. The default content in the home page has four elements, which you can read about in the following list and see in Figure 2-4:

- Two news listings that invite you to explore the QuickStart Guide and welcome you to the portal
- A list of events where appointments and other company events can be added
- Links for You (a Web part that includes hyperlinks to two help resources about SharePoint)
- Portal Owner QuickStart Guide (a Web part that provides a walk-through of the portal)

Page content templates

Page content templates allow the portal pages to have the same look and feel, but they're used in slightly different ways. Here are a few of the common page content templates in SharePoint:

- SPSTOC – The default template for pages such as the Topics page
- SPSNHOME – The News home template used for the News page
- SPSSITES – Template used for the site directory
- SPSMSITE – Template used for the My Site personal site
- SPSTOPIC – Template used for Topics subpages
- SPSNEWS – Template used for News subpages

The content templates are stored in a file directory in

```
C:\Program Files\Common Files\Microsoft
        Shared\web server extensions\60\
        TEMPLATE\1033
```

You can find a manifest of the default content templates at

```
C:\Program Files\Common Files\Microsoft
        Shared\web server extensions\60\
        TEMPLATE\\1033\ SPS\SPSConfig\
        SPSPredefinedCategories.xml
```

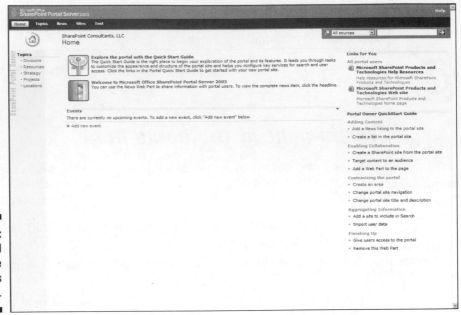

A *Web part* is a specialized container for displaying content. You can find more on Web parts in Chapter 3.

The QuickStart Guide is a good introduction to SharePoint.

Knowing where to go with the Topics page

The purpose of the Topics page is to provide navigation to portal content. As you add content to the portal, you can associate it with a Topic. The Topics page uses the default page content template, which is different from the home page. These differences (which you can see in Figure 2-5) include

 ✔ **Left navigation:** This part of the Topics page changes to show the Current Location in the portal. The bullet items listed below Topics are the default Topics pages created by SharePoint.

   Don't worry about contorting your company to fit the topics provided by SharePoint. You can easily change these topics, and I tell you how in Chapter 3.

 ✔ **Area description:** Describes the purpose of the Topics page.

 ✔ **Browse Topics By:** Shows the default Topics hierarchy created by SharePoint.

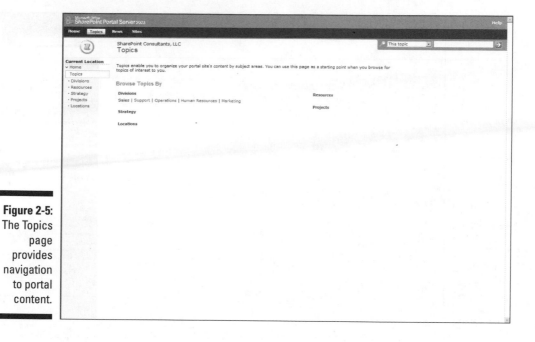

Figure 2-5:
The Topics
page
provides
navigation
to portal
content.

All the news you need

The News page collects portal news, and includes these features:

✔ Three default News pages for categorizing news (Company News, Press Announcements, and External News)

The default News pages are called *subareas* because they are one level below an area page.

✔ The same two news listings on the home page

✔ A news-area Web part that displays news grouped by the three default News-page categories (Company News, Press Announcements, and External News)

Figure 2-6 shows the default News page.

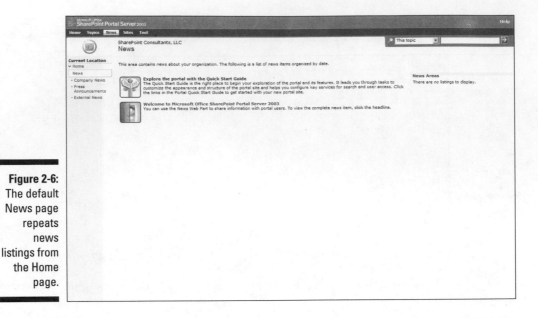

Figure 2-6:
The default
News page
repeats
news
listings from
the Home
page.

The News page usés the news home template, while the Company News,
Press Announcements, and External News pages use the news template.
Unlike the standard SharePoint News page, the company News page doesn't
contain any default content, as you can see in Figure 2-7.

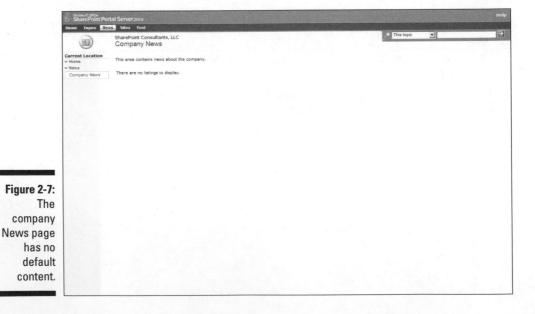

Figure 2-7:
The
company
News page
has no
default
content.

Taking stock on the Sites page

The Sites page shows the site directory. You can use the site directory to list all the sites connected to your portal.

Sites are collections of Web pages. Like portal pages, sites use templates to create a consistent look and feel. Site templates reflect the kind of collaboration that you intend for the site, such as

- ✔ Team
- ✔ Project
- ✔ Meeting
- ✔ Documents

The Sites page has the following elements, which Figure 2-8 illustrates:

- ✔ **Select a view (in the left navigation):** Displays either a summary of sites or lists all sites on the portal.
- ✔ **Search box:** This is for searching the site directory for a specific site.
- ✔ **Browse Sites By:** This section enables you to browse sites by using predefined categories such as Divisions and Region.

  These categories can be changed to suit your organization.
- ✔ **Spotlight sites:** Here's where you find sites that were flagged for special emphasis when they were added to the site directory.
- ✔ **Recently added sites:** These are displayed in the Newest Sites Web part, grouped by time frame (such as by week or month).

Navigating SharePoint

In addition to helping users get around, site navigation provides structure to your portal. SharePoint offers many default navigational elements to help users organize and find content. The portal's search features allow users to bypass structure and zero in on specific content.

Figure 2-8:
The site
directory
lists all
the sites
connected
to your
portal.

Getting around

Navigation helps give users a consistent sense of place so they don't get lost on your portal. Many of the elements described in this chapter orient the user to his or her location on the portal, as follows:

- ✔ **The page title** tells the user what page he or she is on.
- ✔ **Title images** change with the type of page being displayed.
- ✔ **Web part and section headers** direct the viewer's attention to grouped content.
- ✔ **Hyperlinks** (called *listings*) throughout the pages take the user to detailed pages.

The portal uses two *navigation bars*:

- ✔ **The primary horizontal navigation bar** lists all four default portal pages. The currently selected page is in a different color.
- ✔ **The secondary vertical navigation bar** on the left changes hyperlinks with the page.

Chapter 3 covers navigation in more detail.

You can see these elements in Figure 2-9.

SharePoint doesn't use buttons such as *Back, Next,* or *Previous* for navigation. The portal doesn't expect you to navigate it in a linear fashion.

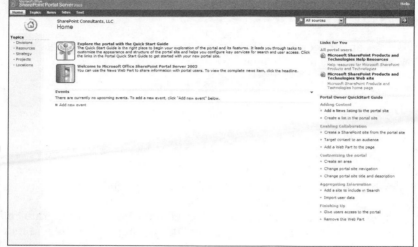

Figure 2-9:
SharePoint
uses many
navigational
elements.

Search and rescue

Sometimes navigational elements can't conveniently find the content you
want. SharePoint's search boxes give the user a way to do a free-form search
while finding content.

The *search box* always appears on-screen just below the page banner and primary horizontal navigation, as you can see in Figure 2-10.

Figure 2-10:
The search
box accepts
free-form
text.

Look at All Those Sites!

Sites are collections of Web pages used for collaboration. Examples of collaboration uses for sites include

- ✔ Projects
- ✔ Teams
- ✔ Meetings
- ✔ Documents

See Chapter 8 to get ideas for using sites for collaboration.

Sites are created with Windows SharePoint Services. A program called Microsoft SharePoint Portal Server 2003 creates the portal and its pages.

Without a portal, sites are just islands of content. The portal helps to

- ✔ Unify the sites.
- ✔ Provide a structured view of (and access to) the sites and their content.

Site layout

All sites have a consistent look and feel. As you can see in Figure 2-11, sites have the following layout elements:

- ✔ Top horizontal navigation
- ✔ Connection to portal in the upper-right corner of the site home page
- ✔ Site name and page title
- ✔ Page-content area

Figure 2-11 shows a site based on the Team template (which includes a vertical left navigation similar to the one on the portal). The vertical navigation bar is called a *Quick Launch bar;* not all site templates include the same navigation bars. (See Chapter 8 for more information about site templates.)

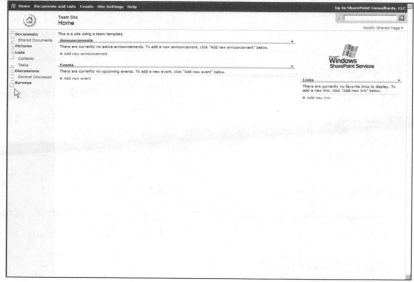

Figure 2-11:
The site
layout
shares
similar
elements
with the
portal
layout.

Site templates

Sites are based on templates. SharePoint installs eight templates by default:

- Team Site
- Blank Site
- Document Workspace
- Basic Meeting Workspace
- Blank Meeting Workspace
- Decision Workspace
- Social Meeting Workspace
- Multipage Meeting Workspace

You choose your site's template when you create the site.

Lists for everyone

I think one of the most exciting features in SharePoint is lists. Lists allow you to capture data on a Web site without any programming whatsoever. Use any of the built-in lists or create your own! You can modify built-in lists to fit your needs. Examples of built-in lists include

- ✔ **Contacts:** A list of contacts that you can link to Outlook

- ✔ **Events:** A calendar of events

- ✔ **Tasks:** A to-do list for your group where you can assign tasks to group members

- ✔ **Issues:** A list that tracks issues and their resolution

Similar to the data displayed in a spreadsheet, list columns can be sorted and filtered by the list owner. Anyone with permission to access the list can create their own personal sorts and filters that only they can view.

Site content

The template you choose when you create the site is what determines the site's default content. A site may have any of the following content installed by default (for more information, see Chapter 8):

- ✔ **Document libraries:** These are places to save version-controlled documents.

- ✔ **Picture libraries:** Here you can view pictures and their properties (such as when and where each picture was taken).

- ✔ **Lists:** These display columns and rows of data similar to a spreadsheet. (See the accompanying "Lists for everyone" sidebar for more information.)

- ✔ **Discussion boards:** These are places to share thoughts about a given topic.

- ✔ **Surveys:** These are tools for getting structured feedback from participants.

The chapters throughout this book offer many suggestions on how to use site content in your company.

Part II
Central Portal Administration

The 5th Wave   By Rich Tennant

"Ironically, he went out there looking for a 'hot spot'."

In this part . . .

I'll show you how to modify your portal, give people access to it (along with its sites), and manage the administration of your portal. I cover the different ways to access SharePoint — and show you how to import user profiles using existing information from your network.

Chapter 3

Configuring the Portal

SharePoint comes with default content and a suggested structure when you install it. Before you can personalize the portal to fit your company, you need to know how to remove the default content.

This chapter covers how to remove default content that SharePoint installs and how to add new content in its place. You also get a look at using the portal site map to display your portal's structure.

Adding Personal Touches to Portal Pages

Four default pages are installed with your portal: Home, Topics, News, and Sites. You can edit each of these pages to remove the default content provided by SharePoint.

The pages are displayed in view mode by default. To remove or add content, you need to put the page in edit mode. To put the page in edit mode, follow these steps:

1. **Browse to the portal home page.**

   You need to access the portal as an administrator. Check with your Information Technology department or help desk to see whether you have administrative permissions to access the SharePoint portal.

   Chapter 4 covers SharePoint security in detail.

2. **Click Edit Page in the vertical navigation bar on the left.**

   If you don't see the Edit Page option, then you don't have administrative access.

The portal page is now in edit mode. Edit mode is different than view mode in these ways, as Figure 3-1 shows you:

✔ The page title changes to Edit: Home.

✔ The Edit Page option in the vertical navigation bar changes to View Page.

✔ You have a new option to Modify Shared Page available.

✔ Web parts have additional options in the header bars.

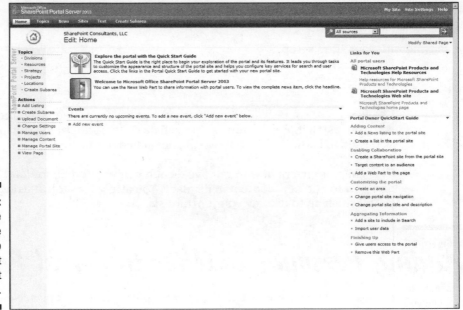

Figure 3-1:
The page title changes to reflect that you can edit the page.

Removing default content

Before you show anyone SharePoint's possibilities, lose that default content installed by SharePoint.

Chapter 2 gives you a detailed walk-through of the default content installed by SharePoint.

Removing listings

There are two listings on the home page that you can remove. To remove listings:

1. In Edit Page mode, place your mouse over the listing heading.

The listing changes to a drop-down box.

2. Click the drop-down box and click Delete, as Figure 3-2 shows you.

A dialog box prompts you to confirm the deletion.

3. Click OK.

The listing is deleted from the page.

You also can remove listings by choosing the Archive option. Archiving keeps the listing on your site but removes it from the display.

Remove listings on other portal pages by repeating the steps in this section for each page.

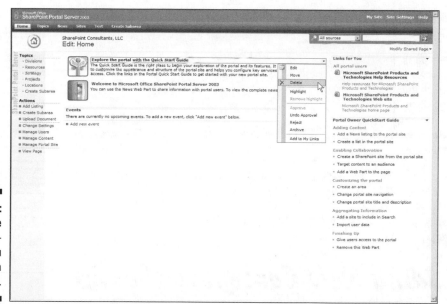

Figure 3-2:
Click Delete on the drop-down menu to remove a listing.

Removing Web parts

The home page has three Web parts that you can remove. To remove any of those Web parts, follow these steps:

1. Click the little arrow in the header for the Web part that you want to remove.

A drop-down menu appears.

2. Click Close in the drop-down menu, as Figure 3-3 shows you.

Don't delete the Web part unless you never want to see that Web part again. Deleting the Web part permanently removes it from your portal.

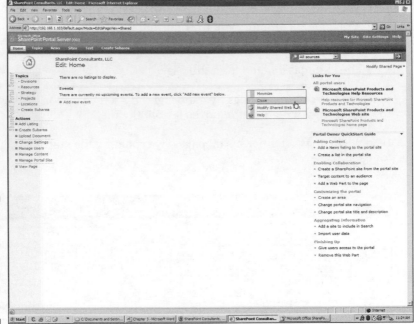

Figure 3-3:
Remove
Web parts
by choosing
Close on the
drop-down
menu.

Remove Web parts on other portal pages by repeating the steps in this section for each page.

You can't modify the layout of the Sites page.

Adding New Content to the Mix

Your portal page looks naked without the default content. You can easily add your own content, and you have many choices.

Playing with Web parts

A *Web part* is a reusable piece of content. All Web parts have

- A title bar
- A frame
- Content

Web parts also have properties that control their appearance, behavior, and whether you can modify them.

The portal page displays Web parts in zones. Pages have four zones for displaying content: top, middle-left, middle-right, and bottom. Figure 3-4 shows the Web-part zones and a Web part.

You add Web parts by first browsing the Web-part gallery and then selecting a Web part to add to the page. The following steps show you how to get to the Web-part gallery:

1. **Browse to the portal home page as an administrator and click Edit Page.**

   The procedure for making yourself an administrator appears earlier in this chapter.

2. **Click Modify Shared Page in the upper-right corner of the page.**

3. **Click Add Web Parts in the drop-down box and then click Browse, as Figure 3-5 shows you.**

   The browse task pane appears. Keep reading to see how to browse the gallery and add Web parts.

Figure 3-4:
The portal page is divided into zones where you can place Web parts.

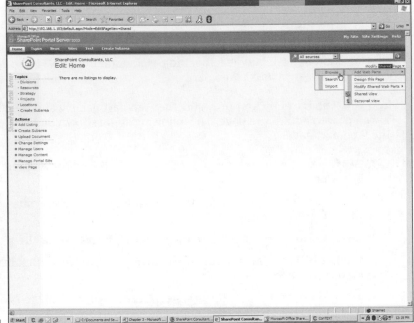

Figure 3-5:
Add Web
parts by
clicking
Modify
Shared
Page.

Browsing Web-part galleries

The Browse task pane lists four galleries at the top of the task pane. The list of Web parts in the selected gallery appears beneath the list of galleries in the task pane. The four galleries available are

- ✔ **Web Part Page Gallery:** Lists the Web parts associated with the page that you're editing

- ✔ **The portal gallery:** Lists the Web parts available in your portal

- ✔ **Virtual Server Gallery:** Lists the Web parts associated with the virtual server that hosts your portal

- ✔ **Online Gallery:** Lists the Web parts available from Microsoft

You also can import Web parts from the Web. Google the Web for "SharePoint Web parts" to find custom Web parts.

To browse a gallery, follow these steps:

1. **Click the gallery that you want to browse.**

   By default, the portal gallery is selected.

2. **Click Filter.**

   A drop-down box with the label *Show:* appears.

3. **Select Web Parts from the drop-down box.**

   The list filters out all content except Web parts.

4. **Click Next to view the next page of Web parts in the list, as Figure 3-6 shows you.**

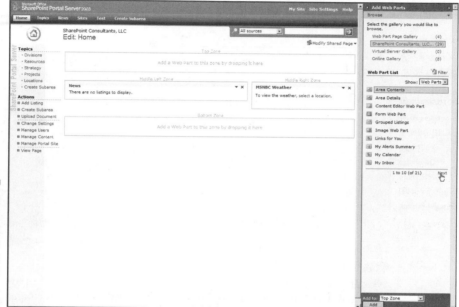

Figure 3-6:
The Web-part gallery lists Web parts that you can add to the page.

Adding Web parts to the portal page

You can add any Web part from any gallery by using the steps in this section. To add the MSNBC Weather Web part from the online gallery, follow these steps:

1. **Click Online Gallery in the Browse Web Parts task pane.**

   Only Web parts available in this gallery are listed, including eight Web parts from MSNBC.

2. **Click MSNBC Weather and drag and drop it to the middle-right zone, as Figure 3-7 shows you.**

   The weather Web part is added to the page.

3. **Click to select a location in the Web part, and enter a city name or zip code to display the weather for that city in the Web part.**

   The Web part displays the weather for the location that you enter.

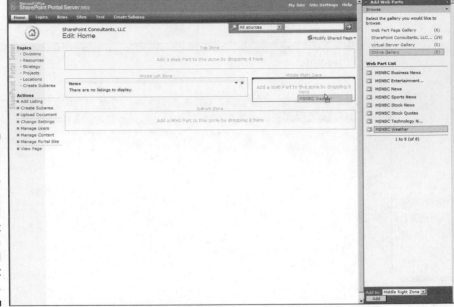

Figure 3-7:
Add a Web part by dragging and dropping it in the desired Web part zone.

Changing Web-part properties

Web parts have properties that affect

✔ Whether you can minimize or close the Web part

✔ How the Web part looks on-screen

You can use the steps in this section to modify the properties for any Web part. To modify the properties for the MSNBC Weather Web part that the preceding section tells you how to add to your home page, follow these steps:

1. **Browse to the portal home page as an administrator and click Edit Page.**

2. **Click the drop-down arrow in the corner of the MSNBC Weather Web part.**

3. **Click Modify Shared Web Part in the drop-down box, as Figure 3-8 shows you.**

   The Web part properties are displayed in a task pane. Keep reading to see how to modify the Web part's properties by using the task pane.

Task panes are windows that appear to the right of a screen and display additional menu options. Office 2003 makes extensive use of task panes.

Figure 3-8:
Change
Web part
properties
by clicking
the drop-
down menu
on the
Web part.

The task pane is divided into four areas:

- ✓ **Content Editor:** Modify content options

- ✓ **Appearance:** Specify the Web part's title, width, height, and frame options

- ✓ **Layout:** Indicate whether you want the Web part visible on the page and where you want it to appear

- ✓ **Advanced:** Specify whether users can minimize or close the Web part, provide a description and icon, and target specific audiences that you want to see the Web part

Chapter 6 describes how to use audiences to create groups of users who can see the Web parts and other content targeted to them.

Change the MSNBC Weather Web part's appearance and advanced properties with these steps:

1. **In the Task Pane, click the plus (+) sign next to Appearance to display the appearance properties.**

2. **Change the title to "Local Weather" and click Apply.**

   The title changes from MSNBC Weather to Local Weather.

3. **Click the plus (+) sign next to Advanced.**

4. **Clear the check marks next to Allow Minimize, Allow Close, and Allow Zone Change.**

   This prevents users from closing, minimizing, or moving the Web part.

5. **Click Apply to save the properties.**

   Figure 3-9 shows the task pane as it appears at this point.

6. **Click OK to close the task pane and return to edit mode of the home page.**

You can change the properties for any Web part by using the steps in this section.

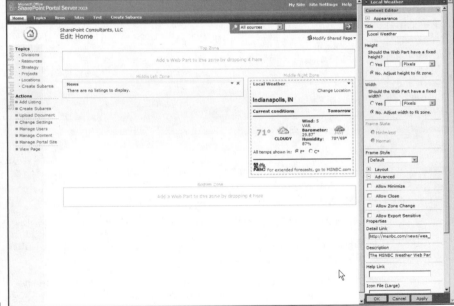

Figure 3-9:
Use the task pane to change the Web part's title and other properties.

Managing portal page content

In addition to Web parts, SharePoint provides many additional content sources such as document libraries and discussion boards. To manage additional portal page content, follow these steps:

1. **Browse to the home page as an administrator.**

2. **Click Manage Content in the Actions list in the vertical navigation bar.**

The Documents and Lists page is displayed. Use this page to add new content to your portal page. The many kinds of content that you can manage for the portal page include:

- ✔ **Listings:** Create hyperlinks to existing or new content in your portal.
- ✔ **Document Libraries:** Create repositories for storing documents and forms.
- ✔ **Picture Libraries:** Create a special repository for storing pictures.
- ✔ **Lists:** Create tabular lists of virtually any kind of business data imaginable. SharePoint includes built-in lists for managing the following:
  - Contacts
  - Events
  - Issues
  - News
  - Tasks
- ✔ **Discussion Boards:** Create newsgroup style discussions.
- ✔ **Surveys:** Create surveys to poll your users on any topic you want.

Each portal page has its own Documents and Lists page for managing content for that page. The portal creates some of this content; you can add to this default content as needed.

Before adding new content, consider carefully where you want to place it. The scenarios covered in chapters 8 through 14 demonstrate these many content types and offer suggestions on where you may want to place those content types.

To add a new portal listing to the Home page, follow these steps:

1. **Click Portal Listings on the Documents and Lists page.**
2. **Click Add Listing on the toolbar.**

   The Add Listing page appears.
3. **Enter a title (such as *Welcome to the new portal*) in the Title field, and then enter a description in the Description field.**
4. **In the Content section, specify the source for the listing by clicking Add a listing by entering text.**
5. **Click the Open Text Editor button and enter a welcome message to your portal users in the text editor.**
6. **Click OK to save the message.**

7. **Click the drop-down in the Group section and select Highlight.**

   This step assigns the listing to the highlight group. You can choose any group for the listing.

8. **Accept the defaults for location and audience.**

9. **Click OK to save the listing.**

When you browse to your home page, your new listing isn't there if you removed the default Web parts. For your listing to show up, you need to add the Web part called Links for You (or the Grouped Listings Web part). Check out "Adding Web parts to the portal page," earlier in this chapter, to find out how to add Web parts.

Finding Your Way with the Portal Site Map

You can add to the structure of your new SharePoint portal. To manage the portal structure, follow these steps:

1. **Browse to the portal home page as an administrator.**

2. **Click Manage Portal Site.**

   The portal site map appears.

The portal site map displays a tree view of the structure of your portal. By default, the portal's main pages (Home, Topics, News, Sites) are displayed. Click the plus (+) sign next to any of the main pages to see the pages beneath the selected page.

SharePoint refers to the portal pages as *areas*.

Creating pages

At the top level in the structure, a page is called an *area*. When you add a page below an area, you say that you create a *subarea*. The Topics and News pages, for example, are subareas to the Home page. However, when a subarea has subareas below it (such as the Topics or News page), you call it an area, and the pages that you add below that area are subareas. (I mean a page. No, wait, I mean an area. Oh, never mind.)

Just remember that you call the pages *areas,* and when you want to add a new page, follow these steps:

1. **In the portal site map, click the page in the tree structure above where you want your page to appear.**

2. **Select Create a Subarea to add the new page.**

To add a new page to the home page, follow these steps:

1. **Click the drop-down box on Home and select Create subarea.**

   The Create Area page appears.

2. **Enter the title Departments in the title field and give the page a description using the description field.**

3. **Accept the default value for publishing dates and location.**

   You can enter a date range for publishing the page if you want. You already chose the location for the page by using the portal site map.

4. **Click OK to create the page.**

   The portal site map shows the new Departments page under Home, as Figure 3-10 shows you. You can use the steps in this section to add pages to your portal, such as pages under the Topics page.

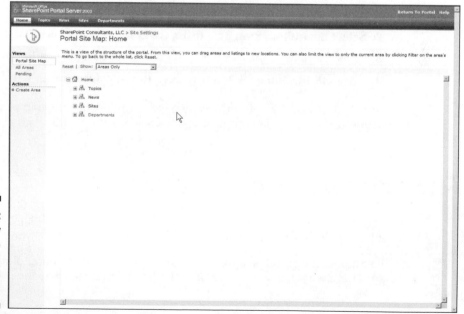

Figure 3-10:
Add a new
page to
the portal in
the portal
site map.

Manipulating page settings

Pages have many settings that you can modify. To modify the settings for the Departments page that you just created, follow these steps:

1. **In the portal site map, click the drop-down box for Departments.**

2. **Click Edit.**

   The Change Settings page appears, offering you five settings tabs:

   - **General:** Change the title, contact, and location

   - **Publishing:** Specify the start date and expiration date, if any, for displaying the page and whether new listings require approval

   - **Page:** Set templates for the page and subarea (pages below the main page)

   - **Display:** Set navigation options, images, and icons

   - **Search:** Specify whether to include the page in search results

To move the Departments page from its present location under Home to the Topics page, follow these steps:

1. **On the General tab in Change Settings, click Change Location in the Area Location section.**

   The Change Location dialog box appears.

2. **Select the radio button next to Topics in the Change Location dialog box.**

3. **Click OK to save the location and close the Change Location dialog box.**

4. **Click OK in Change Settings to save the new location.**

You can use these steps to move any page in the portal site map or change settings for any page in your portal.

Monkeying Around with Sites

The great thing about SharePoint sites is that most of what this chapter tells you about adding and modifying content portal applies to sites.

The SharePoint portal is actually a customized Windows SharePoint Services site. That's why you sometimes hear the portal referred to as the portal site.

Adding sites

Sites are added from the site directory. To add a new site, follow these steps:

1. **Browse to the Sites page on the portal as an administrator.**

2. **In the Actions list in the vertical navigation bar, select Create Site.**

   The New SharePoint Site page appears.

3. **Give the new site a title and description using the title and description fields.**

4. **Enter the URL for the site in the Web site address field.**

   The *URL* is the Web address that you type in the browser's address bar to browse to the site. URL stands for Uniform Resource Locator.

5. **Enter the e-mail address for the site administrator in the e-mail address field.**

   The *site administrator* is the person who has ownership of the site. Any requests for access are e-mailed to the site administrator.

6. **Click Create to create the new site.**

   The Add Link to Site page appears. This page enables you to list the page in the site directory. The site directory lists all the sites that are connected to the portal. To add your site to the site directory, follow the steps in this section.

There may be times when you don't want a site listed in the site directory for all to see. To prevent a site from being added to the site directory, clear the check mark next to List this site in the site directory on the Add Link to Site page. Use the site's URL to access the site directly.

To add a link to the site directory and create the site, follow these steps:

1. **Leave the check mark checked for List This Site in the Site Directory.**

2. **Specify the title, URL, and description as you want them to appear in the site directory.**

   You can make the title and description in the site directory link different from the title and description specified for the site. The site's title and description are displayed on the site itself while the title and description specified in the site directory are displayed on the portal's site page.

3. **Specify whether you want the site link to appear in search results by clicking the check mark next to Include in search results.**

4. **If you want the listing to appear on portal pages besides the site directory, specify those pages in the Areas section by clicking Change location.**

5. **Click OK to save the site directory link.**

6. **Pick the team site template for the site from the Template Selection page by clicking Team Site in the list box.**

7. **Click OK to create the site.**

   As the site is created, the template determines the default content that's offered in the new site.

Modifying the site directory

Any time you create a new site, you have the option to add the new site to the site directory. The site directory — displayed on the Sites page on the portal — asks you for the following information when a site is added to the site directory:

- **Title:** The name of the site as you want it displayed in the site directory.

- **URL:** A hyperlink is created to the site from the URL.

- **Description:** The description should concisely tell what the site is used for.

- **Owner:** The name of the person who is responsible for the site.

- **Division:** A drop-down list that allows you to categorize the site by division such as Sales or Finance.

- **Region:** A drop-down list that allows you to assign the site to a geographic region such as local or national.

- **Spotlight Site:** A check mark here makes the site appear in the list of spotlight sites on the portal's Sites page.

Think of the site directory as a "yellow pages" for the sites on your portal — you want your site directory to help users find information fast. Your site directory will be most useful if it displays site information in a way that is meaningful to your company (for example, division and region may not be useful distinctions in your company). To change the information that your site directory collects when a new site is added, follow these steps:

1. **Go to the Sites page on your portal.**

2. **Click Customize List in the Actions list.**

   The customization page for the site directory list is displayed.

3. **Scroll down to the Columns section and click the Division column.**

   The Change Column page is displayed.

4. **Scroll down to the Optional Settings for Column section. Change the choices displayed in the multi-line text box to whatever divisional choices are meaningful to your company.**

   You can also delete this column if it does not apply to your company. Just click the Delete button at the bottom of the Change Column page.

5. **Click OK.**

   Repeat these steps to modify or delete other columns in the site directory. You can also add columns to the site directory by clicking the Add a new column hyperlink on the site directory's customization page.

By modifying the site directory to fit your company, you give your users quick and easy access to the sites on your portal.

Making new lists (and checking them twice)

Sites have Documents and Lists pages, just like the portal page. To add a new list to a team site that you just created (which you can find out how to do in the preceding section), follow these steps:

1. **Click Create from the primary horizontal navigation bar.**

2. **In the Lists section, click the kind of list to create, such as Tasks.**

   The New List page appears.

3. **Enter a name (such as *Portal Content Ideas*) for the list in the name field.**

4. **Click Create.**

   These steps take you to your new list for sharing portal content ideas with others. (Don't forget to use this list.)

Chapter 4

Accessing SharePoint

- -

- -

*W*hen managing security in SharePoint, you have to remember that there's a difference between portal access and site access.

Granting a user access to the portal isn't the same thing as granting them access to a site. Jim in Accounting may be the administrator for Accounting's departmental site, but he may have read-only access to the portal. And Jim may not have any access at all to the customer service site.

Nevertheless, the portal and its sites use similar concepts for managing user access. But despite their setup similarities, portal access and individual site access are two separate beasts where access is concerned.

Open Sesame

Before a user can access the portal or a site within the portal, you have to grant him or her permission to the portal or site. Permissions determine what a user can and can't do on the portal or site. Examples of permissions include

- ✔ **View Area:** The user can view an area (a page on the portal) and its contents.
- ✔ **Create Area:** The user can add a new page to the portal.
- ✔ **View Items:** The user can view content in lists, libraries, and discussion boards.

SharePoint has dozens of individual permissions. You *could* assign these permissions manually to individual users, but you'd have dozens of permissions to consider for each user. Rather than manage all these permissions and users one by one, use these two tools:

✔ **Sites groups:** SharePoint uses this tool to group commonly used permissions. Users assigned to a site group have all the permissions assigned to that site group.

✔ **Domain security groups:** You can assign these groups of users to site groups.

To manage security, you assign groups of permissions (site groups) to groups of users (domain security groups).

Domain security groups are part of Windows Server Active Directory. Active Directory creates and manages user accounts and security groups. You need to coordinate with your network administrator anytime you need groups of users created.

To see the members of domain security groups, browse the Active Directory.

Resist the temptation to create new site groups as a way to group users together. By assigning users directly to site groups, you end up managing your users in two places: Once in SharePoint and once again in Active Directory. When an Active Directory domain group is assigned to a site group, all the members of that domain group receive the site group's permissions. As new users are added to the domain group, they automatically have the permissions of the site group in SharePoint. Save yourself the headache. There's no need to manually add users to SharePoint if you're using domain groups; use site groups to group permissions and domain security groups to group users.

Granting access with site groups

SharePoint consists of the portal and sites connected to the portal. The user must have access granted to the portal and to any individual sites that you want the user to access. Both the portal and its sites use site groups, but the permissions for each site group are slightly different.

Assigning users to a portal site group gives those users access to the portal pages based on the permissions set for the site group. There are six default portal site groups:

✔ **Reader:** Has view-only access to the portal

✔ **Member:** Can add items and use personal Web parts and My Site

✔ **Contributor:** Can edit and delete items and create sites

✔ **Web Designer:** Can change the look and feel of the portal

- ✔ **Content Manager:** Can modify portal pages and add new pages to the portal
- ✔ **Administrator:** Manage permissions and portal configuration

Assigning users to a site group for an individual site gives them access to only that site and its content. The default sites groups for sites are

- ✔ **Reader:** Can view pages and items on the site
- ✔ **Contributor:** Can add, edit, and delete items on the site
- ✔ **Web Designer:** Can change the site's look and feel
- ✔ **Administrator:** Creates subsites and manages site groups

(Hey, I *said* the portal and individual site groups were similar.) The portal uses two additional site groups that the individual sites don't — Member and Content Manager. The portal's member site group provides an interim set of permissions between reader and contributor that is not necessary for sites. A member can access My Site, which is strictly a portal feature. Similarly, a contributor can manage portal pages. The Web designer manages a site's pages.

The following sections explain how you can use these site groups to grant access to your portal and sites.

Providing basic access

At a minimum, you need to provide users with a way of reading the content on your portal or its sites, without giving them the capability to change content.

There are two kinds of basic access for the portal:

- ✔ **Reader:** This site group provides view-only permissions. You should assign Reader access to any nonpersonnel who may access your portal.

    If you have consultants or contractors on your network, assign them to the Reader site group. As Readers, the consultants or contractors can view content on your portal such as a phone directory without having access to contribute content.

- ✔ **Member:** This site group allows the user to create a *personal site* — a personal Web site within the company portal. (See the "Getting personal" sidebar for more information.) Assign all your employees to the Member site group if you want them to have personal sites.

To set up users with basic access to the portal, follow these steps:

1. **Browse to the portal home page as an administrator.**

2. **Select Manage Users from the Actions list in the vertical navigation.**

    The Manage Users screen appears.

Getting personal

Personal Web sites are a special kind of SharePoint site. A personal site, (also referred to as My Site), has many of the same features of regular SharePoint Web sites, but it's designed for an individual to use. A user accesses his or her personal site by clicking the My Site hyperlink in the portal page banner. A user must at least have Member access to create a personal site.

Personal sites have a private and public view. The public view displays the user's profile along with any content that the user wants to share. Readers can access the public view of a user's personal site by searching for the user in the portal. In the site's private view, a member can store files or display hyperlinks that only he or she can view.

 3. **Click Add Users to open the Add Users screen.**

 4. **Click Select users and groups in the Choose Users section.**

    A dialog box appears.

 5. **Search for a user by entering the user's name in the Starts with text box, clicking the Find button, and then clicking Add.**

    The user's name is added to the list of selected account names on the right of the dialog box, as you can see in Figure 4-1.

 6. **Click OK.**

    Ask your Information Technology (IT) staff or whoever is responsible for maintaining your Active Directory to help you find people in the Active Directory.

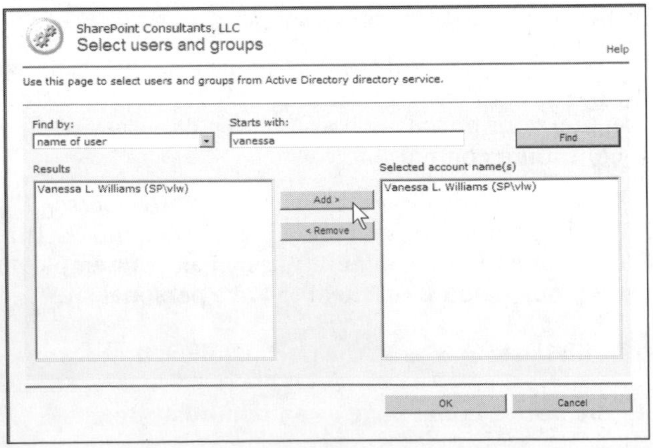

Figure 4-1:
Search for a user and add that person's account to the portal to provide individual access.

SharePoint Consultants, LLC
Select users and groups   Help

Use this page to select users and groups from Active Directory directory service.

Find by: Starts with:
name of user   vanessa   Find

Results   Selected account name(s)
Vanessa L. Williams (SP\vlw)   Vanessa L. Williams (SP\vlw)
                          Add >
                          < Remove

                                     OK   Cancel

7. **Add the user to the site group that you want.**

   The access that you give the user depends on whether the user needs a *personal site:*

   - Choose Reader if the user shouldn't have a personal site.

   - Choose Member if the user needs a personal site.

8. **Click Next, as Figure 4-2 shows you.**

9. **Send the user an e-mail using the e-mail template provided to notify him or her that you have given him or her access.**

10. **Click Finish.**

An individual site that connects to the portal can have two kinds of basic access:

- **Reader:** A reader has view-only access to the site.

- **Contributor:** A contributor can contribute content to a site but can't modify the site's structure. Because sites exist almost exclusively for collaboration, basic site access for most users requires them to be contributors. Otherwise why have the site?

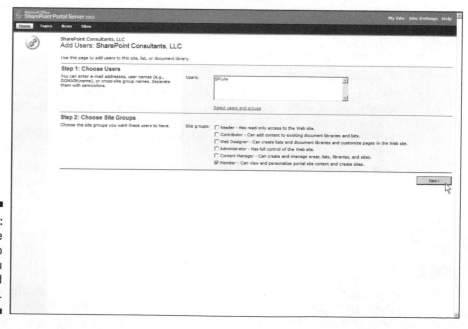

Figure 4-2:
Select the site group to which you want to add this user.

To grant a user basic access to an individual site, follow these steps:

1. **Browse to the site as an administrator.**

2. **Click Site Settings.**

3. **Click Manage Users.**

4. **Click Add Users.**

   The Add Users page for the site appears.

5. **Enter the user that you want to grant access and click the check mark next to the Contributor site group.**

   You can either enter the user's e-mail address or click the Address Book button to select the user from your Outlook address book.

6. **Click Next.**

7. **Send the user an e-mail message by using the e-mail template displayed on the Add Users page.**

   You can add a personalized message welcoming him or her to the site.

8. **Click Finish.**

Always try to assign domain security groups rather than individual users to a site group. This example shows you how to assign individual users. In the section "Site Groups in Action" (later in this chapter), I show you how to use domain groups.

Keeping it current

You have to add, archive, and secure portal and site content. In short, you have to manage it if you want to keep your portal and sites current.

At the portal level, there are two site groups for managing content:

- ✓ **Content Manager:** Can manage content submission requests, archive content, and change the existing structure by adding and editing pages

- ✓ **Web Designer:** Manages the look and feel of the portal

In professional Web development, the look and feel is called the *Presentation Layer.* Someone with skills in graphical and user-interface design usually manages it.

The content manager is usually a member of the business community, and the Web designer is likely a member of the technical staff. Because the business community is more knowledgeable about content, they should take ownership for content management. Web design requires technical skills so it should reside in the technical domain.

The portal's individual sites use a Web designer site group (rather than the content manager) to manage their content. Like a portal Web designer, the site Web designer can also modify the site's structure. A site's Web designer will probably be a member of the team that's using the site. He or she will manage content and the structure of how the site is laid out as well. Unless the site has high visibility in the company, it's not feasible to have your technical staff be responsible for site's Web design.

Most of the examples in this book require you to be at least a member of the Web designer site group.

Chances are that you're mostly concerned with Web design for the portal, not the individual sites. Your portal's Web designer can create templates that keep your site layouts consistent with your portal. Otherwise a site's members can choose a Web designer among themselves.

Special site groups

You can change the permissions for all the site groups discussed so far. (For more about editing existing site group permissions and adding new site groups, see the section "Site Groups in Action" later in this chapter.) Two special site groups have permissions that you can't modify — Guest and Administrator.

Be my guest

You can use SharePoint to assign a user access to a single content item, thereby overriding the entire site group structure. Well, not really. SharePoint creates a special site group called Guest to manage these special one-of-a-kind scenarios. When a user is assigned permission to access a specific item on a site, such as a tasks lists, SharePoint automatically adds that user to the Guest site group. SharePoint automatically removes the user from the Guest site group when the user's permission to access the site item is removed by the site's administrator.

You can't modify permissions for the guest site group.

To see the guest site group in action, follow these steps:

1. **Browse to a site in your portal as the site's administrator.**

   If you created the team site in Chapter 3, use that site. Otherwise use any team site on your portal to which you have administrative access.

2. **Click Shared Documents from the Quick Launch bar at the left of the screen.**

3. **Click Modify settings and columns.**

   The Customize Shared Documents screen appears.

4. **Click Change permissions for this document library.**

5. **Click Add Users.**

6. **Add a user to the document library by entering the user's e-mail address or by clicking the Address Book button to choose the name from the Outlook address book.**

7. **Grant the new user permissions to view the site by selecting the radio button next to View items.**

8. **Click Next.**

9. **In the Send E-mail section of the Add Users screen, enter a personalized e-mail message to send to the user.**

10. **Click Finish.**

You now have a user who has access to one item on your site. To view the guest site group, follow these steps:

1. **Click Site Settings.**

2. **Click Manage Users.**

   The user you added appears as a member of the Guest site group, as Figure 4-3 shows you.

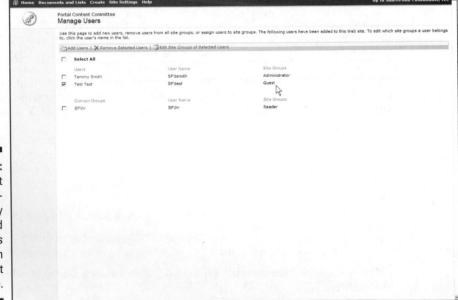

Figure 4-3:
SharePoint automatically adds and removes users from the guest site group.

To revoke a guest user's permissions, delete that user from the Manage Users screen. You don't need to remove their individual permissions because their permissions are removed when the account is deleted. (Aren't site groups cool?)

Administrator accounts

Administrators can do anything to a portal. The administrator site group can't be deleted and must always have at least one member.

To manage the administrator site group, follow these steps:

1. **Browse to the portal as an administrator.**
2. **Click Site Settings in the upper-right corner of the screen.**
3. **Click Go to SharePoint Portal Server central administration.**

   You can also access SharePoint Portal Server central administration by clicking Start⇨All Programs ⇨Administrative Tools on the computer where SharePoint is installed.

4. **In the Security Configuration section, click Set SharePoint administrative group account.**
5. **In the Group Account Name text box, enter the domain group responsible for SharePoint administration in the form domain\name.**

   For example, if the domain name is `MyDomain` and the SharePoint administrator domain group name is `SPAdmins`, type **MyDomain\SPAdmins** in the Group Account Name text box.

6. **Click OK.**

To add a new user as a SharePoint administrator, add that person's username to the domain group in Active Directory that is designated as the SharePoint administrator's group.

When a site is created, SharePoint automatically adds the person who creates the site to the administrator site group for that site. (You *can* add users to the administrator site group of a site by following the same steps in the "Providing basic access" section earlier in the chapter: In Step 5, simply choose Administrator rather than Contributor.)

For more information about administrators, see the accompanying sidebar, "Ghost administrators."

Portal administrators *and* local server administrators have complete access to the portal and all its sites. Know your administrators!

Ghost administrators

The SharePoint environment actually has two kinds of administrators:

- **SharePoint administrators:** These folks can administer SharePoint sites and the portal, but don't have local server access.

- **Local server administrators:** These are the Big Kahunas of the SharePoint environment; they can install Windows SharePoint Services and access SharePoint Central Administration. The local server administrator is usually a member of the Information Technology staff.

Both groups can access and manage all portal and site content. The basic difference between these two levels of administrators is that local server administrators can break more stuff than SharePoint administrators. Make sure your local server administrators have some experience with managing Web servers.

Site Groups in Action

The combination of site groups and domain security groups simplifies managing access to your portal and its sites. You have various ways to use this security model effectively:

- **Assign Active Directory groups to the site groups.** Don't assign individual users to the site groups unless absolutely necessary. Managing security for your portal and site will get complicated and overwhelming if you try to manage security for each individual user.

- **Take advantage of security inheritance.** With security inheritance, a subpage can inherit the security settings of its parent page. For example, if you assign your site group access at the Home page level and let the pages below the Home page (such as Topics, Sites, and News) inherit, you won't have to manage permissions for each of those subpages. This is SharePoint's default behavior. Assign permissions only to sensitive pages (say, a Financial page).

- **Add the domain group-authenticated users to the Readers site group.** This strategy is especially good for using site groups — this setting gives anyone who can log onto your network read-only access to the portal.

- **Add all organizational personnel as members (ideally, by using a domain security group and not by adding each user individually).** This approach allows all your personnel to have personal pages.

- **Set up departmental-power users as Contributors in the portal.** That way they can suggest departmental content for display on the portal.

✔ **Set up individual site users as Contributors to that specific site.** This allows team members to add content to their team site.

✔ **Create a security group in the Active Directory for SharePoint Administrators.** Assign that group to the portal administrator site group, as required by SharePoint.

✔ **Make sure that your content manager and Web designer work closely together, but be wary of having technical folks involved in content management.** Your technical folks can easily become overwhelmed with the volume of content changes that the business community can demand. Your business content managers, however, may be more realistic about how often to change the content if they have to own those changes.

Implementing site groups

This section gives you some examples for implementing portal and site security by using sites groups and domain security groups. The examples in this section show you how to achieve the strategy described previously.

To add a domain group to the Administrators site group, follow these steps:

1. **Ask your network administrator to create a domain group called SharePoint Admins.**

   Because domain groups are part of Active Directory, you'll need your network administrator or whoever is responsible for maintaining your Active Directory to help you. Have the administrator add your SharePoint administrators to the SharePoint Admins domain group in Active Directory.

2. **Click Site Settings on the SharePoint portal.**

3. **Click Manage Security and Additional Settings.**

4. **In the Users and Permissions section of the screen, click Manage Site Groups, and then click the Administrators site group.**

5. **Click the Add Members button.**

6. **Enter the new SharePoint Admins domain group in the Users text box, as Figure 4-4 shows you.**

   You can also click the Select users and groups link to display a dialog box where you can search for domain accounts. (You can see this dialog box demonstrated in "Providing basic access," earlier in the chapter.)

7. **Click Next.**

8. **Enter a personalized e-mail in the template that is provided.**

9. **Click Finish.**

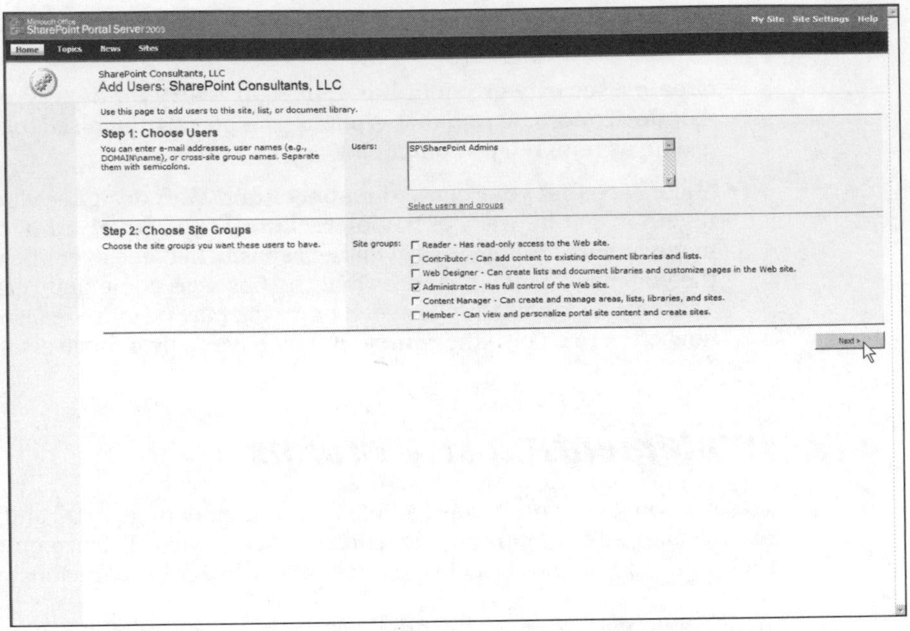

Figure 4-4:
Assign the
SharePoint
Admins
domain
group to
the adminis-
trators site
group.

These steps are very similar to the steps shown in an earlier section
("Providing basic access"), where I show you how to grant access to an individual user. The only real difference is that you are entering a domain group
rather than an individual user. You can repeat these steps to give any domain
group — say, Human Resources — access to the portal.

To give a department (Human Resources, in this example) access to the
portal *and* a departmental site, follow these steps:

1. **Ask IT to create a domain group for HR, if one doesn't already exist.**

2. **Assign the HR domain group to the Members site group on the portal.**

   Follow the same steps listed earlier to add the HR domain group to the
   Members site group.

3. **Create a site for human resources.**

   Creating a site is explained in detail in Chapter 3.

To assign the HR domain group to the contributors site group on the site:

1. **Click Site Settings on the HR team site.**

2. **Click Manage Users.**

3. **Click the Add Users button.**

4. **In the Users text box, enter the HR domain group that your network administrator created.**

   Unfortunately, you can't search the Active Directory when you add users to a site the way you can when you add users to the portal. Instead, you must enter the domain group in the form *domain name\name*. If the domain name is MyDomain and the domain group is HR, then you type **MyDomain\HR**.

5. **Select the check box next to Contributor.**

6. **Enter a personalized e-mail in the e-mail template provided.**

7. **Click Finish.**

Now you have granted contributor permissions to the HR site to all members of the HR domain group. Any time the personnel change in the HR department, the network administrator can make that change in one place — to the HR domain group in Active Directory. You won't have to make any changes to SharePoint because you assigned the entire HR domain group to the Contributor site group, rather than to each individual HR employee. (That's one major headache avoided.)

Working closely with your network administrator — and maintaining that cooperation — saves you from having to manage your users individually.

In addition to the domain groups your network administrator creates, Active Directory provides built-in domain groups. To use built-in domain security groups (in this example, Authenticated Users), follow these steps:

1. **Click Site Settings on the portal.**

2. **Click Manage Users.**

3. **Click Add Users.**

4. **Click Select Users and Groups from the Add Users page.**

5. **In the Select Users and Groups dialog box, click the Find By: drop-down list.**

6. **Select Built-in Accounts from the drop-down list and click Find.**

   A list of the security groups created by default in Active Directory appears.

7. **Choose NT Authority\Authenticated Users.**

8. **Click Add, as Figure 4-5 shows you.**

9. **Click OK to select the built-in group Authenticated Users.**

10. **Choose the Reader site group and click Next.**

11. **Click Finish.**

You have now granted all authenticated network users read-only access to your portal.

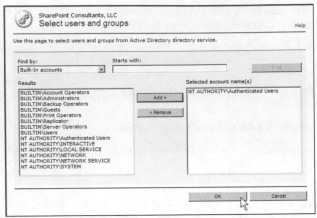

Figure 4-5:
Use the
Select users
dialog box
to select
the built-in
domain
group
authen-
ticated
users.

Authenticated users have access to your portal only. If you want authenti-cated users (or any user) to have access to a specific site, you have to grant them access. (See "Providing basic access," earlier in the chapter, for more information.)

Because you assign the authenticated users to the Reader site group, they can't create personal sites. Users must be members of the Members site group to create personal sites.

Whether or not you already realize it, all the site group assignments made so far rely on SharePoint's use of security inheritance. With security inheritance, when you assign a user or domain group to a site group, they are granted access to the portal or site Home page *and all the pages below;* those sub-pages *inherit* their permissions from the parent page. Using security inheri-tance makes managing permissions very easy.

Sometimes, however, you have to restrict access to a particular area of the portal or site. For example, assume you want to add a new portal page that only executives can view. You don't want that executive page to inherit per-missions from the Home page, because everyone can view the Home page!

To create custom permissions for an Executive page, follow these steps:

1. **Use the portal site map to add a page called Executive under Home.**

   Read more about using the portal site map to add pages in Chapter 3.

2. **Hover your mouse pointer over the new Executive page in the portal site map and click the blue arrow.**

   A drop-down list appears.

3. **Select Manage Security.**

4. **In the Manage Security Settings for Area Executive page, place check marks next to all the site groups.**

   At this point, all the site groups are listed because the portal's home page offers access to all site groups. The executives' page inherited these permissions when it was created. Any user who is assigned to the site groups listed has the permissions associated with that specific site group; it's time to trim those permissions a bit.

5. **Click Remove Permissions.**

6. **Click New User and add the executives domain group.**

   Type the domain group in the Users text box, such as **MyDomain\ Executives**.

7. **Select the radio button next to View listings to grant the Executive domain group access to view the page.**

   You now have a page with custom security settings. Only members of the executive domain group can view and access the page from the portal, as Figure 4-6 shows you.

You may choose to leave your Web designer and Contributor site groups intact for the Executive page if you intend to use the same folks as designers and contributors for the Home page *and* the Executive page. If you want to assign a special person, you can repeat these steps to add that person or domain group. You might want to use a different person any time a page has sensitive information that you don't want your regular content managers and designers to be able to access.

When you've modified the security settings for the Executive page, it no longer inherits permissions from the Home page. To undo your custom settings, click Inherit Permissions from the Parent Area on the Security Settings for Area Executive page.

Assign a content manager by using the Manage Security Settings on the Executive page. The steps are the same.

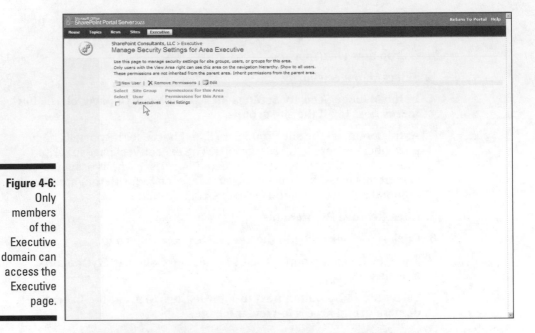

Adding a new site group

With all the options that you have for using the existing site groups, which this chapter does such a fine job explaining, I don't know why you would ever need to add a new site group. But if you insist, just follow these steps to add a site group to the portal:

1. **Browse to the portal as an administrator.**

2. **Click Site Settings.**

3. **Click Manage Security and Additional Settings in the General section of the Site Settings page.**

4. **Click Manage Site Groups.**

5. **Click Add a Site Group.**

6. **Enter a name for the site group in the Site group name text box.**

7. **Select the permissions by selecting the check boxes next to the desired permissions.**

8. **Click OK, as Figure 4-7 shows you.**

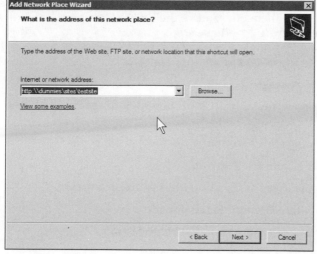

Figure 4-7:
Select the
permissions
that you
want for a
new site
group.

Before you add a new site group, consider whether you need to create either
of these:

- ✔ A new domain security group
- ✔ Custom security access to a special area of the portal (as in the Executive
  example in "Implementing site groups," earlier in this chapter).

To create a new site group in a site, follow these steps:

1. **Browse to the site as the site administrator.**

2. **Click Site Settings.**

3. **Click Go to Site Administration.**

4. **Click Manage Site Groups.**

5. **Click Add a Site Group.**

To add a site group to a portal, follow the steps for adding a new site group
(given earlier in this section), starting at Step 6.

Editing a site group

You may want to seriously contemplate whether you want every Tom, Dick,
and Harry creating sites on your portal. If you want your employees to have

personal sites, they have to be members. But members also can create sites, unless you restrict them. To remove the Create Sites permission from the Members site group, follow these steps:

1. **Browse to the portal as an administrator.**

2. **Click Site Settings.**

3. **Click Manage Security and Additional Settings in the General section on the Site Settings page.**

4. **Click Manage Site Groups.**

5. **Click the Member site group.**

   A list of the users assigned to the site group appears.

6. **Click Edit Site Group Permissions.**

7. **Clear the check mark next to Create Sites.**

8. **Click OK.**

   Now your members no longer have permission to create sites, but they can still create and use the personal site, My Site.

Exploring by Air, Land, or Sea . . .

Or, in the case of SharePoint, by browser, directory, or Windows application. That's right, you have more than one way to use SharePoint.

You can access SharePoint by using a Web browser, probably Internet Explorer. Although you can use other browsers, the reality is that SharePoint is optimized to work with IE, its fellow Microsoft product. Some pages, especially those used by administrators, do not function properly in any browser other than IE.

You can also browse your document libraries in file folders either in Windows File Explorer or the Office 2003 application of your choice. In this section, I introduce you to using SharePoint with Office. See Chapters 8 and 12 for more information about using SharePoint with Office.

You don't need any special access permissions to access SharePoint via folders. When you access SharePoint by using file folders or Office, SharePoint authenticates you in the same way as if you were using Internet Explorer. If you have access to a library or a list by using the browser, you also have access if you're using Office or file folders.

Browsing folders

You can access your document libraries with a feature in Windows called My Network Places.

The folders in My Network Places are called *Web folders* — special file folders that allow you to copy files from your local computer to a Web server (such as SharePoint). To browse your document libraries using Web folders, follow these steps:

1. **Open My Computer.**

2. **Click My Network Places.**

3. **Click Add a Network Place from the Network Tasks task pane on the left of the My Network Places folder.**

   The Add Network Place Wizard appears.

4. **Click Next on the wizard.**

5. **Click Choose Another Network Location.**

6. **Click Next.**

7. **Enter the Web address for a site on your portal in the Internet or network address text box, as Figure 4-8 shows you.**

   To open a site that you normally access through the browser by using the URL `http://dummies/sites/testsite`, enter that URL in the wizard.

8. **Click Next.**

   If you are prompted for a username and password, enter your network username and password. If you are logged into your network, then you should not be prompted.

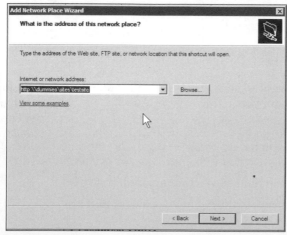

Figure 4-8:
Use the Add a Network Place wizard to browse to your document libraries.

9. **Give your network place a friendly name in the wizard.**

10. **Click Next.**

11. **Click Finish to complete the wizard.**

You can now browse the site, using Windows Folder Explorer like you do with any other directory.

The document library is usually the Shared Documents folder. If you create additional document libraries, you see them listed in the site's folder structure.

If you have problems finding My Network Places or connecting to the site, you can

- **Check with your help desk or whomever it is you call when you need help with your computer or network.** They can help you with this common Windows task.

- **Access the portal by using an application like Word.** The following section leads you through this process.

Using your favorite applications

Using document libraries in a browser like Internet Explorer is painful. You have to open your browser, wait for the page to load, navigate to the library, and find your document. To unleash the power of document libraries, you may want to access them from your favorite Office applications such as Word and Excel. So far, I haven't found any application that can't access my portal's document libraries. Hooray!

To access a document library in Microsoft Word, follow these steps:

1. **Open a Word document (or create one from scratch).**

2. **Click File⇨Save As.**

3. **In the Save As dialog box, click My Network Places at the left of the dialog box.**

4. **Type the address of your site in the File Name box and hit Enter, as Figure 4-9 shows you.**

   If Word can connect to the site, the document library opens.

   Save yourself some time by browsing to the site's home page and then copying and pasting the Web address into the File Name box.

5. **Double-click the Shared Documents folder.**

   Shared Documents is the default document library created when a site is created.

6. **Click Save.**

Saving the Word document connects the creator of the document to the site, creating a link to the document library in My Network Places. The next time you want to save or open a file in this document library, you can use the link in My Network Places, as shown in Figure 4-9.

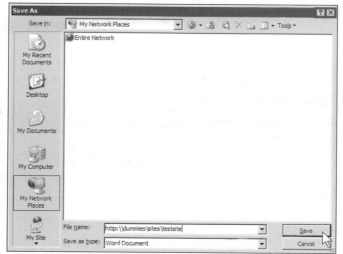

Figure 4-9: Use My Network Places to open a document library in Word.

Importing User Profiles

What's a portal without users? This whole chapter talks about granting users access to the portal and its sites. So you probably want to know how to import user profiles, right?

When you grant access to users in SharePoint, you are actually using the user accounts in Active Directory. For your users to have a presence in SharePoint, each one needs a *user profile* that stores attributes such as

- ✔ The user's name and office phone number
- ✔ The user's picture
- ✔ To whom the user reports

A user's profile appears on the public view of the user's personal site. By creating a user profile, you (or anyone else looking) can find the user in a search.

Instead of adding each user's profile individually, SharePoint enables you to import the user profile data from Active Directory (AD). If you have accurate AD profiles, then you have rich user profiles full of accurate information about your employees. Otherwise you may need to clean up your AD profiles.

Take the time to clean up your AD profiles. The AD profiles can give you a great source of original entry for all your profile information (ideally at the time of hire). By maintaining accurate profiles in AD, you won't have to clean up or completely re-enter profile data in SharePoint. You can just reuse your AD profiles.

To schedule user-profile imports, follow these steps:

1. **Browse to the portal as an administrator.**

2. **Click Site Settings.**

3. **On the Site Settings page, click Manage Profile Database in the bottom section of the page (labeled User Profile, Audiences, and Personal Sites).**

4. **Click Configure Profile Import.**

5. **Accept the default entries for Source Account and Access Account on the Profile Import screen.**

6. **Click the check mark next to Schedule Full Import.**

7. **Specify a schedule by using the controls on the screen or accept the default.**

8. **Click OK.**

   Your user profile information now imports from your Active Directory at the time that you specify. Check back to the Manage Profile Database page to view the import log.

Ask your network administrator for help with this task if you get stuck. He or she can answer your Active Directory questions.

In addition to scheduling your user profile import, you can also use the Manage Profile Database page to

✔ Add and view user profiles.

✔ Add and view user profile properties.

Part III
Portal Design

The 5th Wave   By Rich Tennant

"We need to pimp our storage system."

In this part . . .

1 show you how to match SharePoint to your business. You'll evaluate SharePoint and start building your project team. I help you make your business case and identify candidate projects.

You get the story on how to pick good content for your portal and how to drive people to your portal (no pointed sticks necessary). The content on your portal will be fresh and on-target after you read and apply this part.

As a bonus, you get pointers on making the portal your own with branding options, changes in the color scheme, and the appropriate uses of your company logo.

Chapter 5

Matching SharePoint to Your Business

*I*mplementing SharePoint isn't a trivial matter. Working through the exercises in this chapter can help you determine how ready your company is for SharePoint. And if you decide that your company can use SharePoint, this chapter gives you the tools that you need to convince management, IT, and end users that SharePoint is worth taking a bet on.

How Your Business Shares Information

Your company probably processes information by using expensive software and databases. Some technical department dictates what fancy software the departments have to use, but most departments do the real number crunching and decision making with spreadsheets and small database applications, like Microsoft Access. Everyone usually keeps information like policies and letters in Word documents in a file share somewhere on the network. Sending an e-mail attachment is as close to electronic collaboration as your company gets.

Before you can decide whether SharePoint is right for your company, you have to first understand your information systems and collaboration environment. To know what setup you have to work with, check out the following:

✔ The formal information repositories managed by the internal technical departments such as Information Technology and Information Systems

✔ The informal tools that fall outside the domain of the formal IT/IS infrastructure that employees use a lot

✔ The various ways that people in your company use your IT/IS infrastructure to communicate with each other

✔ The ways in which teams, projects, and meetings use (or can use) your infrastructure

In this chapter, I show you how to check your environment for these elements. By assigning numeric values to your results and plotting them on a graph, you can identify how many projects you have waiting for SharePoint.

Because an information systems environment is more than just hardware and software, you have to also survey your organization. By examining your organization's values and structure, you can determine whether your company can make good use of SharePoint.

Knowing your formal from your informal systems

Information systems come in all kinds of flavors. You can focus on the two classifications of formal and informal information systems. (And no, formal systems don't wear tuxedos and informal systems don't sport Bermuda shorts.)

Formal systems are

✔ Official systems that the IT department supports and manages.

✔ Sometimes called *enterprise systems*.

Examples of formal systems include accounting systems and e-mail software.

Informal systems are

✔ Unofficial systems that IT may support on an as-needed basis.

✔ Usually departmental solutions that someone outside of the IT department creates.

✔ Often the bane of technical support personnel.

✔ Solutions that contain information that you can't easily store in databases, like Word documents and images.

Examples of informal systems include spreadsheets (especially shared), departmental software, and third-party Web sites.

So why does your IT manager care if you use a spreadsheet for tracking how many times your boss ticks you off? Because employees always end up having to ask support personnel to rescue an errant formula or restore a

Word file to a previous version. Support personnel don't hate spreadsheets, but these informal systems can really create a lot of support nightmares. Besides, loads of money and planning go into implementing fancy software (and renting tuxedos, too).

Information systems, formal and informal: Pros and cons

Your IT staff probably tackles informal tools one at a time, as problems in need of solutions bubble up to the surface. When a departmental spreadsheet gets overwhelmed, the department manager often asks IT to take these informal tools and bring them into the formal infrastructure. For example, IT may have to

- Convert spreadsheets into custom Web sites.
- Move Access databases to SQL Server databases.
- Change manual forms into Word documents that users route as attachments via e-mail.

Even so, formal systems aren't necessarily better than informal systems. Each kind of system has its own advantages and disadvantages. Here's a rundown:

- **Advantages of formal systems:**
  - You can budget, schedule, and otherwise control the system.
  - You can base your assignment of resources on a project's priority to the company.
  - You can verify and validate the system.
  - You can back up data.
- **Disadvantages of formal systems:**
  - The system's controlling processes create overhead.
  - Implementation is often a lengthy, time-consuming, and bureaucratic process.
  - Priorities and politics often conflict.

If you take an equally close look at informal systems, here's what you see:

- **Advantages of informal systems:**
  - Anyone can start one.
  - Usually they have low overhead and are simpler to create and use.
  - Informality encourages self-sufficiency.
  - They capture departmental data requirements because they're created by the people who use them.
  - You don't have to worry about third-party scrutiny or prioritizing.
  - They can store information that formal databases can't easily store.

✔ **Disadvantages of informal systems:**

- They may not be on IT's radar so they can easily be neglected.

- They can get complicated very quickly.

- They're difficult to back up and restore.

- They can create unexpected support requirements for IT.

- They may not conform to enterprise standards and data requirements.

- They often store redundant data.

- They're disconnected from the overall information-systems strategy.

SharePoint nicely strikes a balance between formal and informal systems. With SharePoint, you don't need to keep everything under tight control and

A greeting-card mailing list

Say that the executive secretary keeps a mailing list for sending holiday cards in a Word document. The customer service department also has a list, but they keep their list in a spreadsheet. What happens when a new manager decides to consolidate these lists? Some poor soul has to go through each record in the Word document *manually* and compare it to the spreadsheet to eliminate duplicates and merge the data. What a mess! The executive secretary's list is probably set up as mailing labels, each complete with name, address, and zip code — but customer service has separate cells for each name, street address, and zip code in the spreadsheet.

You can implement a single mailing list in SharePoint like this:

✔ Create a single list where each user maintains his or her own records.

✔ Create two separate views of the list, one showing the customers for the executive secretary and another showing the customers for customer service.

✔ Create a second list that links to the first list and allows the executive secretary or members of customer service to enter a record showing that a greeting card was mailed and whether the post office returned it. You can mark addresses as expired when you need to, and you can enter new addresses. SharePoint captures the name of the user who enters each record, so it's easy to find a customer's owner if you need to resolve a duplicate entry.

✔ Down the road — after your employees get accustomed to using SharePoint and you become a SharePoint whiz yourself, you can link the lists to the customer database so that you don't have to manually enter the addresses.

By using SharePoint to manage the mailing list, everyone works off the same list, but they can each look at it their own way. Also, all the records conform to the data entry standards that the list's owner establishes when he or she creates the list. And a common SQL database stores the list, where the list is backed up on a nightly basis. But here's the best part — you don't have to have IT involved at all. Any user with the right permissions can create lists and views.

place everything under the very best practices. Sometimes you just need to get something done. SharePoint can help you with these quick-and-dirty solutions, but it captures those solutions in a common repository that IT can easily monitor. When you need to extend that quick-and-dirty solution beyond the confines of one department, IT already has the basic information that they can use to get started. And because SharePoint uses Microsoft SQL Server, a database already stores the data where you (or your IT staff) can use SharePoint's tools to easily get access to your data.

SharePoint can create a central repository for all of your business's fractured information resources. With SharePoint, you can have your cake and eat it, too: You get access to the positives of a formal repository without creating a stifling, rigid information environment. The accompanying sidebar "A greeting-card mailing list" provides an example.

Spotting your company's formal and informal systems

Use the checklists in the following sections to identify candidate projects — both formal and informal — that may benefit from implementing SharePoint.

Formal systems checklist

You can easily identify formal systems: Most of the company's IT resources flow into them. Here's how to spot them in their natural habitat:

- ✔ Look at the current and future technology and systems budgets. Identify the systems that IT has scheduled for upgrades or implementation. Also check for annual maintenance contracts — formal systems almost always have maintenance contracts.

- ✔ Ask systems and database administrators what systems they're responsible for maintaining. Sometimes managers only remember the bigger systems or the ones that go down the most frequently.

- ✔ Identify all the systems and databases that IT backs up.

- ✔ Ask help-desk support personnel what formal systems they support.

Informal systems checklist

Informal systems typically fly under IT's radar. Conduct a survey of the informal systems that each department uses:

- ✔ Ask help-desk support personnel about all the unofficial tools end users ask them about on a daily basis. They probably know many of them off the top of their heads.

- ✔ Ask users to review their e-mails for attached files. Often these e-mails and their attached files provide clues about how departments are using e-mail to share information.

- ✔ Identify the types of tools that departments use — spreadsheets, Access databases, Word documents, and so on.

✔ Find out the name of and location where the department stores the informal system.

✔ Find out whether users share the informal system. Don't be surprised to find (for example) a homegrown spreadsheet that multiple employees access on a daily basis.

✔ If users share the system, find out whether they share it within the department, with other departments, or outside the company. (Get names for everyone the users share with outside the department.)

✔ Find out how often the department uses the system.

✔ Ask whether the system is confidential or sensitive.

✔ Ask about departmental software that IT may not know about, like banking and communications software. Usually an accounting or payroll department will use banking software to make direct deposits and sweep money out of bank accounts.

✔ Ask about third-party Web sites. Divide those sites into categories such as government, trade association, business partners, and competitors. Be sure to get the URL for each site. Also ask how frequently employees use each site and whether they view or download information.

✔ Get the names and descriptions of paper-based forms. Attach an example to the survey.

Conduct your survey(s) at a time in the business cycle when employees don't have a billion jobs on their plates. Asking an accounting department to take a survey at the end of a month doesn't make you any friends. However, employees in the accounting department do use these tools at month's end. For this reason, think about conducting a follow-up survey either during or immediately following their busy time. You may want to allow up to six weeks for a department to finalize their surveys. If you rush your survey subjects, you risk missing many tools that people just forgot about because they only use them during a certain time in the business cycle.

After you complete the survey of your formal and informal systems, you have a better picture of how the people in your company are using these kinds of systems. Everything you identified as an informal system is a candidate for moving to SharePoint. Don't be surprised to find a few formal systems that you can eliminate by using SharePoint instead.

Going beyond e-mail

Every company has a bunch of policies and procedures that it needs to communicate to its employees. You want to celebrate and share news of new hires, new babies, and new jobs. You also share form templates, company logos, licensing images, and pictures from the company holiday party.

Think about how your company shares this information. No, don't tell me — let me guess . . . e-mail! When a procedure changes, you send out an e-mail. When someone has a new baby, you send out an e-mail.

E-mail gives you great opportunities to communicate, but most companies overuse and abuse it. Here are a couple of e-mail's many advantages:

- ✔ Quick and easy use
- ✔ Low overhead

Now, think about these disadvantages:

- ✔ Anyone can send e-mail.
- ✔ You easily overuse it.
- ✔ E-mail can bring some nasty worms and viruses into your company's e-mail system.
- ✔ You can't easily archive e-mails in a useful way.

SharePoint to the rescue! Imagine being able to store these various documents and images in a safe, secure repository where only the people who need to update the documents can and only the people who need to view them do. You can communicate and archive all that news in a consistent manner.

Complete this checklist to identify the kind of communications that your company uses:

- ✔ Identify departments that issue policies and procedures. These departments probably include human resources, administration, accounting, and operations. Try to get electronic or hard copy samples of their communications with employees.
- ✔ Figure out what approval protocols Human Resources uses to get employees to actually use new policies and procedures.
- ✔ Look in your e-mail inbox. See who sends you all those communications in the first place.
- ✔ Divide up communications based on whether they're version-controlled documents or files, one-off files, or some kind of announcement or message.

  ✔ Figure out how often these departments send a communication or make a change to a policy.

  ✔ Identify the audience who receives each communication.

  ✔ If your company has a public relations or marketing department, ask about press releases and product promotions.

Hold on to this communications checklist and refer to it as you work through the examples in this book. The departments creating these communications may become members of your content management team.

Everyone working together

You need to figure out how much collaboration goes on in your company. You want to find out how often (and how well) people work together in teams or on projects. Any time two or more people pass a document between themselves, you have collaboration.

To find examples of collaboration in your company, look for these characteristics:

  ✔ Any task forces, projects, or teams

  ✔ Frequent or regularly repeated meetings

  ✔ Product lines, service areas, sales territories, or other criteria that group people together for a common goal

  ✔ Business processes that require document workflow, such as submitting expense reports

Figure out the who, what, when, where, why, and how frequent for the items in this list. The groups you identify here could make good use of SharePoint's site templates for teams, meeting workspaces, and document workspaces.

Diving into the personal side of your office

Your company's information systems and collaboration environment don't exist in a vacuum. You also have to take into account office politics, cliques, gossip, and sometimes hair pulling and eye scratching. (Or, wait, was that the episode of *Jerry Springer* I watched last night?)

If you work in an office for any length of time, then you know what I mean. Remember that SharePoint is a collaboration tool — collaboration, as in, people working together. Before you can justify implementing any collaboration tool, you have to take an honest look at politics, power, and culture in your company:

- ✔ **How does your company handle hiring, promotions, and training?** Do employees have the skills that they need to perform their day-to-day jobs? If your company hires anyone with a pulse, you may need to do some training before you ever get started with SharePoint.

- ✔ **How professional is your organization?** A large number of professionals who all have a lot of letters after their names may mean that you have a nice brain trust. You need to find out how invested they are in your company — and in a project such as SharePoint.

- ✔ **Does your company set its wages at, above, or below the market average?** If everyone in your company is overworked and underpaid, then you have an uphill battle to get those folks working together. Threats and coercion don't lend themselves well to collaboration.

- ✔ **How long have employees worked at their current jobs?** Don't assume that the longer they've been there, the better. Long-timers may be turf oriented and stuck in their ways.

- ✔ **Is your company privately owned, family owned, or a public company?** The answer to that question has a bearing on how involved the owners and executives are — and you'll also want to know that.

- ✔ **How does your company structure incentives?** Do your incentives encourage teamwork and cooperation or backstabbing and cutthroat behavior?

- ✔ **Does the executive team have visible power struggles?** If so, look into your crystal ball and predict which executive will likely prevail — *before* picking him or her to sponsor your project.

- ✔ **What is your company's commitment to technology?** Are your systems constantly going down?

Take a look at the physical structure of your company:

- ✔ **Do your employees have access to computers?** It also makes a difference whether the computers are standalone or networked.

- ✔ **What are the different kinds of computers used in the company?** For example, identify how many desktops, laptops, handhelds, or other size computers employees use.

- ✔ **What kind of software do you use?** For example, are you primarily a Microsoft shop, or are you strictly open-source?

> ✔ **How many of your employees are permanent, temporary, full time, and part time?** You can have a real problem creating excitement among temporary workers.
>
> ✔ **What is the geographic makeup of your company?** Are people in different time zones?

The questions in the preceding lists help you figure out whether your company's environment can support SharePoint. If some of these questions make you think twice, don't despair — you may still make SharePoint work for your company. You just need to identify problem areas in advance — and be prepared to deal with them. Whatever you do, don't make the mistake of assuming that implementing a software product can solve "people problems" in your company.

What Projects Does Your Business Need?

You can use SharePoint in a number of ways. The following list shows you a few of those uses. (And each use includes a chapter reference where you can find out more about it.)

> ✔ Convert spreadsheets and Access databases to custom lists (Chapter 10)
>
> ✔ Convert paper-based forms and Word forms to InfoPath forms or custom lists (Chapter 12)
>
> ✔ Place hyperlinks to third-party Web sites in a central location (Chapter 3)
>
> ✔ Make third-party Web sites searchable (Chapter 11)
>
> ✔ Create a custom Web page that groups together the lists, forms, and Web sites that you need to complete a business process (Chapter 12)
>
> ✔ Use the version-control features of a document library to make sure you have all public views of policies and procedures up-to-date (Chapter 9)
>
> ✔ Organize information by product line, sales territory, or business process (Chapter 11)
>
> ✔ Use e-mail alerts to tell users when you update information (Chapter 10)
>
> ✔ Set up a meeting workspace so that users can store meeting agendas, minutes, and other related documents (Chapter 8)
>
> ✔ Store training and installation documents for a formal system or a business process in a document library (Chapter 9)

You need some rhyme or reason for deciding how to tackle these projects. Using the answers you get from the questions in preceding sections of this chapter, you can assign levels of difficulty, prioritize your projects, and determine your return on investment.

Rating your project ideas

To determine which projects to tackle and how to make your business case for implementing SharePoint, create a spreadsheet that contains the following information (which you collect in the "How Your Business Shares Information" section in this chapter):

- ✔ List all the tools, software, communications, and collaboration efforts that you discover in the spreadsheet.

- ✔ Categorize these elements of your information and collaboration environment according to whether one department uses them, departments share them, or departments share them with third parties.

- ✔ Assign a number to each of these categories, with more difficult to implement categories having a higher number. For example, assign tools shared with third parties a higher number because you will probably have more difficulty implementing them.

- ✔ Assign extra points if a tool is time sensitive or confidential.

- ✔ Assign points based on the kind of tool that you currently use for a given solution — spreadsheet, Word document, Web site, manual form, or e-mail.

- ✔ Be subjective. Assign points based on your assessment. If something looks hard, it probably is.

Add all the points together for each row and sort in ascending order. You can easily implement those solutions with the lower scores first.

Figuring out which projects will give you the least trouble

For each item that you list on the consolidated spreadsheet that you create in "Rating your project ideas" section earlier in this chapter, list the feature in SharePoint that you can use to implement that item. If you don't know the SharePoint feature or level of difficulty, then make your best guess. Anyone with some IT/IS experience can help you out. Then, using Table 5-1, mark the feature's level of difficulty. Use the numeric values so you can sort the features more easily.

Table 5-1	Task Difficulty	
Feature	*Level of Difficulty*	*Numeric Value*
Custom List	Medium	20
Custom Web page	Medium	20
Document Library	Low	10
Indexing	High	30
InfoPath	High	30
Links	Low	10
Team Site	Medium	20

Sort the assessment in ascending order by the level of complexity (the tool's total point value you calculate in the preceding section) and in ascending order by the level of difficulty. You can now see the least complex projects that you can most easily implement at the top of the list.

Finding projects that give back

As with any business decision, you have to consider the return on investment for implementing SharePoint. Sure, you can easily create a custom list to manage the names of the owner's pet snakes. But if no one ever uses the list, then why bother? And if you tackle all the hard projects first, you can quickly overwhelm your company's resources.

Before making your decision, add another column to the spreadsheet that you create in the section "Rating your project ideas," earlier in this chapter, and label it "ROI" (for Return on Investment). When deciding the return on a given task, consider the following:

✔ **Influence of people affected:** If a given feature affects an influential person, you can get some powerful support on your side. Unless, of course, that person tends to influence your business in a negative way.

✔ **Number of people affected:** If this feature only benefits a few people, you may not have a very large return. However, if it affects the entire organization, you have real problems if something goes wrong.

✔ **Profile of change:** A high-profile implementation usually means a higher return, but not without higher risk.

When considering return, think of the return to the department that uses SharePoint, the organization as a whole, and the SharePoint implementation project. Early in the project, you may want to select tasks that reflect positively on the project, even if they don't give a very high return to the organization.

After assigning ROI to the tasks, plot them on a graph. The graph just provides a quick visual representation of which projects you should tackle.

Now that you've plotted tasks, use the graph to help you pick your implementation strategy:

- **Quadrant I:** Low risk, high returns. Implement one or two projects from this quadrant and increase your star power.
- **Quadrant II:** Low risk, low returns. You can test the waters with this low-hanging fruit. Implement several of these tasks so the returns pile up.
- **Quadrant III:** High risk, low returns. Why bother?
- **Quadrant IV:** High risk, high returns. You're betting the farm with these projects.

Building an Implementation Team

If your organization has already installed SharePoint, then you know that installing it isn't the same as implementing it. Because SharePoint is a software product, many organizations make the mistake of leaving the whole shebang to the realm of IT. SharePoint is a collaboration tool — consider it a red flag if nobody in your company wants to collaborate on its implementation. A collaboration tool needs teamwork to really succeed; it's not a one-man show.

The many phases of SharePoint

A SharePoint implementation has many phases in its life cycle. Typical IT projects include phases for planning, installation, testing, and maintenance. Although a SharePoint project has all these steps, you have to also consider the entire product life cycle, including day-to-day use and how you may retire the product five years down the road.

Table 5-2 outlines the phases of a typical SharePoint project and lists some activities that usually occur in each phase. As you move from left to right in this table, both your implementation and the SharePoint product itself mature.

Table 5-2		SharePoint Project Phases		
Planning	*Implementing*	*Operational*	*Transition*	*Retirement*
Selling the idea	Installing software and hardware	Administration	Upgrades to software	Planning for a replacement product
Building a team	Building the portal and adding content	Maintenance	Adding hardware	Starting over at the planning phase
Identifying content sources	Training	Support	Evaluating software	
Determining hardware and software requirements	Testing	Training		
Budgeting		Content management		
		Archival		

You need people with different skills for each of the phases in Table 5-2. To assemble a good team, first take into consideration the many skills that you need:

- ✔ **Content Experts:** Your functional departments — such as human resources, public relations, and other operational and support departments — should drive most of your content.

- ✔ **Creative:** You need people to plan the look and feel of the site, way beyond just logo placement.

- ✔ **Data:** You need a database administrator who understands SQL Server, a systems analyst to elicit and analyze requirements, and programmers to create advanced solutions.

- ✔ **Editorial:** You need someone to edit, index, categorize, and eventually archive all that content. You may also need writers who can convert your company's print-based communications to material suitable for viewing in a Web browser.

- **Legal:** Every project needs lawyers! Seriously, you need help drawing up policies, privacy statements, and terms-of-use agreements.

- **Management:** You need a project manager to manage the schedule and define milestones for the project. Oh, and if you want anyone to give you funding, then consider finding a cheerleader among the executive team.

- **Quality Assurance:** To make sure that everyone plays by the rules, you need to develop and execute test plans, as well as check for compliance with your enterprise's look-and-feel style guides.

- **Technical:** You need specialists in networking and security, as well as people to administer the server hardware and software.

You don't need people with *all* these skills just to get started. In fact, if your project is small enough, you may never need all these skills. For example, you can skip the legal stuff if you know only internal employees use your site. Or, better yet, have your human resources professionals draft the policies.

Finding your company's skill gaps

So you say that you don't have a staff librarian? Although most organizations don't have librarians and editors, you still need the skills that come with those jobs. Don't worry — you don't have to hire someone with the job title "editor," but you do need to define an editorial process. Without someone paying attention to how you organize content and whether that content conforms to portal styles, your portal looks like spaghetti very quickly. Have you ever tried to do a search at a Web site and been frustrated by the number of clicks it takes to find what you're looking for — *if* you ever find it at all? Your site may frustrate users in the same way if you try to blindly add content without thinking about the editorial process.

To identify gaps where you may need additional help, try these suggestions:

- Conduct a skill survey. With the help of Human Resources, identify people in your company who may have writing skills or artistic abilities.

- Check out Table 5-3 to figure out the points in SharePoint's life cycle that call for certain skills.

  Look for people who can do double duty, performing one role early in the project and another later.

Table 5-3		Skill Sets			
Skills	*Planning*	*Implementation*	*Operational*	*Transitional*	*Retirement*
Content Experts	Medium	High	High	Medium	Medium
Creative	Medium	High	Medium	Low	Low
Data	High	High	Medium	Medium	High
Editorial	Medium	High	Medium	Medium	Medium
Legal	Medium	Low	Low	Low	Low
Manage-ment	High	High	Low	Medium	High
Quality Assurance	Medium	High	Low	Low	Medium
Technical	High	High	Low	Medium	High

Your skill gap may look like the Grand Canyon. You may want to outsource some roles, especially if outsourcing prevents your staff from becoming over-whelmed. You can quickly neglect the vast amount of writing and editing that you need to do. You can find many highly skilled freelance writers and edi-tors willing to work for you. Hire one if you can't find the skills that you need in-house.

In a perfect world, software would automatically implement and administrate itself. Unfortunately, the world that you and I live in doesn't even come close to that fantasy. SharePoint is an enterprise-server application; approach it with the same planning and budgeting techniques you use for any server product.

Many companies make the mistake of only budgeting for the hardware and software, assuming that the software somehow magically runs itself. Or, they assume that their existing staff can handle the extra burden of managing one more server.

But SharePoint is a product about people. And people aren't cheap.

Before moving forward with your implementation, take these tips into consideration:

- ✔ Be sure to shop around when outsourcing. Fees from a national consulting firm may be three times higher than a local consulting firm or freelancer.

- ✔ Think about hiring temporary workers or a college intern to help your permanent staff with day-to-day processing tasks. This extra help gives your staff time to do SharePoint project work.

✔ Don't forget about the costs associated with not implementing SharePoint. Choosing not to use SharePoint doesn't necessarily mean that your company saves money. In fact, it may cost you more in the long run to keep all your fractured systems running. Also, if your people can't find the information they need because you don't have it well organized, that wasted time costs you, too.

If your company has a finance department, ask them to compute the net present value (NPV) for this project.

NPV is a financial calculation that determines whether the company can benefit financially from a project. This NPV number tells the finance professional the value of this project in dollars and cents. Many companies use NPV to objectively figure out which projects they want to implement. They can select projects based on each project's relative worth to the company.

I often hear IT professionals say IT projects have no return because those projects don't generate revenue. But even though something doesn't make money, it can still have financial incentive to the company. Although calculating NPV goes beyond the scope of this book, you can easily adapt many of the exercises in this chapter to provide input for NPV calculations.

Putting your team together

Over the years, companies have found out the hard way that large teams don't make for successful projects. Assembling 30 people in a room and throwing them at the task of implementing SharePoint surely leads to mayhem. Instead, you can create a workable hierarchy of teams:

✔ **Core Team:** Your core team is at the top of the hierarchy. This team remains intact throughout the project, ideally throughout the product's life cycle. You want to include a Project Manager, SharePoint Administrator, Content Representative, and Editorial Representative. (You can combine the content and editorial into a single representative.) The core team creates excitement about the project, delegates tasks to subteams, and assigns goals and milestones.

✔ **Technical Team:** In-house and outsourced specialists who deal with the hardware and software issues for SharePoint make up your technical team. They have a lot of work to do in the planning and implementation phases, but their work peters out as you move into the day-to-day operations of SharePoint.

✔ **Content Team:** The content team can start out small during the planning phase. As you move into the implementation and operations phases, you may want to appoint content representatives from each functional department. If you can't appoint that many reps, then at least give each functional area a representative and make sure that functional departments know their representative. The content team can take care of artistic concerns, or you can create a separate team to deal with branding.

✔ **Process Team:** This team defines the project processes that the other teams follow to get their work done. For example, this team defines how the technical team moves software into production. The process team also defines the business and quality assurance processes that your company uses for adding content to the portal after you have it operational.

You may decide to create additional teams, depending on how you want to structure your portal. For example, if you have a large company, you may want to offer advertising space on your portal to offset your costs. You can create a team that looks for ways to use your portal to generate revenue or cut costs.

As you assemble your teams, keep these points in mind:

✔ Keep teams to no more than six people. Your content team is your only exception. Rather than having one large content team, consider breaking it into a hierarchy of teams.

✔ You may have only one person on a team when you first get going.

✔ Be sure to account for double roles that people may fill, but don't overload any one person.

✔ You can outsource, especially your technical and editorial roles. Use internal people to drum up content ideas and define how to add new content.

Building Your Case for SharePoint

After you complete the exercises in this chapter (or do your homework just as thoroughly on your own), you should have a pretty good picture of

✔ **Some candidate projects for SharePoint:** What you need to know here is how much effort it'll take to implement these projects, which human resources are required, and what the business stands to gain.

✔ **What you have now, what you need to get, and where you want to go:** Be sure you know how to structure your team, what it's going to take to keep SharePoint up and running, and what the long-term vision is for the implementation.

The next step is to get your company on board. As you prepare your SharePoint business case, keep the following points in mind:

- **Remember your audiences.** Be ready to present your business case to multiple stakeholders many times over your project's life cycle. You won't just sell SharePoint once. Consider the different perspectives of executive management, operations, technical staff, and end users as you prepare your case. Each of these stakeholders has a different set of criteria with which they evaluate this project.

- **Get buy-in.** If you know ahead of time that a particular individual or department will be a roadblock, court them early and often. If possible, get them to take a stake early in the planning phases, and don't let people or departments drop out of this process at any time.

- **Know your politics.** Be aware of the formal and informal power structures in your company. If you think that politics may hinder your project's success, consider outsourcing your project-manager role. A third party can much more easily point out problems to management than an employee can.

- **It's all about business value.** You have to show your stakeholders how this project adds value to the business. Again, remember your audience. To executive management, business value often means financial return. Operations may see value as a tool that streamlines business processes, while a line worker may like SharePoint because he or she perceives it as easier to use than Word or Excel.

Finally, you may very well come to the conclusion that your organization just isn't ready for SharePoint. If you work through the exercises in this chapter and get little or no cooperation anywhere in your company, then that's a red flag — especially if your company expects to command SharePoint from the top down. Tell the company not to throw its money away. Instead, submit a plan for what your company needs to do be better prepared for implementing SharePoint. Then offer to quit your job, become a management consultant, and ask for big bucks to implement the plan for your company. (Okay, just kidding there. I think.)

Chapter 6

Managing Portal Content

Your SharePoint portal site is the hub of your SharePoint implementation. You use sites connected to the portal site for team collaboration — and for executing business processes efficiently — but the portal site tells people how to get to where they want to go.

The portal is the directory; the site is the destination.

The Content Is the Message

You need a lot of content planning and management to get your SharePoint portal up and running. Without good content on your sites and an easy way to get to those sites from your portal, your portal is dead in the water.

Your portal content can come from anywhere, not just your SharePoint sites. A good portion of your content probably comes from inside your own business, but it can also come from

- ✔ Competitors' Web sites
- ✔ Government Web sites
- ✔ Industry associations
- ✔ News sources
- ✔ Services, such as marketing-research tools, to which your company subscribes

In Chapter 11, you can find out how to display content from around the Web on your SharePoint site.

Knowing what content you want

Regardless of your content sources, you need some kind of litmus test to determine whether you want to use the content on your portal. As with any good resource, you want the content on your portal to be

- ✔ **Accurate:** Bad information ruins your portal's credibility.
- ✔ **Interesting:** Humdrum content doesn't attract your employees.
- ✔ **Relevant:** Cluttering the page with useless information turns employees off.
- ✔ **Timely:** Stale information makes you look lazy.
- ✔ **Unique:** Information that employees can't get elsewhere makes them want to use your portal.

In short, you have to make your portal *useful* to your employees. After all, if they can find all the information on your portal more easily elsewhere in the company, why should they use the portal at all?

Drawing in the crowds

Good content alone can't bring your employees to your portal. Here are some ways to actively promote your portal:

- ✔ **Provide executive sponsorship.** If your executives and management refuse to use the portal, then why is anyone else going to use it?
- ✔ **Create incentives for using the portal.** People do what you reward them for doing. Offer coupons or special offers available only through the portal.
- ✔ **Reference your portal in all your employee communications.** Talk up your portal every chance you get, including in print communications. Be sure that your portal content is consistent with the communications that reference it.
- ✔ **Use the portal for all electronic communications.** Don't use e-mail to attach new policies, forms, or directions to the company picnic. Make users click-through to the portal to get the details of the communication.

Click-through is a term used in Web advertising. When a company places an advertisement on a Web site, it's how they find out the number of times that the ad gets clicked.

Chapter 14 shows you how you can view what pages your employees are viewing in SharePoint.

Not everyone sees self-service as a good thing. Make sure that you evaluate your audiences before moving content to the portal. Your company picnic may be a lonely event if your employees resent using the portal to get directions.

Think about how people access your portal. Chapter 4 covers your access options. If someone calls Human Resources to ask about a form, how does HR tell him or her to access the portal to get the form? A user can access the portal in several ways; HR can tell the user to do any of the following:

- ✔ Go through My Favorites
- ✔ Use the home page on their browser
- ✔ Use a shortcut on the desktop or Start menu
- ✔ Type the URL in the browser address bar
- ✔ Start at the Outlook Today start page
- ✔ Go through the Outlook public folder's home page

Don't assume that everyone acts the same way when told to access the portal Web site. Be prepared for

- ✔ Employees wanting to access the portal in different ways
- ✔ Employees who don't know how to use a Web browser

Your best bet is to pick one way to tell people how to access your portal and be consistent with that message.

See www.microsoft.com/technet/prodtechnol/sppt/reskit/ c4061881x.mspx for more information on setting the home page for either Outlook Today or an Outlook public folder.

Displaying Content on the Portal

A SharePoint implementation has the following two major parts:

- ✔ The portal site
- ✔ All the sites connected to the portal site

The portal site and its connected sites create a hierarchy of sites. You store the majority of your content on individual SharePoint sites, not on the portal site itself, which sits at the top of the hierarchy. The portal provides an entry to the content stored on the sites.

You have three options for displaying site content on your portal:

- **Listings:** These are essentially hyperlinks on steroids.
- **RSS feeds:** This technology is used on the Internet for sharing news headlines. (See Chapter 11 for more information about RSS.)
- **Web parts:** These are Web site building blocks.

You can use these three display options on almost any of the built-in pages on the portal, or you can add custom portal pages (which you can read all about in Chapter 3).

The SharePoint portal and its sites are Web pages. You can use anything you know about building Web pages to add content to SharePoint. For example, in Chapter 11, you can find out how to use Javascript to create a rolling product banner.

Using Web parts

In Chapter 3, you can see how to add and remove Web parts from the portal home page. You do run into one major problem with using Web parts — you can only display Web parts on the portal for content that you actually have stored on the portal site. You probably don't want to store all your content on the portal. You probably have content stored on SharePoint sites that you want to *display* on the portal.

If you follow the examples in this book, you have separate sites for

- Accounting
- Human resources
- Marketing
- Project teams

In order to display this content on your portal, you need other tools besides the standard list and library Web parts. You don't have access to the Web parts for the lists and libraries from sites on the portal, only on the sites where the lists and libraries are stored.

You can, however, use the Page Viewer (the Web part that displays Web pages) to show the content you've stored on your sites. You can see the Page Viewer Web part in action at various places around the book:

✔ Chapter 8 tells you how to use the Save As Web Page feature in Office.

✔ Chapter 9 shows you how to display a slide show in a Web part page.

✔ Chapter 10 shows you how to create an organization chart with Visio, and then save the organization chart as a Web page.

You can display any of the examples in the preceding list in a Page Viewer Web part that you add to a page on the portal.

Showing the world your listings

You can display news and links to your SharePoint site content on your SharePoint portal by using a listing. A listing is a fancy hyperlink that lets you specify

✔ Where SharePoint displays the listing on the portal.

✔ Who can see the listing.

You can create listings directly from a portal page or from the site content that you want to display. Figure 6-1 shows what a listing looks like on the portal.

Figure 6-1:
A portal list-
ing creates
a hyperlink
to the
destination
content.

Check out Chapter 3 to see how to create a listing on the portal. Chapter 9 shows you how to create a listing on the portal when adding site content.

Keeping your syndication simple

You have one display option that's actually not part of SharePoint, but you can use it in Web-site development — Really Simple Syndication, or RSS. Figure 6-2 shows an RSS display for an announcements list. Compare Figure 6-2 with Figure 6-1, which shows the same announcements list as a portal listing.

You use Really Simple Syndication to share content on Web sites. (I cover RSS in more detail in Chapter 11.)

Figure 6-2:
An RSS
display of an
announce-
ments list.

In the RSS feed that Figure 6-2 shows, you can actually see the contents of the announcements list. With the portal listing, you only get a hyperlink to the list. When you need only a hyperlink, use a listing. If you want to display the list's actual contents, RSS is the only way to go.

In Chapter 10, you can find out how to create the announcements lists that you can see in Figure 6-2. You store the list itself on the HR site and have someone in Human Resources maintain the list.

RSS isn't part of SharePoint, so you have to install a few tools to help you use it. RSS has two elements:

✔ You need a tool to create the RSS feed from your site content.

✔ You need a tool called an *RSS viewer* to convert the feed from RSS to HTML so you can view the feed in the Web page.

You call creating a feed *syndication*.

Even if you don't want to create your own RSS feeds based on site content, you probably need an RSS viewer on your site. Having this viewer lets you display feeds from third-party Web sites. (Chapter 11 shows you examples of displaying external Web sites by using RSS.)

Creating feeds

Before you can display the feed, you have to create it. You can use several third-party tools to perform this task, or you can build your own tool. I show you how to use a tool from Bluedog Limited called Syndication Generator.

The Bluedog Syndication Generator takes a list on your site and spits it out as an RSS feed. You can use this generator easily, and it gives you reliable results.

Creating feeds by using the Bluedog tool has four basic steps:

1. **Download the tool.**

2. **Install the tool on your SharePoint server.**

3. **Drop Blue Dog's Syndication Web part on the site where you want to store the content.**

4. **Tell the Syndication Web part for which list you want it to create a feed.**

You can find plenty of RSS generators available on the Internet. I like a generator that you can find on the U2U Web site at

```
www.u2u.net/tools.aspx?T=RSSFeed
```

To download and install the tool from Bluedog, follow these steps:

1. **Download the Syndication Generator from Bluedog Limited onto your SharePoint server from**

   ```
   www.bluedoglimited.com/Downloads/pages/SyndicationGenerator.aspx
   ```

2. **Double-click the `SyndicationGeneratorSetup.exe` file.**

3. **Follow the installation instructions.**

If you accept all the defaults, the tool should install just fine. If you have problems, post a message on the Bluedog Web site asking for help.

To use the Bluedog Syndication Generator on your site, follow these steps:

1. **Navigate to a site on your portal.**

   Choose a site where you have a list or library you want to syndicate using an RSS feed.

2. **Click Modify Shared Page⇨Add Web Parts⇨Browse.**

3. **In the Virtual Server Gallery, drag and drop the Syndication Generator Web part onto the page.**

   See Chapter 3 for more information on adding Web parts.

4. **In the Syndication Generator Web part, click Open the tool pane.**

   A task pane for configuring the Web part appears at the right of the screen.

5. **Enter a title and description for the RSS feed.**

6. **In the Information Link text box, enter a hyperlink that returns the user to the syndicated list.**

   Enter the URL for a list or library that you want to syndicate. When the user clicks on the title for the RSS feed, this URL is used to take the user to the list or library.

7. **Enter an identifier to create the RSS feed.**

   An identifier is a name for the RSS feed. The identifier appears in the URL for the feed. For example, type the identifier **HRNews** for a feed that displays news from the HR announcements list.

8. **Below the Syndicated Lists memo box, click the Browse button.**

   A list of all the lists, libraries, and discussion boards appears.

9. **Double-click the list you want to syndicate from the memo box.**

   This step enters the list into the Syndicated Lists box, as Figure 6-3 shows you.

10. **Click OK to save the configuration.**

    You now have a syndicated list, as you can see in Figure 6-3.

You can create a new Web part page (I named mine `Rssfeeds`) in your site to store all your syndicated lists in one place.

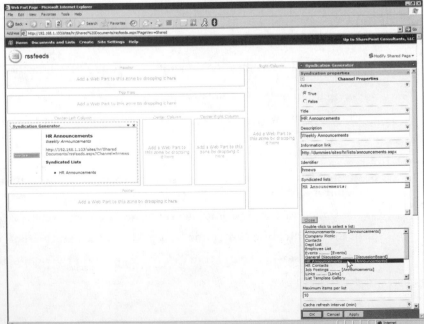

Figure 6-3: Specify the list that you want the RSS generator to syndicate.

The hyperlink in the Syndication Generator Web part displays the RSS feed for the HR Announcements list. Figure 6-3 shows the Syndication Generator Web part with the hyperlink for the syndicated list. Figure 6-4 shows what the RSS feed looks like when you click the hyperlink.

Consuming feeds with help from a Smiling Goat

The feeds that the Syndication Generator creates aren't very user friendly. You need to transform them into a nice list that you can display on the Web. This section shows you how to use a tool from Tim Heuer at Smiling Goat called FeedReader.

In Chapter 11, you can find out how to use another RSS reader from George Tsioko's Web site. You can find readers available all over the Web.

To use the Smiling Goat FeedReader, follow these steps:

1. **Download FeedReader from the Smiling Goat Web site (at www. smilinggoat.net/stuff.aspx) to your SharePoint server.**

2. **Double-click the file that you download in Step 1.**

3. **Follow the instructions in the installation wizard to install FeedReader on your SharePoint server.**

4. **Use SharePoint's command-line tool stsadm to complete the installation.**

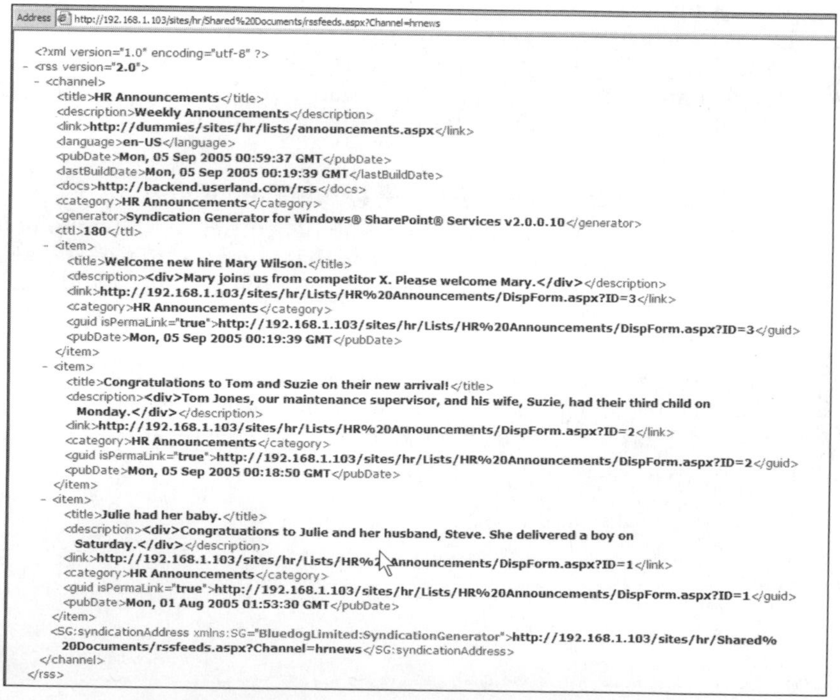

Address http://192.168.1.103/sites/hr/Shared%20Documents/rssfeeds.aspx?Channel=hrnews

```
<?xml version="1.0" encoding="utf-8" ?>
- <rss version="2.0">
  - <channel>
      <title>HR Announcements</title>
      <description>Weekly Announcements</description>
      <link>http://dummies/sites/hr/lists/announcements.aspx</link>
      <language>en-US</language>
      <pubDate>Mon, 05 Sep 2005 00:59:37 GMT</pubDate>
      <lastBuildDate>Mon, 05 Sep 2005 00:19:39 GMT</lastBuildDate>
      <docs>http://backend.userland.com/rss</docs>
      <category>HR Announcements</category>
      <generator>Syndication Generator for Windows® SharePoint® Services v2.0.0.10</generator>
      <ttl>180</ttl>
    - <item>
        <title>Welcome new hire Mary Wilson.</title>
        <description><div>Mary joins us from competitor X. Please welcome Mary.</div></description>
        <link>http://192.168.1.103/sites/hr/Lists/HR%20Announcements/DispForm.aspx?ID=3</link>
        <category>HR Announcements</category>
        <guid isPermaLink="true">http://192.168.1.103/sites/hr/Lists/HR%20Announcements/DispForm.aspx?ID=3</guid>
        <pubDate>Mon, 05 Sep 2005 00:19:39 GMT</pubDate>
      </item>
    - <item>
        <title>Congratulations to Tom and Suzie on their new arrival!</title>
        <description><div>Tom Jones, our maintenance supervisor, and his wife, Suzie, had their third child on
          Monday.</div></description>
        <link>http://192.168.1.103/sites/hr/Lists/HR%20Announcements/DispForm.aspx?ID=2</link>
        <category>HR Announcements</category>
        <guid isPermaLink="true">http://192.168.1.103/sites/hr/Lists/HR%20Announcements/DispForm.aspx?ID=2</guid>
        <pubDate>Mon, 05 Sep 2005 00:18:50 GMT</pubDate>
      </item>
    - <item>
        <title>Julie had her baby.</title>
        <description><div>Congratuations to Julie and her husband, Steve. She delivered a boy on
          Saturday.</div></description>
        <link>http://192.168.1.103/sites/hr/Lists/HR%2Announcements/DispForm.aspx?ID=1</link>
        <category>HR Announcements</category>
        <guid isPermaLink="true">http://192.168.1.103/sites/hr/Lists/HR%20Announcements/DispForm.aspx?ID=1</guid>
        <pubDate>Mon, 01 Aug 2005 01:53:30 GMT</pubDate>
      </item>
      <SG:syndicationAddress xmlns:SG="BluedogLimited:SyndicationGenerator">http://192.168.1.103/sites/hr/Shared%
        20Documents/rssfeeds.aspx?Channel=hrnews</SG:syndicationAddress>
    </channel>
  </rss>
```

Figure 6-4:
The
RSS feed
created
by the
Syndication
Generator.

5. Enter this command on the command line:

```
stsadm.exe -o addwppack -filename "C:\Program
        Files\Smiling
        Goat\FeedReader\smilinggoat.feedreader.cab" -
        globalinstall -force
```

You can find the `stsadm` command-line tool at

```
C:\Program Files\Common Files\Microsoft Shared\web
        server extensions\60\BIN
```

After you install the tool, you can use it as you would any other Web part. To use the FeedReader Web part on your portal, follow these steps:

1. Browse to your portal home page.

2. Click Edit Page.

3. Click Modify Shared Page➪Add Web Parts➪Browse.

4. In the Virtual Server Gallery, drag and drop the FeedReader Web part to the portal page.

5. In the FeedReader Web part, click Open the tool pane.

The task pane displays configuration options for the Web part.

6. Paste the URL for the RSS feed that the Syndication Generator creates in the preceding section, as you can see in Figure 6-5.

7. Click OK.

You now have a Web part on your portal that displays information from a list on a SharePoint site. As the list is updated on the SharePoint site, the FeedReader Web part updates with the new listings.

Getting your feeds just the way you like them

The Syndication Generator displays all the entries in a SharePoint list. It doesn't let you pick a certain list view that you want to use. It does, however, have a mapping configuration that lets you specify a filter and which fields to display.

The U2U generator that I mention in the section "Creating feeds," earlier in this chapter, lets you select a view. It requires more work to install and set up, but it has a slicker user interface than the Syndication Generator.

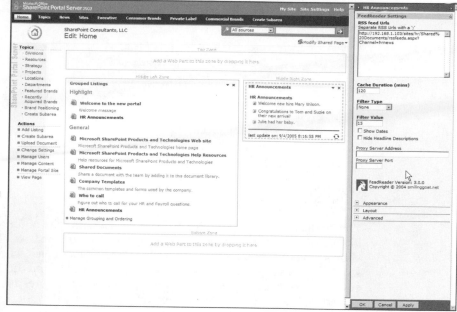

Figure 6-5:
Paste the
URL for the
RSS feed in
the Web
part.

The HR list that I syndicate in the section "Creating feeds," earlier in this chapter, shows all the announcements in the HR list. To configure a filter so that the Syndication Generator displays only list items that haven't expired and that relate to a new baby announcement, follow these steps:

1. **Navigate to the site where you manage the syndicated list.**

2. **Modify the Syndication Generator Web part that you added in the section "Creating feeds."**

   a. **Click the drop-down arrow on the Web part's title bar.**

   b. **Choose Modify Shared Web Part from the drop-down menu.**

3. **In the task pane, scroll down and expand the Mapping Properties option.**

4. **Click the View Field Names button that appears below the List Filter Mapping box.**

   All the fields and their data types for the list appear in the task pane.

5. **In the List Filter Mappings box, create a filter by entering the following code, as you can see in Figure 6-6:**

```
HR Announcements=
<Where>
  <And>
    <Geq>
      <FieldRef Name="Expires" />
      <Value Type="DateTime">
        <Today />
      </Value>
    </Geq>
    <Eq>
      <FieldRef Name="Type" />
      <Value Type="Choice">Baby</Value>
    </Eq>
  </And>
</Where>;
```

This code uses a field named Expires with a data type of date/time. It uses another field called Type with a data type of choice. The filter shows only those entries from the HR Announcements list where the Expires field is greater than or equal to today's date *and* the Type field equals Baby. You can see how to create this list in Chapter 10, or you can adapt this filter to suit another list.

This code is written in CAML, Collaborative Application Markup Language. See the sidebar "CAML" to find out more about this code.

6. **Click OK.**

The RSS feed on the home page displays the filtered list.

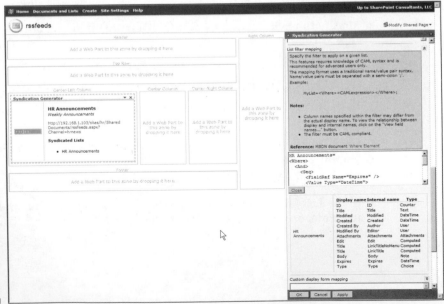

Figure 6-6:
Filter the list by using the List Filter Mappings option.

CAML

Collaborative Application Markup Language, CAML, is a language that you use to specify the templates for SharePoint sites and lists. You create SharePoint sites and the lists, libraries, discussions, pages, and other content in those sites by using templates. A site template, for example, specifies what kind of lists, libraries, and other content you create when you create the site.

You can use CAML to modify existing templates to make them look the way you want.

In the example in the section "Getting your feeds just the way you like them," earlier in this chapter, you use CAML to specify a filter for a list by using a where statement. To find out more about building where clauses in CAML, check out

```
http://msdn.microsoft.com/library/default
        .asp?url=/library/en-us/spptsdk/
        html/tscamlovIntroduction_SV010
        29856.asp
```

Keeping Your Content in Good Shape

As any Web master can tell you, Web sites don't maintain themselves. If you want your portal to stay fresh, you have to put some work into it.

Approving and archiving

You need a way to get content on and off the portal and its sites. You can't allow content managers to display just anything. Thankfully, SharePoint provides several options for managing content.

Approving content with listings

You can turn on content approval for portal listings. Content approval allows you to approve content *before* it's displayed on the portal. Here's how to turn on content approval for a portal listing:

1. **Navigate to a page on the portal, such as the News page.**

2. **Click Change Settings in the Actions menu.**

3. **Click the Publishing tab.**

4. **In the Listing Approval section, click Yes next to Require Approval to Publish New Listings.**

When a contributor adds a new listing to this page, that listing isn't displayed until the site administrator approves it. To approve the listing, follow these steps:

1. **Navigate to a page on the portal, such as the News page.**

2. **Click Manage Content in the Actions menu.**

3. **Click Portal Listings.**

4. **Click the title for the listing that needs approved.**

   You know a listing needs approval because you can see the listing has a status of pending.

5. **Choose Approve from the menu (as Figure 6-7 shows you).**

Figure 6-7:
Approve a new listing to display it on the page.

You can use the menu in Step 5 of the preceding list also to reject or archive a news listing.

Approving content in lists

You can configure lists and libraries for content approval. I show you how to set up the portal's site directory to use content approval. You access the site directory by using the portal's Sites page. The site directory is a special kind of SharePoint list.

Enabling content approval on any SharePoint list or library is a pretty quick process. It uses the same steps that enable content approval for the site directory — namely, these:

1. **Navigate to the Sites page on the portal.**

2. **Click Customize List in the Actions menu.**

   To enable content approval in a list or library other than the portal's site directory, click Modify settings and columns in the Actions menu of the list or library.

3. **Click Change General Settings.**

4. **In the Content Approval section, click Yes under Require Content Approval for Submitted Items.**

5. **Click OK.**

You can also approve entire sites. Here are the steps:

1. **Navigate to the Sites page as a Web Designer or above.**

   See Chapter 4 for more information about access permissions.

2. **Click Manage Sites from the Actions menu.**

   All the sites in the site directory appear in a list.

   When content management is enabled for lists or libraries on a SharePoint site, a special Approve/Reject Items view is created to allow you to approve and reject items.

3. **Click the title of the site that you want to approve.**

4. **Choose Approve/Reject from the drop-down menu, as you can see in Figure 6-8.**

5. **Click Approved to approve the site.**

   The pending site is approved and appears in the site directory.

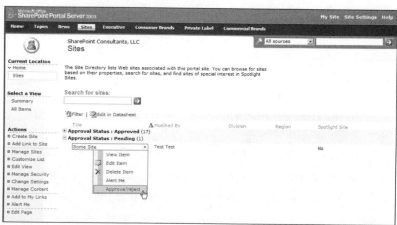

Figure 6-8: Choose Approve/ Reject from the menu to approve or reject an item.

Follow these same steps to reject an item, choosing Rejected rather than Approved in Step 4.

Giving your content a lifespan

SharePoint lets you specify the date range over which you want to display an area or listing. This feature lets you ensure that content doesn't

- ✔ Appear before you want it to be available.
- ✔ Remain after you want it to disappear.

To specify publishing dates, you need to

- ✔ Enter the publishing dates when you create a new portal listing.

   See the previous section, "Showing the world your listings," for more about portal listings.

- ✔ Edit an existing portal listing and change the publishing dates.

- ✔ Edit the publishing dates on a portal area — in particular, the Home, Topics, News, and Sites pages — by using the Change Settings link.

Approved content appears in search results regardless of its publishing dates. *If you absolutely don't want the content to be seen, keep it off the portal.*

To approve and expire content, you only need to have fields for the right statuses in the list. In Chapter 10, you can find out how to create status and expiration fields for your custom lists.

Playing to the right audiences

You can use audiences to target content to a specific group of users. For example, you can create a Manager audience to make sure that only members of the Manager audience see meeting notices for a meeting of managers.

To create an audience (hey, if only it were that easy in showbiz), follow these steps:

1. **Click Site Settings on the portal.**

2. **In the User Profile, Audiences, and Personal Sites section, click Manage Audiences.**

3. **In the Audience Settings section, click Create Audience.**

4. **Enter a name and description for the audience.**

5. **Specify to include users who satisfy all rules.**

6. **Click OK.**

7. **On the Add Audience Rule page, select the radio button next to User in the Operand section.**

8. **In the Operator section, click the drop-down list and choose Member of.**

9. **In the Value section, type the name of a domain group or distribution list, as you can see in Figure 6-9.**

   See Chapter 4 for a discussion of domain groups.

10. **Click OK.**

The Audience Properties appear. You can add additional rules from this page, and you can also view audience membership here.

You have to compile audiences periodically so you have an accurate list of membership. You can start audience compilation whenever you feel the need, or you can schedule periodic compilations by using the Manage Audiences page.

You can use audiences in two ways. You can target

✔ Portal listings to a specific audience.

✔ A Web part to a specific audience.

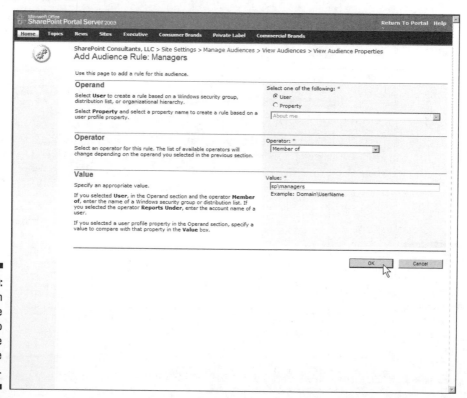

Figure 6-9:
Add an Audience rule to define audience membership.

Suppose, for example, you want to target the RSS feed created earlier in this chapter (see "Consuming feeds with help from a Smiling Goat") to a specific audience. Here's the drill:

1. **Modify the FeedReader Web part.**

2. **In the task pane, expand the Advanced features.**

3. **Scroll down to Target Audiences and then click Select.**

4. **Add audiences by using the Select Audiences dialog box, as you can see in Figure 6-10.**

You can add the same Web part to a page a number of times and target each instance of that Web part to a different audience. For example, you can target a FeedReader Web part directed to new hires and add another FeedReader Web part for all announcements *except* those for new hires.

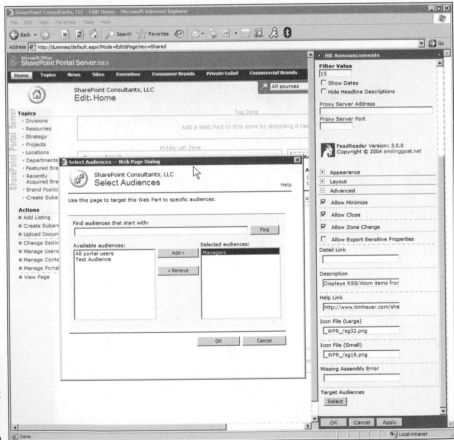

Figure 6-10: Target content to an audience by using the Select Audiences box.

Chapter 7

Branding the Portal

Your company probably has gobs and gobs of marketing brochures describing its products, people, and mission. Chances are your company's logo is emblazoned on everything from shirts to pens to coffee mugs. (If your company is *really* cool, it has a Pez dispenser with a logo.)

Such tchotchkes are one way to convey your company's identity — or at least proclaim that it has one. Even if your company doesn't own some strong brands or consider itself *branded* (associated with a copyrighted name), visual designs such as logos and color themes convey your company's image to the outside world.

Branding and company identity aren't just for the outside world. The mojo that sells your company's products also affects the people who sell, produce, and account for those products.

You wouldn't dream of going to a trade show without your corporate-logo polo shirt (right?) — so why leave your portal undecorated? If your company has a branding strategy, you can make your SharePoint portal part of it — or even a starting point for branding. This chapter shows you how.

Solving an Identity Crisis

Whether your company has an actual brand (used to communicate your company's identity) depends on whether your company already has standards in place for how it's perceived publicly — if it does, you have two possible starting points in the quest for a branded portal:

✔ If your company has a strong brand used to communicate corporate identity, there may be design or identity standards for how the company wants its image represented in print and online. Ask your Public Relations or Marketing departments for them.

✔ If your company doesn't have a corporate identity, the following sections show you how to look around both inside and outside your company and snoop out its identity.

Okay, company identity is important, but let's not go overboard here: Your SharePoint portal is for an internal audience. Flashy visual branding may not be appropriate for the way you use SharePoint within the company — but the portal should reflect your organization's existing *identity standards* and *values,* while still loading fast and working efficiently. The following sections show you how to reach that balance.

Sniffing out identity standards

Let's face it — for a lot of people, fascination with a product or service starts with visual appeal. Your corporate identity probably has a face; here are some places you can get a closer look at it:

✔ **Corporate graphics:**

   • Logos, color themes, marketing brochures, and letterhead

   • Freebies your company gives away at trade shows

   Look for freebies in the sales, marketing, public relations, and licensing departments.

   • Company office decoration

✔ **Industry characteristics:**

   • Your company's position within the industry

   • Whether the industry is expanding or contracting

   • Whether your company deals primarily with the private or public sector

   Look at the marketing messages of your competitors.

✔ **Corporate communications:**

   • Mission and vision statements

TIP

If these statements don't exist in print form, ask the executive team to give you these statements.

- Company press releases

- Corporate legal structure

A *public company* has a different legal identity from that of a *private company*. (As a rule, if your company has no shareholders of publicly traded stock, it's private.) The tenor and frequency of your company's communications are influenced by its legal structure.

Using the preceding impressions you've gathered, evaluate your company's identity. How does it come across to you? For example, is it

✔ Serious and stiff (but reliable)?

✔ Fun and whimsical (but dynamic)?

✔ Fast-paced (but focused)?

What your company values

How employees are rewarded (monetarily and otherwise) can speak volumes about what an organization considers valuable. The company's real values — not only its business objectives, but also how it "walks the walk" for its own people — provide an important key to its identity.

TIP

Let Human Resources help you evaluate how your company's compensation practices reflect the company's values.

A firm's compensation structure says a lot — usually in terms of how much time, money, and prestige attach to particular jobs — about what it values. Here are some questions that can help make that picture clearer:

✔ To what extent do incentives encourage teamwork or individuality?

✔ How is company loyalty measured and rewarded? (For example, do years of service result in more pay and more time off?)

✔ To what extent do incentives reward quantity over quality (or vice versa)?

✔ Short of micromanagement, how available is "face time" with decision makers?

✔ Does the workflow (and workload) leave room for home life?

✔ Are company goals and objectives realistic and attainable?

✔ Are some departments valued over others? (For example, are sales higher up on the compensation scale than accounting?)

The emerging picture of your company's identity, style of working, sense of purpose — and even character — suggests how your portal should be branded. For example, suppose your company has stockholders and its image depends on (say) reliability and the responsible use of resources. In that case, you may have to work a financial disclosure into your portal — and that usually depends on the company's legal structure:

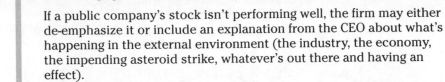

- A **public** company often includes the company's stock performance on the main page — especially if it's something to brag about.

    If a public company's stock isn't performing well, the firm may either de-emphasize it or include an explanation from the CEO about what's happening in the external environment (the industry, the economy, the impending asteroid strike, whatever's out there and having an effect).

- A closely held, **family-owned** business usually doesn't release financial information. (Guess they figure it's nobody else's business. So to speak.)

To be sure, a corporate identity can encompass some pretty sensitive issues. Logos and colors can help inspire a sense of community and common purpose — for example, the official color scheme on an airline's fleet is called its "livery" — but that's more of an outward face. The real value in branding a SharePoint portal is internal: communicating the company's goals, objectives, and strategies to the people responsible for implementing them. (Yep, that's you!) But those goals, objectives, and strategies aren't always shared in equal detail (or with equal verve) throughout an organization. To identify opportunities to present a united, upbeat image to the rank and file, look to the company's *executive team* and *internal departments*.

The sidebar "Setting the tenor with SharePoint" suggests how you can use your company's internal departments to help communicate values.

You can find goals and objectives in every department in your organization. The question is how to emphasize them individually and coordinate them visually so they all make sense to an online visitor.

Your portal is a hub — and an opportunity to promote internal goodwill. You can use it to direct people's attention to specific areas of your company. How you lay out your pages — and how employees navigate through your site — could actually foster positive feelings about being part of the company, and further encourage employees to reach company goals.

Chapter 6 has examples of portal navigation and adding content to your portal.

Setting the tenor with SharePoint

What you communicate to your employees speaks volumes about what you value. Use SharePoint to make the company's priorities transparent by turning to your internal departments for ideas on content:

✔ Finance

Toot your horn about good news! (But consider whether confidential financial information is *safe* to post. A portal user may make it public.)

✔ Sales and marketing

Communicate about such marketing opportunities as new product lines, product lines on promotion, sales regions that need emphasis, and adding revenue through add-on sales (such as warranties).

✔ Accounting

Highlight process improvement benchmarks, such as reducing billing errors or processing cycle times.

✔ Human resources

Consider communicating the total value of compensation — you know, salary-plus-vacation-time-plus-stock-options-plus-rides-in-the-Lear-Jet — expressed either generally in terms of the relative value they add or by providing users individualized views of their total compensation picture. Or use the portal to hawk underutilized benefits such as short-term disability and 401k matching.

Brand This

Branding your SharePoint portal is more than just putting a logo online. It's a large, complex undertaking that requires manpower and information.

 Consider creating a *branding subcommittee* to handle branding the portal. This section is an introduction to branding in SharePoint. Your committee should research all the available SharePoint branding techniques before formulating a strategy.

Portal, areas, or sites?

Before you can brand anything, you must know what to brand. Deciding what to brand depends on the Web page's *function* and *audience*.

Function

SharePoint uses four terms for the different kinds of Web pages and sites it creates: *portal, portal site, portal area,* and *site.*

These function terms are confusing because they are often used interchangeably. To eliminate confusion, remember that the whole enchilada is called the portal. Anything with the word *portal* in front of it — portal site, portal area — is part of the portal. SharePoint sites — team sites, Meeting and Document workspaces — are separate Web sites whose content is accessed by using the portal.

Portal

A *portal* works like a folder; it's a container for many sites. A portal can bring together content (say, several departmental or team sites) in the same place, usually to simplify navigation. The portal lets your employees search and navigate through several sites that wouldn't otherwise be connected.

Focus most of your branding and customizing efforts at the portal level. The portal is the hub for accessing your SharePoint sites so everyone sees the portal first.

Portal site

The portal site is the portal's Web site. All the pages that make up the portal — Home, Topics, News, Sites, Site Settings — are the portal (Web) site. I like to use the term *portal* to describe a *logical* portal — navigation, content, search. The term *portal site* describes the physical makeup of the portal.

Portal area

A *portal area* is a container within the portal — like a room in a building — that serves to keep information (often of various types or from various departments) in the same place. Areas *provide navigation to SharePoint site* and *group similar information.* In previous versions of SharePoint, an Area was called a category. The physical manifestation of an area is a Web page, so this book uses the term portal pages when referring to areas.

Although the terms *portal* and *area* are often used interchangeably, this book uses *portal* to mean anything related to the logical portal and *portal pages* to mean portal areas.

Site

For the purposes of this book, a *site* is an internal Web site that an organization creates by using SharePoint. Sites are often built around teams or documents. A site can also contain other sites. Without a portal, sites aren't usually connected to each other.

SharePoint sites can be branded, but that's usually left to the site administrator.

Design tips and best practices

Over the years, design professionals have developed many tips and best practices. If your company isn't familiar with Web design, I suggest your committee invest some energy in this topic. Here are a few ideas that may help get them started:

✔ **Follow user-interface guidelines:** If your company already has a Web site or other custom applications, then hopefully you have a set of guidelines for designing user interfaces. These usually specify color schemes, font families, and the usage of images.

✔ **Usability, usability, usability:** Having a fancy Web site means nothing if it isn't usable. Consider having end users test your design.

✔ **Accessibility:** Consider whether your site needs to be accessible to people with disabilities. Implementing this special access could be challenging in SharePoint, but not impossible. Better to make this decision upfront instead of waiting till after the portal is implemented.

If your company isn't well versed in Web design, it's not alone — and help is available:

✔ There are many great resources for Web site design on the World Wide Web.

✔ *CSS Web Design For Dummies* covers many Web design topics.

Audience

There are two kinds of Web pages on a SharePoint portal site and SharePoint sites:

✔ *User-facing pages* are the Web pages viewed by the employees who access your portal.

Only brand the user-facing pages.

✔ *Administrative pages* used by administrators to configure the portal.

Don't apply branding to administrative pages. It might be hard to administer your portal if you break your administrative pages.

Laying out pages like a professional

The look and feel of SharePoint pages follow the usual pattern of other Web pages. Normally they show the standard characteristics:

✔ **Page banner or header:** This usually goes across the top of the page and includes the company logo.

✔ **Site navigation:** Pages often have two ways to get around:

• *Horizontal navigation* below the page banner

• *Vertical navigation* on the left or right

✔ **Page body:** The body is often where the site's most dynamic content is found. The body may also be further divided into zones such as top, middle, right, left, and bottom.

✔ **Page footer:** The footer may include *horizontal navigation* and *contact and copyright information.*

As you think about how you want to customize your portal, think in terms of its look and feel. It should be versatile enough to accommodate various types of information, but consistent enough to provide visual continuity from one page to the next.

Branding exercises

You can brand your SharePoint portal through Site Settings, the portal's centralized administration screen.

Follow these steps to customize your portal with Site Settings:

1. **Click Site Settings in the upper-right corner of the portal site header.**

   If you don't see the Site Settings hyperlink, then you probably don't have sufficient security permission. To see this hyperlink and access the page, you must be a SharePoint administrator. If you aren't, get with Information Services pronto.

   The Site Settings screen is divided into several administrative areas. From this screen, you can manage users, content, searching, and audiences.

2. **In the General Settings section, click the hyperlink Change portal site properties and SharePoint site creation settings.**

   The Change Portal Site Properties and SharePoint Site Creation Settings screen appears. You can change such settings as

   • The name of the portal site that appears on the main page and in navigation

   • Your company logo

   • A special style sheet for spelling out font colors and sizes

Using Your Company Logo

In the Change Portal Site Properties and SharePoint Site Creation Settings page that you access in the preceding section, you'll notice a value in the Custom Portal Site Logo section for specifying a custom logo — and that it doesn't look like an ordinary file path. That's because the path *isn't* a regular file path. It's actually part of a hyperlink to the site logo.

If you paste the value in the Custom Portal Site Logo section in front of the portal server name then you have the URL for your site logo — like this:

```
http://dummies/_layouts/images/sitelogo.gif
```

You can see your site logo in the browser by pasting the entire URL in the address bar of your browser.

To change the site logo, you need to copy a new image file to the path where the default image is stored.

A default SharePoint installation stores image files, including the default SharePoint logo, at:

```
C:\Program Files\Common Files\Microsoft Shared\
            Web server extensions\60\TEMPLATE\IMAGES
```

As you browse around the portal, you notice that the site logo appears at the top of the page.

Open your file directory to SharePoint's image path and place your company logo there. For this example, I use a logo from the Dummies Web site and save the logo to the folder directory where the default SharePoint logo is stored.

In the Change Portal Site Properties and SharePoint Site Creation Settings page, type in the name for the file at the end of the path listed in the Custom Portal Site Logo section, and then click OK. (For this example, type **dummies.gif**, as shown in Figure 7-1.)

Figure 7-1:
Type the filename for your company logo to change the portal site's logo.

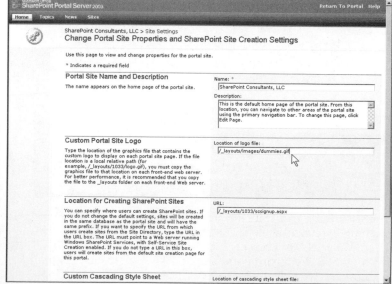

The site saves your settings and returns you to the Site Settings page. You should now see your company logo (rather than the default SharePoint logo) in the upper-right corner.

If instead of having a logo, you have an ugly red X inside a square with the words Site Logo next to it, then SharePoint couldn't find your file. (Welcome to the wonderful world of Web design!) As with many Web-development tools, SharePoint gladly saves whatever information you give it — but it doesn't verify that your file exists. Then along comes the browser to build the Web page — and when it can't find your picture and the exact address specified, it doesn't know what to do. Figure 7-2 shows the browser displaying a placeholder image — a red X — because it can't find your logo file.

Figure 7-2:
SharePoint displays a placeholder image when an image can't be found.

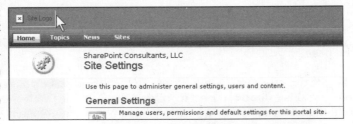

To correct the problem, you identify the exact location where you stored the file. Make sure you typed it the same way as in the Change Portal Site Properties and SharePoint Site Creation Settings page.

After you have the path correctly entered, you should see your company logo on-screen, as in Figure 7-3.

Figure 7-3:
Display a custom logo using the Change Portal Site Properties and SharePoint Site Creation Settings page.

Customizing SharePoint with Style Sheets

Your company's logo probably doesn't match the default SharePoint color scheme. The easiest way to change the colors of elements on SharePoint's pages is to use a custom *style sheet* — a configuration file that can control the look and feel of every page on your Web site.

Style sheets aren't unique to SharePoint. In fact, they're a standard feature used on most professionally developed sites. The sidebar "Basic style-sheet syntax" offers a look at how to tell a style sheet what to do.

Here are some common style-sheet commands:

```
background-color
color
font-size
font-family
```

A great way to see style-sheet commands is by looking at an existing style sheet. There are also many references available online. (My favorite is www.htmlhelp.com.)

Basic style-sheet syntax

Style sheets use their own *syntax* (sequence of code elements). SharePoint mostly uses *classes* — in effect, containers for properties — to control formatting.

When you've defined the properties of a *style* (a specialized class), you can then apply to anything on the Web page that you want to use that style. For example, the following syntax is for a class called `MyStyle`. Anything given the `MyStyle` class is displayed *in bold with a green color on a yellow background*. Here's the syntax that makes it look that way on-screen:

```
.MyStyle
{
Font-weight: bold;
Color: green;
Background-color: yellow;
}
```

The basic syntax for a style-sheet class looks like this:

✔ **First line:** A *period,* followed by the *name* of the class, like this:

```
.MyStyle
```

✔ **Second line:** A *left curly brace* ({)

✔ **Command lines:** Each command must be followed by a *semicolon,* like this:

```
Color: green;
```

There is no limit to the number of lines in a class.

✔ **Last line:** A *right curly brace* (})

The amount of spacing used between the lines and braces in the class isn't important.

Stylin' with SharePoint

When you've created a class, you have a versatile and reusable tool. After you've used a class to override the default styles provided with SharePoint, you can redefine the class as needed — in fact, reuse it many times. What better way to customize SharePoint?

Style sheets can — and do — take up books of their own. But let's not get carried away here;

this chapter contains some of the common styles you need to customize SharePoint's look and feel. Okay, it's just the tip of the iceberg — Cascading Style Sheets are powerful and versatile — but if you want to get a lot handier with style sheets, I recommend *CSS Web Design For Dummies*. It covers all the ways that style sheets can make a Web site look pretty.

To apply a style-sheet class to a paragraph in a Web page, I use this line of HTML:

```
<p class="MyStyle">This text is bolded, green in a yellow background.</p>
```

The sidebar "Stylin' with SharePoint" shows how classes work in SharePoint.

The official name for a style sheet is *cascading style sheet* (or *CSS*). Style sheets are called *cascading* because a single site can use information from many style sheets. When the style sheets contradict each other, they are applied in a hierarchical fashion: Whichever style sheet gets applied *last* is what the user sees.

Style-sheet files

By default, SharePoint uses two style sheets for controlling fonts, colors, and other look-and-feel elements of the page:

- ✔ `sps.css`: This file is used by SharePoint portal pages such as Home, Topics, News, and Sites.
- ✔ `ows.css`: This file is used by SharePoint team sites that you add using SharePoint's site directory.

SharePoint's style sheets are stored in their own directory:

```
C:\Program Files\Common Files\Microsoft Shared\web server extensions\60\
                TEMPLATE\LAYOUTS\1033\STYLES.
```

For customizing SharePoint's style sheets, I recommend adding a custom style sheet that gets applied *after* the sps.css and ows.css style sheets. This custom sheet overrides whatever styles were already applied by SharePoint's style sheets. Figure 7-4 shows a directory listing of SharePoint's style sheets.

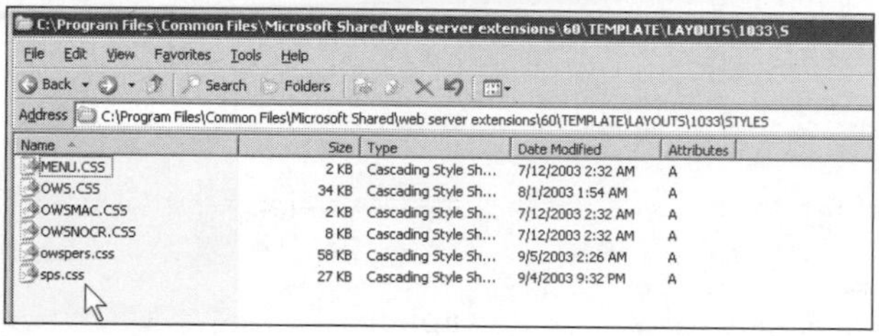

Figure 7-4:
SharePoint
uses style
sheets to
control the
look and
feel of the
portal and
its sites.

You can create a custom style sheet in three quick steps:

1. **Open Notepad or the text editor of your choice.**

2. **Type your style-sheet classes in the Notepad file.**

3. **Save your custom style sheet to the file directory where SharePoint's style sheets are saved.**

TIP

If you're nursing a hunch that style sheets are essential tools for branding your portal, you're right on target — but make sure you use them correctly. When you brand your portal, be sure to decide on your color scheme up front so you aren't surprised by how many changes are necessary to put it all on-screen.

Get some class and modify your portal

You can take advantage of the *cascading* characteristic of style-sheet classes to modify the look and feel of your SharePoint portal. When you create a custom style sheet that uses the same classes found in SharePoint's style sheets, the fonts and colors you specify in your custom style sheet will override any properties specified in the SharePoint style sheet for the same class. The trick is getting the right classes.

Here's the sequence when you start inserting classes into your Notepad file for your custom style sheet: Start by modifying the page banner, add your modified classes, and then apply your custom style sheet. Doing so applies your modified classes; they'll override SharePoint's default classes.

Modifying the page banner

SharePoint uses a *page banner* across the top of all of its pages. Chances are SharePoint's default blue color scheme doesn't match your company's logo, so you'll have to change the background and font color of the page banner. To do that, you modify the style-sheet classes used by the page banner.

Follow these steps to add modified page-banner classes to your custom style sheet:

1. **Enter the following page-banner classes into your Notepad file:**

```
.ms-banner, .ms-GRHeaderText
{
    color: black;
}

.ms-banner a:link
{
    color: black:
}

.ms-banner a:visited
{
    color: black;
}

.ms-bannerframe, .ms-GRHeaderBackground, .ms-storMeFree
{
    background-image: none;
    background-color: yellow;
}
```

These classes set the following look-and-feel elements of SharePoint's page banner:

   • Make the font color `black` for the classes `ms-banner` and `ms-GRHeaderText`.

   • Change the color of the hyperlinks in the upper-right corner.

   • The background color is set to `yellow`.

2. **Save the custom style-sheet file to the default style-sheet directory:**

```
C:\Program Files\Common Files\Microsoft Shared\
        Web server extensions\60\TEMPLATE\LAYOUTS\1033\STYLES
```

3. **In the file directory, create a new folder called Custom.**

Using a separate folder to store your custom style sheets allows you to see at a glance which style sheets are custom and which are not.

4. **In the Custom file folder, save your custom style-sheet file as** *custom.css*, **as Figure 7-5 shows.**

   You don't *have* to change the file extension from .txt to .css, but it's common practice. (Always helps to know which files are style sheets.)

Figure 7-5: Save the custom style sheet in a custom folder in SharePoint's default Style Sheets directory.

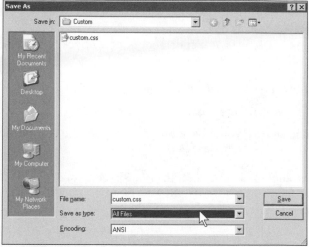

Applying your custom style sheet

To actually override the SharePoint default styles, you apply your custom style sheet. To do that — and to make sure the new style sheet works — follow these steps:

1. **From the portal's home page, click Site Settings.**

2. **On the Site Settings page, click the <u>Change portal site properties and SharePoint site creation settings</u> link.**

3. **Locate the section labeled Custom Cascading Style Sheet.**

4. **Enter the path to the custom style sheet you created, as Figure 7-6 shows.**

   If you used the preceding example, the path should be

   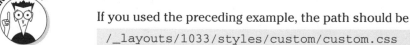
   ```
   /_layouts/1033/styles/custom/custom.css
   ```

5. **Click OK.**

   The page banner should now reflect the changes specified in the custom style sheet.

Figure 7-6:
Enter the
path to the
custom style
sheet.

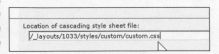

Location of cascading style sheet file:
/_layouts/1033/styles/custom/custom.css

If you don't see the changes you specified, double-check to make sure you typed the following configuration settings exactly:

- ✔ Check the path to the custom style sheet.

- ✔ Check the classes in the custom style-sheet file.

- ✔ Check to make sure you have a *semicolon* (;) at the end of each command in the style-sheet classes.

You can see the effects of your custom style sheet by clicking the Refresh button on your browser. Figure 7-7 shows a SharePoint portal with a custom style sheet applied to it.

Figure 7-7:
A Share-
Point portal
using a
custom style
sheet to
change the
page
banner.

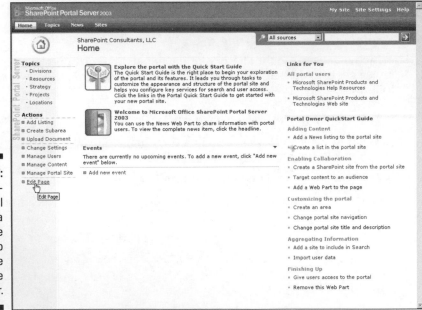

In the SharePoint portal, the My Site hyperlink in the upper-right corner is still white. To change this, add the entry shown here to your style sheet:

```
#hlMySite
{
        color: black;
}
```

The preceding command starts with a *pound sign* (#), not a period. The # sign denotes this is an *ID*, not a class. An ID can be used only once in a Web page. (By contrast, a class may be used many times, even on the same page.) Here it makes sense to use an ID rather than a class because the My Site link should appear only once on the portal's home page.

Modifying horizontal navigation

The horizontal navigation is the on-screen bar that's just below the page banner. The default hyperlinks are Home, Topics, News, and Sites.

To specify colors and fonts to use for navigation, you have to create navigation classes that override the default fonts and colors that SharePoint uses. To change the color from blue to black, for example, type the code in Listing 7-1 into your custom style sheet.

Listing 7-1: Navigation Classes for Fonts and Colors

```
.ms-phnav1wrapper, .ms-navframe
{
        background-color: black;
        background-image: url();
        width: 100%;
        border-top: 1px yellow solid;
}

.ms-phnavmidc1sel, .ms-phnavmidc0sel

{
        background-color: yellow;
        background-image: url();
        BORDER-top: #FF9933 1px solid;
        BORDER-left: #FF9933 1px solid;
        BORDER-bottom: #CC6600 1px solid;
        BORDER-right: #CC6600 1px solid;
}

.ms-navheader, .ms-pvtbt, .ms-pvnavmidC1
{
        color: yellow;
```

(continued)

Listing 7-1 *(continued)*

```
}
.ms-pvnavmidC1 a:link, .ms-pvnavmidC1 a:visited, .ms-pvtb
        a:link, .ms-pvtb a:visited
{
        color: yellow;
        text-decoration: none;
}
.ms-pvtb a:hover, .ms-pvnavmidC1 a:hover
{
        color: orange;
        text-decoration: underline;
}
```

The background for the horizontal navigation is actually a blue image file. To make SharePoint (actually Internet Explorer, which is showing the image) display the background color as black, we have to override the background image property. The command background-image: `url()` takes care of that problem.

This style also uses the `border-top` shorthand command to specify three properties on one line, using the following syntax:

```
Border-top: <color> <size> <style>;
```

If you aren't familiar with picking colors for use on a Web site, run a search on the phrase *Web-safe colors*. There are many online resources with *color pickers* — programs that convert the color you see on-screen to the cryptic code you type into a style sheet.

After you apply these changes, the left vertical navigation's style changes. (You can style the horizontal and vertical navigation differently, but it's much easier to pick one scheme for both.)

Styling the search box

Tweaking the search box shows how complex styling can be. There are several styles that must be updated. You end up with a *boxier* search box than the default. (If you want to preserve the curvy style of the default box or replace the blue background images with your own images, you can find resources on the Web that show how.)

To change the style for the search box, add the following code to your custom style sheet:

```
.ms-searchform, .ms-sbtable
{
        background-color: black;
```

```
}

.ms-sblbcorner, .ms-sbtopcorner
{
        background-color: black;
        background-image: url();
}

Div.ms-titleareaframe
{
 border-top: 3px solid black;
}
```

Keep these handy points in mind when you're tweaking custom style sheets:

✔ It isn't necessary to close the style-sheet file when you make changes to the file. Just type in your changes, save the file, and refresh the portal's home page to apply your changes.

✔ To see the effects of your custom style sheet, you can click your browser's Refresh button after you save your latest changes in the style-sheet file.

✔ If you need to refresh your memory about applying custom style sheets, see the "Applying your custom style sheet" section earlier in this chapter.

Going beyond copy and paste

The easiest way to customize SharePoint is to dig into the SharePoint style sheets. Of course, "easy" is relative. There are many other ways to customize the look and feel of your SharePoint portal. So fill your toolbox and get a strong cup of Joe. The following resources help you fill your toolbox. (You'll have to get the brew yourself.)

Using Microsoft resources

The best place to find information about SharePoint's style sheets is the Microsoft Web site. You're in luck: They have an article that lists all the styles used in sps.css — and even gives examples. To find this article, go to www.microsoft.com and search for *customizing SharePoint style sheets*. You want the article titled "Customizing SharePoint Sites and Portals: Style-sheet class Reference Tables, Part 3."

Sniffing styles with Firefox

Mozilla Firefox is a handy Web browser with tools that let you load a style sheet, manipulate it, and view the changes.

You can download Firefox free from www.getfirefox.com.

Installing Web Developer

After installing Firefox, follow these steps to install Chris Pederick's Web Developer:

1. **Click Tools⇨Extensions.**

2. **Click the** Get More Extensions **hyperlink in the lower-right corner.**

   This opens the Firefox Web site.

3. **On the Web site, find the Developer Tools category.**

   All of the developer tools are listed in alphabetical order.

4. **Browse to the last page of developer tools and select Web Developer.**

5. **Click Install and follow the instructions for installing Web Developer.**

   You must close and reopen your browser after installing Web Developer for the installation of Web Developer to take effect.

   When Web Developer is installed, you should see a toolbar above the tabs where you view Web pages.

One of the things that makes Firefox so cool (besides being totally cool in general) is the horde of custom extensions you can download for it.

An *extension* is a software tool developed by a third party for use with a particular program. And for figuring out SharePoint's style sheets, no Firefox extension is better than Web Developer. The sidebar "Installing Web Developer" shows how to set it up.

Although this tool does many cool things, you most need three specific tools — the ones described next. Open your portal home page in Firefox and then use any of the following tools to see details about SharePoint style sheets:

Viewing styles

Before you can make changes, you have to know what you're changing. Get a look at the portal's existing style sheets before you modify them. You have several possible ways to sneak a peek:

✔ **Click CSS⇨View CSS.** Doing so displays all the style sheets in use.

   Using this technique opens the SharePoint style sheets in a new tab behind the portal page. Click the tab that displays the CSS. As you scroll down, several style sheets are listed. If you apply a custom style sheet, it appears at the bottom of the tab.

- ✔ **Click Information⇨Display ID & Class Details.** This procedure displays the style-sheet classes in use on the portal page. This tool shows where each class is applied.

- ✔ **Click CSS⇨Edit CSS.** This is what you do when you want to actually edit the various CSS files in the browser environment and apply your changes immediately.

Keep all your *permanent* changes in `custom.css`. Otherwise you lose those changes if Microsoft upgrades their style sheets.

Google it!

If you need more help figuring out exactly which SharePoint style you want to tweak, try Googling *"SharePoint CSS"* (include the quotation marks) — and don't forget to appreciate your luck: A large community of bloggers and sites is puzzling out the SharePoint style sheets. They probably have what you need.

When you've tweaked all the styles you need to present your company image on your portal, don't be surprised if various departments and administrative levels get into the act, but keep in mind that *branding is usually applied at the portal level, not the site level.* Consider letting the site administrators handle how much branding is practical for their sites. Sites are for departments, teams, or other users who need to collaborate around something specific like a document or project. Plus, sites are easier to customize than the main portal.

Creating Vision and Mission Statements

If (like many employees) you've ever wondered what that fine-sounding mission statement was really for, here's the answer: It's the very thing to put on the company portal. (Okay, just kidding there. But that is one use for it.) Here's the rationale:

- ✔ The company's vision and mission statement belong at the portal level.

    These statements are an example of giving SharePoint Portal Server its own identity (plus it wins bonus points with the executives, another excellent reason for its existence . . . kidding again).

- ✔ Individual department's statements can be listed at the site level.

    Site-level statements can be rolled up to the portal level for display.

Finding a home for mission and vision statements

To add a place to navigate to your company's vision and mission statements, follow these steps:

1. **Browse to the portal home page.**

2. **Under Actions in the left navigation, click Edit Page, as shown in Figure 7-8.**

   Your home page should now be in Edit mode. Make sure the title of the page reads Edit: Home. Figure 7-9 shows the home page in Edit mode.

3. **Click Create Subarea on the horizontal navigation bar, as shown in Figure 7-10.**

   The Create Area page appears. Use the Create Area page to add a new page to the portal.

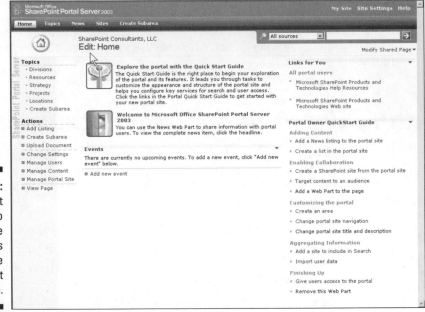

Figure 7-8: Click Edit Page to place the portal's home page in edit mode.

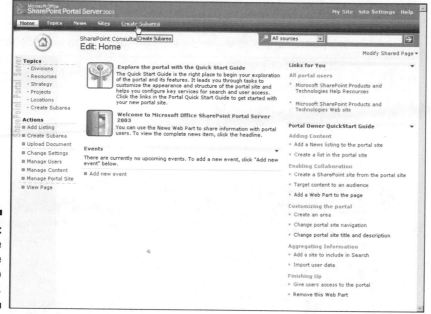

Figure 7-9:
The home page's title changes to Edit: Home.

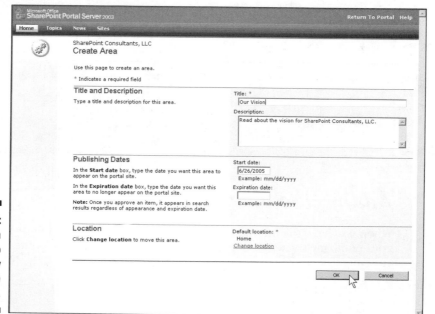

Figure 7-10:
Create a subarea to add a new page to the portal.

4. In the Create Area page, enter a title and description, as shown in Figure 7-11.

- The title appears on the new page's navigation header bar.

- The description is viewable from the portal's search screen.

5. Click OK.

A new page is added to the portal using the title you enter in Step 4.

You should now have a highly visible means of displaying your company's vision and mission statements.

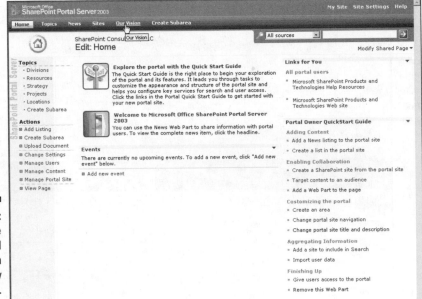

Figure 7-11:
Enter a title
and
description
for the new
portal page.

Adding the vision

When you have the new portal page in place, you can prominently display your company's vision statement (hey, it looks so nice next to the mission statement). You need to enter the text and format it.

Entering text

Follow these steps to add the text of your vision statement:

1. **Browse to the newly created Our Vision page on the portal, as shown in Figure 7-12.**

2. **Click Edit Page.**

3. **Add a new Web part:**

   a. **Click Modify Shared Page in the upper-right corner.**

   b. **Select Add Web Parts⇨Browse.**

   Figure 7-13 shows how to access the Add Web Parts menu.

   SharePoint presents a task pane that lists a Web part gallery.

4. **Select the Content Editor Web Part, as shown in Figure 7-14.**

   This is a generic Web part that enables you to add text.

5. **Click the Add button on the bottom of the screen.**

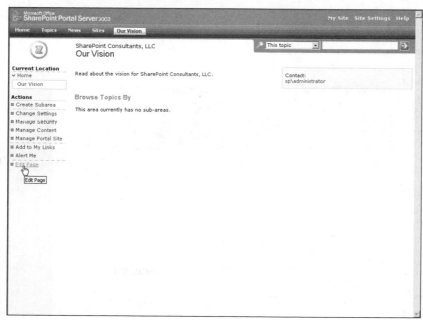

Figure 7-12:
Click the Our Vision link on the navigation bar to access the new portal page.

Figure 7-13:
Use the
Add Web
Parts
menu to add
Web parts
to the page.

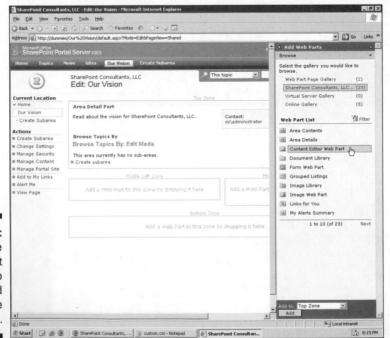

Figure 7-14:
Use the
Content
Editor Web
Part to add
text to the
page.

6. **Close the Add Web Parts task pane (click the little X in the upper-right corner), as shown in Figure 7-15.**

   The Content Editor Web Part is added to the top of the page, just below the banner.

7. **Click the words Open the Tool Pane in the Content Editor Web part.**

   Doing so opens a tool pane that enables you to add content to the Web part.

8. **Click Rich Text Editor in the tool pane, as shown in Figure 7-16.**

9. **Enter the text of your vision statement into the rich text editor, and then click Save.**

   Your statement should now appear in the Web part.

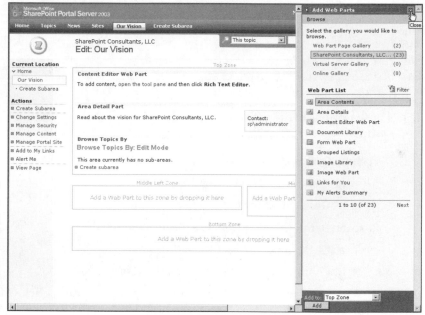

Figure 7-15:
Close the task pane by clicking the X in the upper-right corner.

Modifying a Web part's configuration

The Web Part task pane offers several options for modifying the appearance and layout of the Content Editor Web part.

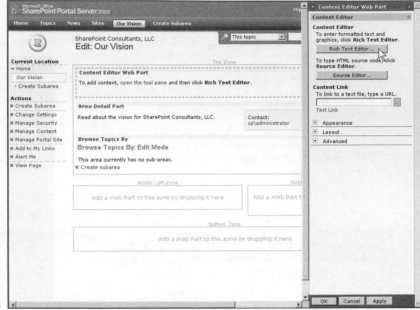

Figure 7-16:
Use the Rich
Text Editor
to enter text
into the
Content
Editor Web
part.

These options in the task pane are similar for any Web part you use. The procedure for changing a Web part's settings is similar for all Web parts:

1. **Specify that the Web part may not be closed:**

   a. **Click the Advanced option.**

   b. **Deselect Allow Minimize and Allow Close.**

2. **Change the title that appears in the Web part:**

   a. **Click Appearance.**

   b. **Change the title to Vision Statement.**

3. **When you're done changing the Web part's settings, click OK to save your changes.**

   Figure 7-17 shows the Web part task pane where all this takes place.

Removing irrelevant content

Obsolescence happens — and if your content is lucky, that's *all* that might make it irrelevant. To remove such Web parts from the page, follow these steps:

1. **Click Modify Shared Page⇨Modify Shared Web Parts.**

2. **Select the Area Detail Part, as shown in Figure 7-18.**

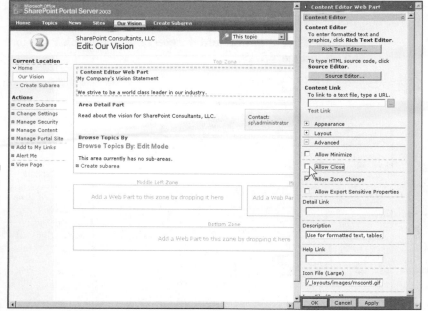

Figure 7-17:
The Web part task pane allows you to change a Web part's settings.

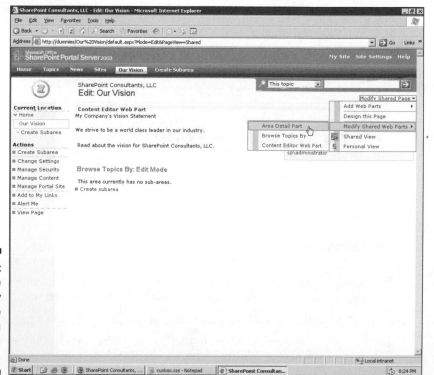

Figure 7-18:
Use the Modify Shared Web Parts menu to select a Web part.

TIP

The Area Detail Part tool pane offers the same appearance and layout options as the Content Editor Web part.

3. **Click the Layout option and deselect the Visible on Page option, as shown in Figure 7-19.**

4. **Click OK to save.**

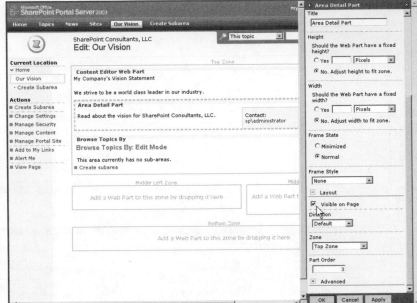

Figure 7-19: The Visible on Page setting tells SharePoint whether to display the Web part on the page.

Advanced Branding Tools

After you've successfully branded your portal, you may want to try out the many additional ways to brand a SharePoint portal or SharePoint sites. You can use the style-sheet tweaks to get started, but if you really want to get serious about it, consider using one of these techniques:

WARNING!

✔ **Use Microsoft Front Page — carefully:** You can open sites in Front Page and customize them, but a word to the wise: Don't make a habit of it.

You can use Front Page to do some pretty fancy stuff to your sites, but the extra bells and whistles come with a couple of cautions:

• Modifying a site in Front Page may reduce the site's performance.

• Never use Front Page to modify the main portal pages — Home, Topics, News, Sites.

✔ **Modify an existing theme on a SharePoint site:** SharePoint sites use themes to provide a visual style (also called a *skin*) to the whole site. You can use this feature in a couple of ways:

- Apply a canned theme

- Open the theme in Front Page and customize it

These techniques don't apply to the portal.

✔ **Add Web parts:** If the Web parts you have aren't getting the job done, you can add other Web parts for the purpose; some are even ready-made.

Before trying to create everything from scratch, browse the Web for existing Web parts. A large gallery of Web parts is available online.

✔ **Modify area-page templates in ASP.NET:** You can open the portal pages in ASP.NET and make minor tweaks — or do a complete overhaul. You don't need an expensive editor such as Visual Studio to modify the portal pages. You can open the pages in any text editor.

Many of the changes we made by using style sheets can also be done by modifying the templates.

If you modify area-page templates, *always save a backup of the original template* so you can restore the original version if necessary.

✔ **Manipulate the SharePoint server-side controls:** SharePoint's default Web parts are called *server-side controls.* For example, the vertical navigation on the portal home page is a server-side control. It can be modified to display horizontally.

Branding your SharePoint portal gives your portal users a sense of identity and place. Your branding strategy can be as simple or as sophisticated as you need for your company. When you choose a strategy, remember there are many good articles available on the Web (and, in particular, the Microsoft Web site) to help you. Happy branding!

Part IV
Build It, and Hope They Come

The 5th Wave   By Rich Tennant

SPAM KING
MASS EMAIL MARKETING
A Limited Canker on the Butt
of Society Partnership

In this part . . .

The features demonstrated in this part are good for introducing SharePoint to your company. You get a handle on using SharePoint to improve the management of meetings and documents. You're also introduced to using Office 2003 with SharePoint. You get the lowdown on creating document libraries on the portal for storing fax cover sheets and other standardized communications templates. And if you've ever wondered about the best ways to use company logos and branding images, this part shows you how to manage them using an image library.

Chapter 8

Collaborating with SharePoint Sites

In This Chapter

▶ Creating sites and workspaces for team collaboration

▶ Organizing your meetings with Meeting workspaces

▶ Bringing users together to work on a document in a Document workspace

▶ Matching SharePoint's site templates to the task ahead

▶ Using Microsoft Office 2003 with SharePoint

SharePoint is a tool that lets you create Web sites. You can build blank sites — sites without any content — or you can use one of the many site templates that SharePoint provides.

A *site template* is a boilerplate that you use for making a certain kind of Web site. (You can even make your own site templates, but that's another book.)

SharePoint comes with three site templates:

- **Document workspace:** Centered around a single document
- **Meeting workspace:** For managing meetings and all the files that support meetings
- **Team site:** For managing projects, departments, or any group activity

SharePoint provides four variations of the Meeting workspace:

- **Blank Meeting workspace:** An empty Meeting workspace that you can customize
- **Decision Meeting workspace:** Adds lists for managing decisions and tasks
- **Social Meeting workspace:** A site for managing get-togethers complete with a groovy party hat clip art
- **Multipage Meeting workspace:** Same as the Meeting workspace with a few blank Web pages thrown in for fun

A site template is a configuration file that specifies all the content that makes up a site. For example, the site template for a team site specifies the lists, libraries, Web parts, and other features that appear by default on any Web site based on that site template.

You may hear a Web site called a *site* or a *workspace*. In SharePoint, both terms refer to the same thing — a Web part page that includes Web parts.

This chapter walks you through the major highlights of the main site templates. To get really acquainted with the features of all the site templates, you can simply create a new team site and then create subsites that use each site template. So . . .

To create a new top-level team site, follow these steps:

1. **On the portal home page, click Sites.**

2. **In the Actions navigation list on the left of the screen, click Create Site.**

   The New SharePoint Site page appears.

3. **On the New SharePoint Site page, enter the title "My Team Site" in the Title text box.**

4. **Enter the URL "myteamsite" in the text box URL name.**

5. **Click Create.**

6. **On the Add Link to Site page, accept the defaults.**

   By accepting the defaults, you get your site listed in the site directory and included in searches.

7. **Click OK.**

   The Template Selection page appears.

8. **Click Team Site.**

   On the Template Selection page, you select the template you want SharePoint to use when building your site.

9. **Click OK (as you can see in Figure 8-1).**

   Now you have a new team site.

You call a site *top-level* if it's the first site that you create in a site hierarchy. You call any sites that you create within the top-level site *subsites*.

See Chapter 6 to find out how to add subsites to the portal's site directory.

Figure 8-1:
Choose
Team Site
from the
Template
Selection
page to
create a
new team
site.

To create subsites within the team site created in the preceding number list, follow these steps:

1. **Click Create on the primary horizontal navigation bar in your team site.**

2. **On the Create page, scroll down to the Web Pages section.**

   The Create Page displays the templates for all the items you can add to the team Web site (in this case, the one created in the previous steps).

3. **Click Sites and Workspaces.**

   The New SharePoint Site page appears.

4. **Enter the title "My Document Workspace" and the URL "mydoc".**

5. **In the Permissions section, select the radio button next to Use same permissions as parent site.**

   Permissions are settings that determine how much access your users have to the site and its content. A site can either manage its own permissions or inherit them from its parent site. By default, the site inherits permissions from its parent site. You can change this setting later. Inheritance is explained in Chapter 4.

Being the astute reader you are, I'm sure you noticed that the New SharePoint site page used in the previous section did *not* include this "permissions" business. That's because we were creating a top-level (or *parent*) site. As in real life, inheritance applies to children. Here the children inherit the same permissions as the parent (naturally that applies *only* to sites).

6. Click Create.

7. Choose Document Workspace from the Template Selection page.

8. Click OK.

You have a new Web site based on the Document workspace template.

Repeat these steps to add sites based on each of the site templates. Specify a descriptive name and URL for each of the sites. (Oh, while you're at it, play around with the sites and get a feel for how they differ. I'm in no hurry.)

Go Team!

A *team site* is the most versatile of all the sites that you can create. You can use a team site to host

- ✔ An entire project or committee
- ✔ A department
- ✔ A group of similar processes, such as a self-service site for human resources forms

Team sites can include every kind of SharePoint content, including subsites. By default, a SharePoint team site displays the following content on its home page:

- ✔ Announcements
- ✔ Events
- ✔ Links
- ✔ A site image

Figure 8-2 shows a team site.

Chapters 10 through 13 describe various scenarios for using SharePoint team sites.

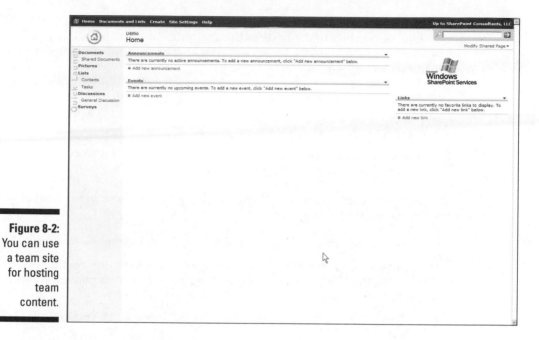

Figure 8-2:
You can use
a team site
for hosting
team
content.

Another Meeting?

SharePoint's Meeting workspace is like a beefed-up Outlook meeting request. In addition to storing a meeting's date, time, and attendees, your meetings have their very own document library, task list, and any other SharePoint library or list your little heart desires.

Even without SharePoint, the Outlook calendar folder gives you some useful capabilities:

- ✔ Create an appointment on your calendar
- ✔ Invite attendees and view their schedules
- ✔ Tell attendees whether their attendance is optional or required
- ✔ Allow users to respond to meeting invitations

It's sad, but true — many users don't know how to respond to meeting requests in Outlook. Your users need to know how to respond to Outlook meeting requests before they can use Meeting workspaces in SharePoint. (If you're laughing, then I'll bet your users don't know how to use Outlook.)

Although I have used the Outlook meeting request feature for years, I still find attaching documents to the body of the appointment a real pain. Okay, you can attach an agenda pretty easily, but attaching to the appointment can be a bigger headache than it's worth:

- Invitees don't always know how to open attachments.
- Attachments are stored in the e-mail server, where they can't be stored forever.
- You have to know the date of the meeting to retrieve any documents stored in that meeting's appointment.

Meeting workspaces correct all these problems by creating a permanent storage repository for meeting documents:

- Agendas and other documents open via hyperlinks.
- Files are stored on a Meeting workspace dedicated to the meeting. Creating the Meeting workspace within a team site gives context to the Meeting workspace.
- A Meeting workspace can store multiple documents in a version-controlled library.

Until we meet again

Using Microsoft Outlook 2003, you can create a Meeting workspace within your meeting appointment, or you can link to an existing workspace.

To create a Meeting workspace, using Outlook 2003, follow these steps:

1. **Create a new appointment in Outlook 2003.**

   The appointment's subject becomes the title for the new Meeting workspace. If your meeting appointment's subject is lunch hours, then your Meeting workspace is *titled* lunch hours. (You might want to rethink that one.)

2. **Click Invite Attendees from the toolbar or the Actions menu.**

   The Meeting Workspace button appears below the reminder information on the Outlook Meeting window.

3. **Click the Meeting Workspace button.**

   The Meeting Workspace task pane appears in the right of the Outlook Meeting window.

4. **In the Meeting Workspace task pane, click Change Settings in the Create a workspace section of the task pane.**

The task pane now gives you two options:

- **Select a Location:** Here you specify the site where you want the workspace created. You can use any site, including the portal site.

- **Select a Workspace:** You have the option to create a new workspace or link to an existing workspace. If you choose to create a new workspace, you can select the site template to use for the workspace.

5. **In Select a Location, click Other.**

6. **Type or paste in the URL of the top-level site where you want to create the workspace in the Other Workspace Server dialog box and click OK.**

To create the Meeting workspace on the portal, enter the URL for the portal. Otherwise, enter the URL for a site that's connected to the portal. (For example, you can use the team site created at the beginning of this chapter.)

7. **Select the Basic Meeting Workspace template type from the Select a template type drop-down list.**

8. **Click OK.**

The task pane summarizes your choices.

9. **Click Create, as Figure 8-3 shows you.**

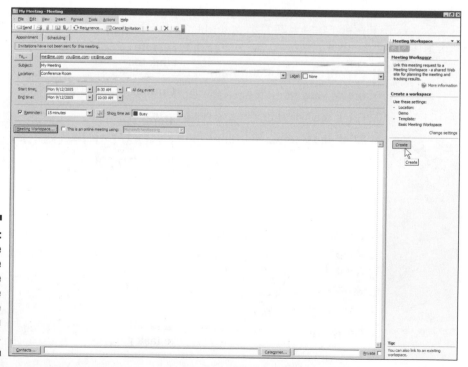

Figure 8-3:
Click Create
to create
the
workspace
on the site
that you
specify.

Outlook sends a request to SharePoint to create the Meeting workspace on the specified site. The Outlook appointment is linked to the workspace, and a hyperlink to the workspace appears in the body of your appointment, as you can see in Figure 8-4.

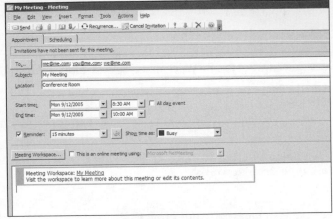

Figure 8-4:
A hyperlink to the newly created workspace appears in the appoint-ment.

You can link a recurring meeting to a Meeting workspace; there SharePoint lists each meeting with its own specific content.

To link an Outlook 2003 appointment to an existing Meeting workspace, follow these steps:

1. **Create a new appointment in Outlook 2003.**

2. **Invite your attendees in the Outlook Meeting request.**

3. **Click the Meeting Workspace button.**

4. **Click the Change Settings in the Meeting Workspace task pane.**

5. **In the Select a Location section of the task pane, enter the site location where you have the existing Meeting workspace stored.**

   See Steps 5 and 6 in the previous instructions (for creating a Meeting workspace with Outlook) if you need specific instructions.

6. **Select the radio button next to Link to an existing workspace.**

7. **Select the workspace to which you want to add the appointment link from the drop-down list.**

8. **Click OK.**

   The task pane summarizes your choices.

9. **Click Link.**

   Now you have a link between the new meeting appointment and the existing Meeting workspace.

In the Meeting workspace, SharePoint adds a Meeting Series pane to the left side of the page, as you can see in Figure 8-5. All the meetings associated with the workspace appear in the Meeting Series page. By clicking a meeting link, you see only the content associated with that meeting.

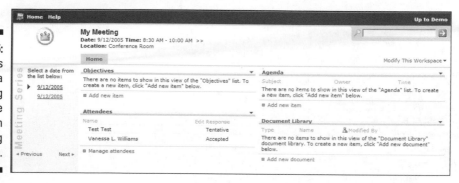

Figure 8-5:
All meetings
linked to a
Meeting
workspace
appear in
the meeting
series pane.

You can remove a meeting link between an Outlook appointment and a Meeting workspace in either of two ways:

✔ **Remove the link from the Outlook 2003 appointment, using the task pane of the Meeting workspace:** Just display the Meeting Workspace task pane and click the Remove button.

✔ **Delete the appointment from your Outlook 2003 calendar:** The meeting still appears in the Meeting workspace, but the workspace is no longer linked to the appointment in Outlook. You can still find any content associated with the meeting in the workspace.

The Meeting workspace lets you choose from three options for a meeting that you no longer have linked to an Outlook appointment:

✔ **Move:** Move the meeting's content to another meeting on the same workspace. You might do this to consolidate two meetings into one meeting.

✔ **Keep:** Keep the meeting's content.

✔ **Delete:** Delete the meeting's content.

To choose one of these options, follow these steps:

1. **Browse to the Meeting workspace.**

2. **Click the meeting from which you removed the appointment link.**

   You'll recognize it because it has a big red exclamation point next to it.

3. **Click Move, Keep, or Delete from the drop-down menu, as Figure 8-6 shows you.**

You cannot remove a link that connects a single occurrence of a recurrent meeting to a SharePoint Meeting workspace. You can, however, remove the link from the entire *series* of recurrent meetings in Outlook. Removing a link to a recurring meeting doesn't give you the option to move, keep, or delete that series of meetings in the Meeting workspace. (Looks like you'll still have to go.)

Figure 8-6:
Choose what you want to do with the content of a meeting whose appointment link you remove.

Anatomy of a Meeting workspace

The basic Meeting workspace displays these Web parts on the home page by default:

- ✔ Agendas
- ✔ Attendees
- ✔ Document library
- ✔ Objectives

In addition to the basic Meeting workspace, you can use any of four additional variations on the Meeting workspace in SharePoint. Each of these workspaces differs only a little from the basic Meeting workspace:

- ✔ **Blank Meeting Workspace:** You guessed it — this workspace is blank.

- ✔ **Decision Meeting Workspace:** Includes Web parts for tracking decisions that must be made in the meeting, as well as a task list.

- ✔ **Multipage Meeting Workspace:** Displays Web parts for objectives, agendas, and attendees, and provides two blank pages.

- ✔ **Social Meeting Workspace:** Adds a Things to Bring list, along with a list for directions, additional pages for discussions, and a really bad clip-art image of some party doodads — the ultimate in party planning.

Web parts

Meeting workspaces and the Web parts that they contain are nothing special by themselves — until you make them work for you. You can

- ✔ Create special lists for the Meeting workspace with built-in list templates, or make a custom list. (See Chapters 10 through 13 for examples that use the built-in list templates and custom lists.)

- ✔ Add all the regular team-site Web parts to a workspace. (You can take a tour of those Web parts in Chapters 10 through 13.)

To add more Web parts to a basic Meeting workspace, follow these steps:

1. **Browse to the Meeting workspace.**

2. **Click Modify This Workspace in the upper-right corner of the page.**

3. **Click Add Web Parts from the Modify This Workspace drop-down menu.**

   A filtered list of workspace Web parts appears.

4. **Drag and drop a Web part from the list into a Web part zone.**

   The page is divided into rectangles (at left, center, and right) called *Web part zones*.

Click Show All Lists to display the workspace's Create Page page. From the Create Page page, you can select any kind of list, library, discussion board, or survey that you want to add to your Meeting workspace.

To add Web parts from the top-level site or other Web part gallery, follow these steps:

1. **Click the drop-down arrow next to Create Lists in the Add Web Parts task pane.**

2. **Click Browse from the Create Lists menu to view all available galleries.**

   You can also use the Create Lists menu to import Web parts. You can find Web parts to do almost anything you can imagine on the Web.

3. **Select a Web part from the gallery; drag and drop it into a Web part zone.**

Content

You add objectives, tasks, or other content to your workspace very much like you do when adding content in a team site. To add new content, follow these steps:

1. **In a Web part such as the Objectives or Document Library Web parts displayed on the Home page of a Meeting workspace, click the Add New Item or Add New Document link.**

Web parts that display lists such as Objectives or Agendas provide an Add New Item link. Web parts that display document libraries (such as the Document Library Web part) show the Add New Document link. The Attendees Web Part displays a link called Manage Attendees. No matter what kind of information is displayed with a Web part, it provides a hyperlink to add new content. Clicking the hyperlink takes you to a form for the underlying list or library where new data can be entered.

2. **In the list or library, click the New Item or New Document button.**

3. **Click the title of any of the Web parts displayed on the Meeting workspace to go to the list or library where you can add new content.**

   Lists such as Objectives show a New Item button that you click to add a new list item (in this case, a new objective — lose ten pounds, maybe?). Document libraries have a New Document button and the Attendees list has a Manage Attendees button. See a pattern?

Attendees

SharePoint automatically adds attendees invited in the original Outlook appointment as meeting attendees and site users.

If you set up a person as a site user, he or she gets permission to access the Meeting workspace where he or she is added. All the rules that you can find in Chapter 4regarding access to SharePoint sites apply to workspaces as well.

Meetings

Meeting workspaces are special because they do, after all, help you handle meetings — and they display meetings linked from Outlook 2003. You can add agendas, objectives, documents, and anything else you want to a specific meeting on a Meeting workspace. Meeting workspaces can even host multiple meetings on a single workspace. The meetings serve as a way to organize the content on the Meeting workspace.

Your Meeting workspace could have ten meetings. You're only going to see the objectives, agenda, and documents for the first meeting when you look at the first meeting. Everything isn't muddled together.

What if you want to see all your agendas across all meetings in a Meeting workspace? Piece of cake. Follow these steps:

1. **Browse to a list, such as Agenda, on the Meeting workspace.**

2. **Click the All Meetings button on the toolbar.**

   All the agendas stored on the Meeting workspace are displayed, regardless of the meeting. To go back to seeing the agenda for a single meeting, click the This Meeting button.

Just so you know: Attendees can use the All Meetings button to see content from a meeting they didn't attend — even if they weren't invited to that meeting.

You can share a list's content across all meetings by changing the Series Items setting from no to yes in the list's General settings. To access a list's general settings, follow these steps:

1. **In a list such as Agenda, click Modify Settings and Columns.**

2. **Click Change General Settings.**

3. **Click the radio button next to Yes in the Share List Items Across All Meetings (Series Items) section.**

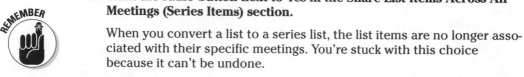

   When you convert a list to a series list, the list items are no longer associated with their specific meetings. You're stuck with this choice because it can't be undone.

Pages

You can easily add additional pages to your workspace. You can also reorder and rename pages. To add pages to your basic Meeting workspace, follow these steps:

1. **Click Modify This Workspace.**

2. **Click Add Pages from the Modify This Workspace menu.**

3. **In the Pages task pane, enter a descriptive name for the page in the Page Name text box.**

   This name appears in a tab next to the Home tab on the Meeting workspace.

4. **Click Add.**

   A tab to access the new page appears next to the Home tab, as you can see in Figure 8-7.

5. **Add Web parts to the page from the Add Web Parts task pane (displayed on the right when the page is created).**

To rename your pages or change the order in which they appear, choose Manage Pages from the Modify This Workspace menu.

You can also add any kind of site or workspace as a subsite to your basic Meeting workspace. To add a subsite, follow these steps:

1. **Click Modify This Workspace.**

2. **Choose Site Settings from the Modify This Workspace menu.**

3. **Click Manage Sites and Workspaces.**

   The Sites and Workspaces page appears.

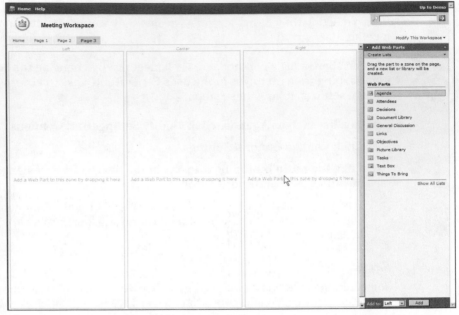

Figure 8-7:
Pages
added to a
workspace
appear
next to the
Home tab.

4. **Click Create.**

   The New SharePoint Site page appears.

5. **Follow the instructions to create the new site or workspace.**

   See the steps at the beginning of this chapter for specifics on how to complete the New SharePoint Site page.

Document Central

Document workspaces are geared around document collaboration — you know, when two or more documents work together to write an award-winning novel (just kidding). Actually, it's your team members who do the collaborating on a document — working together to write a killer sales presentation or a litigation-proof policy manual. A Document workspace makes that possible in several ways:

✔ You can store a single master copy of a document.

✔ Members of a team can modify their working copies of a document.

✔ You can accept (or reject) changes from the working copies into the single master copy.

A new Document workspace displays these Web parts by default:

- ✔ Announcements
- ✔ Links
- ✔ Members
- ✔ Shared Documents
- ✔ Tasks

You use these Web parts to add information that's related to the document. For example, use the Tasks list to assign tasks such as proofreading, researching, and formatting the document to members of the team.

You can create Document workspaces in SharePoint using a Web browser, like you can any other SharePoint site, or from Word 2003. Figure 8-8 shows an example of a Document workspace.

As with Meeting workspaces, you can add any kind of Web part, list, library, or subsite to a Document workspace. (See the previous section on Meeting workspaces for the details of adding content to a workspace.)

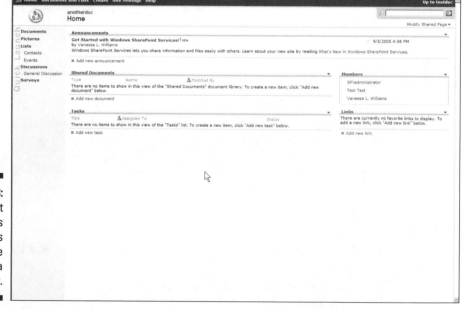

Figure 8-8:
Document workspaces help users collaborate on a document.

Joining the club

You call the users of a Document workspace *members*. How new members are added depends on whether the workspace manages its own permissions or inherits them from its parent site.

You specify permissions when you create the workspace. (I discuss permissions management in more detail at the beginning of the chapter, where I show you how to add document and Meeting workspace subsites to your team site.)

If the workspace is set up to manage its own members and their permissions when it's created, then you see an Add New Member link in the Members Web part, as Figure 8-9 shows you. Otherwise you must go to the Document workspace's parent site to add members and set their permissions; to do so, click the link in the upper-right corner of the screen (the one that starts with Up to), and there you are.

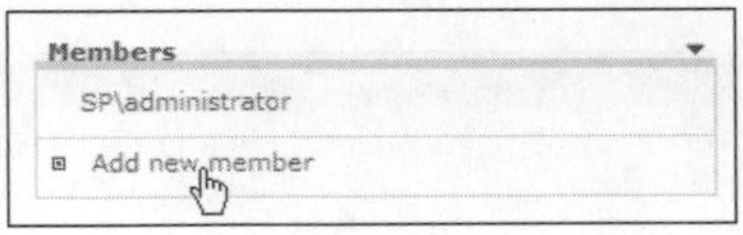

Figure 8-9:
The Add
New
Member link
means the
workspace
manages
its own
permissions.

To change the way a Document workspace manages its members and their permissions, follow these steps:

1. **Click Site Settings on the primary horizontal navigation bar of the workspace.**

2. **Click Go to Site Administration.**

   The Site Administration page appears.

3. **Click Manage permission inheritance from the Users and Permissions section.**

4. **Select the radio button next to Use unique permissions.**

5. **Click OK.**

You can now add users to the site by using the Manage Users link in Site Administration or with the Members Web part. (See Chapter 4 for more about adding users to a site.)

Managing documents

A Document workspace includes a document library with version control turned off. With version control disabled, you overwrite the document every time you save it, similar to what happens with a regular network file share. With version control turned on for a document library, a new version of the document is created each time the document is saved. (I cover document libraries and version control in more detail in the next chapter; later in this chapter, I show you how to enable document versions in the Document workspace's document library.)

Compare and merge documents

Using the built-in features in Microsoft Word, team members can create local copies of a document and merge their changes later with the version in the document library. To create a new Word document by using the library, follow these steps:

1. **On the home page of the Meeting workspace, click Shared Documents.**

2. **Click New Document from the toolbar.**

    A new Word document opens.

    The New Document button opens a document based on the file template that's defined for the library, usually a Microsoft Word document. Chapter 9 explains how you can change the file template for a library to another type, such as Microsoft Excel.

3. **Type your document in the new Word document.**

4. **Click Save.**

    The document is automatically saved to the document library because you create it from that library.

About that document just created in the preceding steps: Don't close it right away. Leave it open until I tell you to close it later on in the chapter. If you close it now, you won't see how another user can open the same document for editing. (And I *know* you're dying to see that.)

To open another local copy of the document that you're still editing (you left it open, right?), follow these steps:

1. **Open the document from a different computer than the one that you use in the preceding steps.**

    Browse to the document library on another computer that's running Microsoft Office, and hover your mouse pointer over the document listing in the document library. Click the drop-down menu that appears, and then click Edit in Microsoft Word.

    Word tries to open the document and displays the File In Use dialog box.

2. **Select the radio button next to Create a local copy and merge your changes later.**

3. **Click OK.**

   The document opens in read-only mode.

4. **Enter text on the local copy of the document.**

   Pretend that you are adding text to a document and enter anything you want in the Word document.

5. **Save the file by clicking File⇨Save in Word.**

   Word displays a dialog box telling you that the file is locked and cannot be saved at this time. It's locked because you have it open another computer. The dialog box explains how to merge the local file with the library file later on, when the file is no longer locked by another user.

6. **Click OK.**

   The Save As dialog box appears.

7. **Save the file on your local computer.**

If the locked file becomes available while you are editing the document in read-only mode, Word notifies you and gives you the option to merge your changes.

To merge the changes in the local copy with the original library file, follow these steps:

1. **Save and close the original file in the library.**

   Click File⇨Close in Word. Save the document if prompted. The file is automatically saved in the SharePoint document library because you created it by using the New Document button in the library.

2. **Open the local file in Microsoft Word that you saved in the preceding example.**

3. **In the Tools menu, click Compare and Merge Documents.**

   The Compare and Merge dialog box opens. It should open in the document library folder where the original file is saved. If it doesn't, you have to browse to the document library and select the file (as I show you in Chapter 4).

4. **With the original document selected in the Compare and Merge dialog box, click Merge.**

   Word displays the merged documents for editing.

The Compare and Merge feature in Word is very powerful, especially when you use it with Word's Track Changes feature. You may want to study up on Word before you use either or both of these features.

Instead of having multiple people working on one large document, consider creating a Master Document that points to subdocuments that you have stored elsewhere on SharePoint. Individuals can work on their subdocuments without tripping all over each other. Check out Bil Simser's post on his Weblog, `http://weblogs.asp.net/bsimser/archive/2005/01/11/350518.aspx`, to find out how to use Word's Master Document feature with SharePoint.

To check out or not to check out

SharePoint document libraries offer two strategies for managing document editing, depending on how you want SharePoint to manage the locked document while you're editing. (Another person can't edit a locked document.)

Without check out

If you need to make a quick change to a document, you can edit documents without checking them out. With this strategy, the latest and greatest version of the document is always available:

✔ A document is locked only while you have that document open.

✔ After you close the document, any user with permissions to edit items in the document library can edit the file.

Edit without checking out if you plan to change a document quickly.

With check out

Checking out a document when you make changes indicates to other users that the document may be unavailable for editing for a while:

✔ When you check out the document, you're the only person who can change the checked-out copy until you explicitly check it back in.

Document checkout creates an exclusive lock on the file that's checked out. No other user can update the file until you explicitly check it back in.

✔ Other users can

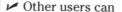

• View the last checked-in version of the document.

Other users can't see any changes that you make in the checked out document before you check it back in.

• Edit a local copy of the last checked-in version of the document.

• Merge other users' local copies with the library copy after you check in the copy you finished editing.

Check out the document if you're making extensive changes for at least a few days.

The Check In and Out feature works very well with Word's Compare and Merge Document features.

To check in and check out a document while you make edits to that document, follow these steps:

1. **Click the document title in the library.**

2. **Choose Check Out from the drop-down menu (as Figure 8-10 shows).**

   The document's Checked Out To property updates. The Checked Out To property records the name of the person who has the file checked out.

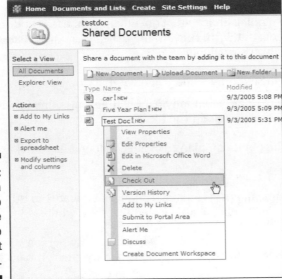

Figure 8-10:
Check out a document to make changes to that document.

3. **Make your modifications to the document.**

4. **Save the document in Word.**

   If Word prompts you to check in the file, select the radio button next to *Keep checked out* and click OK. As you work with the document (opening and closing it over a period of a few days, for example) Word prompts you to check your document in — annoying, but it keeps you from forgetting to check the document in when you're done editing.

   During this time, other users can't view your changes to the document; they still see it in its last checked-in version.

5. **When you're ready to check your document in, use the following steps to check in your document by using Word:**

   a. **Open the document file in Word.**

   b. **Choose File⇨Check In from the menu in Word.**

   c. **Enter comments to describe this version of the document in the Check-In Comments dialog box.**

   d. **Click OK.**

If other users try to edit the checked-out document, Word prompts them to create a local copy. Other users have to save any modifications locally and merge those modifications with the Master Document after it's checked in.

In the event someone checks out a document and never turns it back in, you can override the check out, provided you have the right permission. (See Chapter 4 for more about permissions.)

Creating document versions

Another option for document collaboration is to enable document *versioning* — you create a new copy of the document every time you update it, and each copy is a new version of the document. Versioning lets you

✔ Save the entire version history for a document

✔ Store comments along with each version

✔ Revert to a previous version of a document

To enable document versioning, follow these steps:

1. **Click Modify Settings and Columns in the document library.**

2. **Click Change General Settings.**

3. **In the Library Settings page, select the radio button next to** Yes **in the Document Versions section.**

SharePoint creates a new document version in two cases:

✔ The first time you add the file to the library

✔ When you (or any other user) check in a file after modifying it

You can create new versions in other ways, but these two instances are the best and most pertinent.

You can always check a file in just *before* you make major modifications to the file. For example, if you decide to delete several paragraphs, then you probably want to check in first. You can then revert to the previous version (the one you create by checking in) if you change your mind later about the paragraphs.

To view or restore a previous version of a document, follow these steps:

1. **Hover over the document's title in the library.**

2. **Choose Version History from the title's drop-down menu.**

   All the saved versions of that document appear.

3. **Click one of the versions to restore, view, or delete.**

4. **Choose View, Restore, or Delete from the menu (as you can see in Figure 8-11).**

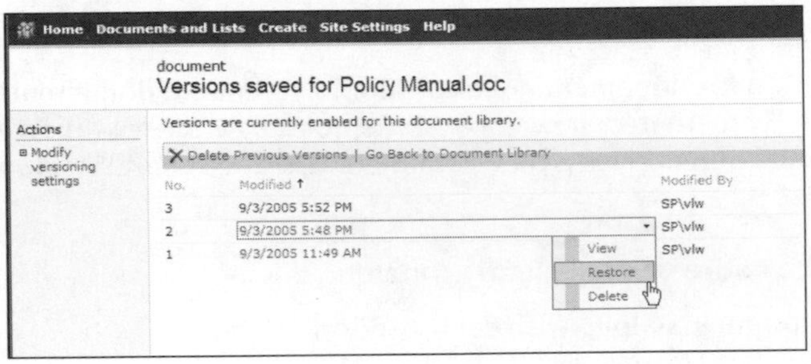

Figure 8-11:
Click a document version to restore it.

Using the Right Template for the Job

You don't get a hard-and-fast rule to tell you which of the SharePoint site templates to use when. More often than not, you combine templates to create an optimum solution. For example, you can add a

✔ Document workspace to a team subsite

✔ Meeting workspace to a project team site

✔ Team site to another team site

The entire SharePoint portal is a combination of site templates — and so are all its sites. The portal is a special kind of team site that has team sites attached to it.

Here are some suggestions for using site templates:

✔ Use a Meeting workspace any time that you need to keep meeting-specific content and you don't need that content connected to another site.

✔ Use a Document workspace to collaborate on a specific document, such as a policy manual. Plan on publishing the final document to another site but maintaining all the support content for the policy manual in the Document workspace.

✔ Use any workspace template for more intimate collaborations when a smaller number of team members collaborate on a single solution or document.

✔ Use sites when participants have less frequent (or even anonymous) contact with each other.

You can't easily share content among different workspaces and sites in SharePoint. Be sure to plan for content that you want to use across sites before breaking things into too many subsites.

Prototype your solution — build and try out a few throwaway sites — before you implement the real thing. I often start a project thinking that I should implement something one way, then change my mind after walking through some scenarios.

Making Friends with Office

I've shown you how to use Outlook and Word in the context of Meeting and Document workspaces. That's just the tip of the iceberg where SharePoint's integration with Office is concerned. In this section, I expand on using Office with SharePoint for team collaboration by showing you

✔ Which versions of Office play nice with SharePoint

✔ How to use the shared workspace task pane in Word and Excel

✔ How to link contacts and events in SharePoint to Outlook

✔ How to link Excel lists to SharePoint lists

✔ How to save an Office document as a Web page that you can display in SharePoint

Got Office (2003)?

SharePoint works best with one particular Office version: Microsoft Office 2003. In fact, SharePoint Portal Server 2003 (SPS) is actually *part* of the

Office 2003 System (although you have to buy SPS separately from client Office 2003 applications like Word and Excel).

If you don't have Office 2003 (or wonder whether you can squeak by without it), here's what to expect from the different Office versions:

- **Office 2000:** You can open and save files in document libraries using Office 2000.

  Unless your company's help desk has a lot of stamina, don't even think about using Office 2000.

- **Office XP:** You can export lists to Excel.

  If you expect your users to access SharePoint mostly through the Web browser, you can get by with XP.

- **Office 2003:** Out-of-this-world integration with SharePoint.

  Trust me: To get the most from your SharePoint investment, you really need Office 2003. And from what I hear, the next version of Office will work even better with SharePoint.

 Okay, sure, you can still make the most of your SharePoint money without upgrading to Office 2003. Just be sure that your version of Office has all the features needed to achieve your business goals. Then study the upcoming section and the specifics about version differences, which you can find in the Microsoft article "Good, Better, Best" at

```
http://office.microsoft.com/en-us/assistance/HA011726401033.aspx
```

Making Office and SharePoint work together

Some Office 2003 applications, such as Word and Excel, give you a special Shared Workspace task pane for working with SharePoint. There you can

- Create a new workspace
- Link a document to an existing workspace
- View or add tasks to a workspace
- View and open other documents in a workspace
- View or add links in a workspace
- View document history and check out a document

The Shared Workspace task pane gives you access to the Document workspace content from inside your Office application. To view the Shared Workspace task pane, follow these steps:

1. **Open Word or Excel.**

2. **On the Tools menu, click Shared Workspace.**

   The Shared Workspace task pane appears.

To link a document to a new workspace, follow these steps:

1. **Open Word or Excel.**

2. **Create a new document or spreadsheet.**

3. **Click Tools⇨Shared Workspace.**

   The Shared Workspace task pane appears.

4. **In the Shared Workspace task pane, enter a name for the Document workspace in the Document Workspace name text box (such as My Document Workspace if you're feeling creative).**

5. **Choose a location on your SharePoint portal or site where you want to store the workspace from the Location for new workspace drop-down list.**

   If you don't see the site listed in the drop-down list, click (Type new URL) and type (or paste) the URL to the site.

6. **Click Create.**

   Office prompts you to save the document.

7. **Save a copy of the file locally.**

   You can delete the local copy of the file when you know you've successfully created the workspace.

SharePoint creates a new workspace with your document saved to the document library. The Shared Workspace task pane updates to show the name of your new workspace at the top. (Figure 8-12 shows an example of the Shared Workspace task pane in Excel.)

To add new members to the workspace, follow these steps:

1. **Click the Members tab on the Shared Workspace task pane.**

   The Members tab has two people on it. It's selected by default.

2. **Click the Add New Members link at the bottom of the Shared Workspace task pane.**

   The Add New Members dialog box appears.

 3. **Enter members' names in the multi-line text box; separate them with semicolons.**

 You can enter e-mail addresses or domain accounts if those are needed. (For more information, see Chapter 4.)

 4. **Choose a site group for the members by clicking the drop-down box.**

 The Contributor site group is already selected for you.

 5. **Click Next.**

 6. **Verify each member's name, e-mail address, and display name in the confirmation screen.**

 Make any appropriate changes.

 7. **Click Finish.**

 Office prompts you to send e-mail invitations to your new members. After you've done that, you have new members in the workspace — and they're listed in the task pane.

To add a new task in the Shared Workspace task pane, follow these steps:

 1. **Click the Tasks button in the Shared Workspace task pane.**

 The Tasks button looks like a clipboard with a check mark on it.

 2. **Click the <u>Add New Task</u> hyperlink at the bottom of the task pane.**

 The Task window appears.

 3. **Enter a new task in the task window.**

 4. **Click OK.**

 The task is entered in the SharePoint Document workspace and appears on the Shared Workspace task pane, as you can see in Figure 8-12.

Bringing SharePoint to Outlook

SharePoint can link and import data from contacts and events lists into Outlook 2003, so you can

 ✔ Export SharePoint events to the Outlook calendar

 ✔ Import contacts from Outlook to SharePoint

 ✔ Export SharePoint contacts to Outlook contacts

 ✔ Link SharePoint contacts or events to a folder in Outlook 2003

SharePoint team sites include events and contacts lists by default. Use the events and contacts lists in a SharePoint team site to practice importing, exporting, and linking to Outlook.

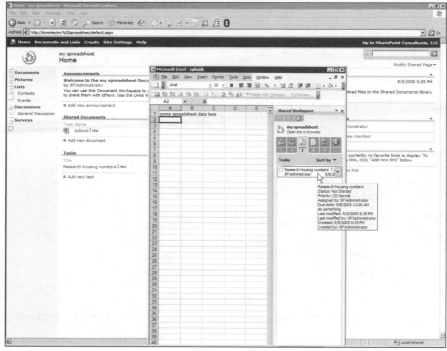

Figure 8-12:
Enter tasks
by using the
Shared
Workspace
task pane.

To export SharePoint events to Outlook, follow these steps:

1. **Browse to an events list in SharePoint.**

2. **Click an event in the list to display that event.**

   If your list doesn't have any events, click New Item to add a new event to the list.

3. **Click Export Event from the toolbar.**

   A prompt appears to download an iCalendar file.

4. **Click Open, as you can see in Figure 8-13.**

   The file opens as an appointment in Outlook.

You use the iCalendar file format to specify calendar appointments.

To export contacts, follow these steps:

1. **Browse to a contacts list.**

2. **Click a contact in the list to display the contact.**

3. **Click Export Contact from the toolbar.**

4. **When prompted, click Open to open the vCard file as an Outlook contact.**

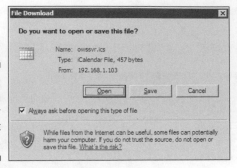

Figure 8-13:
Open the
iCalendar
file to save it
in Outlook.

You use the vCard file format to define contacts.

To import contacts, follow these steps:

1. **Browse to a contacts list.**

2. **Click Import Contacts on the toolbar.**

   The Outlook address book appears.

3. **Select the contacts that you want to import from the Outlook address book.**

4. **Click OK to import the contacts.**

To link a list of contacts or events to Outlook 2003, follow these steps:

1. **Browse to the list.**

2. **Click Link to Outlook in the toolbar, as you can see in Figure 8-14.**

Figure 8-14:
Use the Link
to Outlook
button
to display
the listed
contacts or
events in an
Outlook
folder.

Outlook displays a dialog box to tell you that the folder is being added.

3. Click Yes to add the folder.

The folder is added to the folder list in Outlook, as in Figure 8-15.

None of these approaches creates an actual *synchronized* link between your Outlook calendars or contacts and a SharePoint list. Chapter 13 gives you pointers on how to create a synchronized link.

Figure 8-15: You can display Contacts and Events folders in Outlook.

For more information on how to integrate Outlook 2003 with SharePoint, see the Sample Resource Kit on Microsoft's Web site at

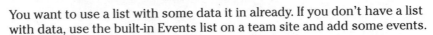

www.microsoft.com/technet/prodtechnol/sppt/reskit/c4061881x.mspx

Linking Excel lists to SharePoint lists

One of the coolest features in SharePoint is the capability to link Excel spreadsheets to custom lists: Adding or updating data in a linked Excel spreadsheet updates the underlying SharePoint list accordingly. In effect, the spreadsheet is a data-entry form for your SharePoint list. You can create a link between an Excel list and a SharePoint list in two ways:

✔ Use the List feature on the Excel Data menu to create a link between an Excel list and a SharePoint list.

✔ Create the link by using the Datasheet view in the SharePoint list.

The term *list* has a special meaning in Excel. Designating a set of data on an Excel worksheet as a list adds some features to the data; one handy one is that it becomes a lot easier to link that data to a SharePoint list.

You can link an Excel list to a SharePoint list by using the list's Datasheet view. Just follow these steps:

1. **Browse to a list in SharePoint.**

   You want to use a list with some data it in already. If you don't have a list with data, use the built-in Events list on a team site and add some events.

   You can also create a link between an Excel spreadsheet and a SharePoint document library.

2. **Click the Edit in Datasheet button on the toolbar.**

   The list appears in a Datasheet view.

3. **Click the Task Pane button on the toolbar.**

   The Office Links task pane appears.

4. **Click Export and Link to Excel in the task pane, as you can see in Figure 8-16.**

   The Opening Query dialog box appears. SharePoint sends the list data to Excel in the form of an `iqy` file, which Excel knows how to open.

5. **Click Open.**

   The data from the SharePoint list is imported into an Excel list.

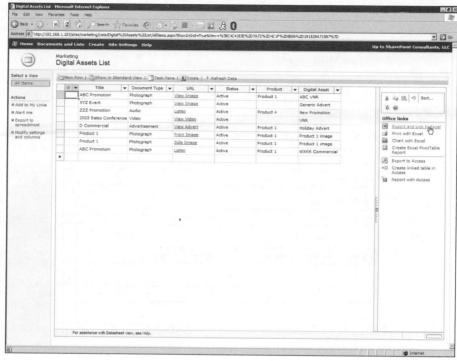

Figure 8-16:
Create a link
between a
SharePoint
list and
Excel with
the Office
Links task
pane.

You can enter data right into the spreadsheet and update the list on SharePoint because the Excel list is linked to the SharePoint list. A couple of quick steps update the list:

1. **Place your mouse on any cell in the list in Excel.**

2. **Click Data⇨List⇨Synchronize List from the menu in Excel.**

You can link a SharePoint list to tables in Access with the Office Links task pane. (Chapter 13 shows you how.)

Saving your Office document as a Web page

All Office applications offer the Save as Web Page feature. Saving as a Web page is a quick, simple, nontechnical way to create content for a site. Each Office application has a slightly different approach to this operation, but the basic steps for saving an Office document as a Web page look like this:

1. **In an open Office application, choose File⇨Save as Web Page from the menu.**

2. **Enter the location on the SharePoint site to which you want to save the Web page.**

   If you're using a pre-2003 version of Office, you can save your document as a Web page on your local computer and *then* upload it to the SharePoint document library.

3. **After saving the document as a Web page, use a Page Viewer Web part to display the page on the site or portal.**

   I show you how to add the Page Viewer Web part in Chapter 11. If you're using Visio, Chapter 10 describes how to save a Visio document as a Web page.

Playing nice with others

SharePoint is part of Microsoft Office 2003, so you can expect SharePoint to integrate with all Office 2003 applications.

Here are a few resources that can help you get a better grasp on Office 2003 and SharePoint:

- ✔ **Microsoft Office InfoPath:** See Chapter 12 for an example of using InfoPath with SharePoint.

- ✔ **Publishing an Excel spreadsheet as a Web page:** `http://office.microsoft.com/en-us/assistance/HP052673981033.aspx`

- ✔ **Integrating SharePoint and Office 2003:** `www.microsoft.com/technet/prodtechnol/windowsserver2003/technologies/sharepoint/spoffint.mspx`

- ✔ **Using Office 2003 and SharePoint for collaboration:** `www.microsoft.com/office/editions/prodinfo/technologies/sharepoint.mspx`

Chapter 9

Document Libraries

*E*very company has standard communications templates used for fax cover sheets and memos. Your company may even have templates for Excel spreadsheets and other kinds of Office files.

Some of those files are images; your company has company logos and branding images that must be managed. Where I work, we have new images each year because our products have a different theme each year. The branding images must be updated accordingly.

How do you manage these templates and images? Are they stored in a common folder (file share) on the network? Maybe in a public folder on your Exchange server? Or does each department handle images in its own way?

Chances are you have some combination of approaches. Regardless of your repository, can it manage versions? After all, how do you *know* you have the latest logo, branding image, or template?

SharePoint to the rescue. SharePoint libraries give you a central place to store all these company-wide templates and images. This chapter introduces the wonderful world of document and picture libraries in SharePoint with a few simple examples. Richer examples are presented in other chapters in this book (for example, Chapter 12 covers form libraries).

In SharePoint, a *library* is a file that serves as a repository for storing other files. Each SharePoint library has a different purpose:

▸ **Document library:** Here you can store files of any kind.

▸ **Picture library:** This one includes special commands and viewers for managing image files.

▸ **Form library:** This is the place to store documents that manage XML data.

Although you can use any kind of library you want, it's best to match a library's purpose with its intended use.

Standardizing Communications

Every business has standards (or should have) for internal and external communications. Such standards show up in document templates for items such as

- Fax cover letters
- Memo and letter templates
- PowerPoint templates
- Spreadsheet templates

Storing all these templates in various places — and keeping track of the latest versions — can make even the best administrative assistants a little batty. You can use document libraries in SharePoint to consolidate and manage all your shared communications templates.

Having all these templates in a single repository is helpful for new hires. (The old hands usually like it too, after they get used to it.)

A document library works much like a normal file share or a directory on your local hard drive. Any kind of file can be saved to a document library, but SharePoint libraries work best with Microsoft Office files (products from the same maker usually play nice together). What's so neat about document libraries is what they can do:

- Save all the versions of a document
- Limit who has access
- Allow the document to be checked out for revision
- Provide multiple modes of access, either through the Web browser or the file system
- Store custom properties along with the file
- Provide custom views of other files stored in the same document library

Creating a new document library

Before you create a new document library, you must decide where the document library will live — and in most cases, that means a site. For example, if you have a team site, then a document library on that site would be an ideal place to store the team's files. Or you may create a document library on a departmental site; who'll be using it is a big hint about where to put it.

To create a library on a site, follow these steps:

1. **Browse to the site.**

2. **Click Create on the primary horizontal navigation bar.**

   You see templates of all the documents, lists, and other items that can be created for the site.

3. **Click Document Library.**

For more information about team sites, see Chapter 8.

Document libraries can also be created on the portal itself — and provide a central place to store enterprise-wide communications templates. To create a document library on the portal, follow these steps:

1. **Browse to the portal home page.**

2. **Click Manage Content from the Actions list on the vertical navigation bar.**

   The Documents and Lists page appears.

3. **Click Create to access the Create Page.**

   A list of all the items that can be created appears.

4. **Click Document Libraries to create a new document library.**

5. **Enter** Company Templates **as the name.**

6. **Click Yes to display the document library on the Quick Launch bar.**

7. **Click Yes to create versions.**

   For more about document versions, see the sidebar, "To control or not to control . . . what is the version?" later in the chapter.

8. **Accept the default document template and click Create.**

   A new document library is created. (See "Using document templates to create a new document," later in this chapter, for more information.)

A document library's *default document template* determines which Office application is launched when the user clicks New Document in the document library.

Cruising the document library

Across the top of the library, a toolbar lists the actions available in a document library. Figure 9-1 shows the document library toolbar. The available actions are

✔ **New Document:** Create a new file, using the default document template for the document library. (For more about this feature, see "Using document templates to create a new document," later in this chapter.)

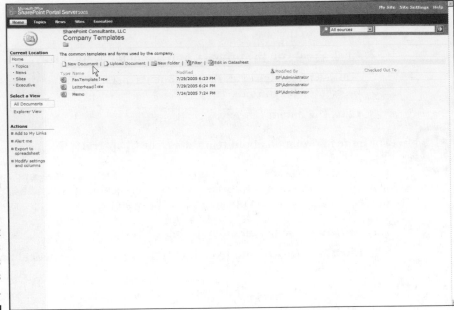

Figure 9-1:
The
document
library's
toolbar lists
the actions
available.

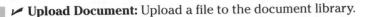

✓ **Upload Document:** Upload a file to the document library.

✓ **New Folder:** Create a new subfolder within the document library.

Resist the urge to re-create your network file structures in a document library. Your document library should never have more than one level of folders. There's a better way: See the "Custom properties" section (later in this chapter) for pointers on using properties instead of folders to organize your document libraries.

✓ **Filter:** Change the list of documents displayed by filtering a file property.

✓ **Edit in Datasheet:** Display the list of documents in a spreadsheet-like datasheet. The default view is called *Standard view*.

The Datasheet view allows quick and easy editing of file properties.

The vertical navigation bar along the left side of the document library contains a couple of handy options:

✓ **Select a View:** Choose to display the list in Summary View, Explorer View, or a custom view you create.

For more about views, see the section "Get a new view."

✓ **Actions:** This section shows a list of actions you can perform with this document library, such as these:

  • **Add to My Links:** Allows you to add a hyperlink to this document library on your personal Web site.

- **Alert me:** Tells SharePoint to send you an e-mail any time files are added or removed from the document library.

- **Export to spreadsheet:** Export the columns and rows you see on the screen to an Excel 2003 spreadsheet.

- **Modify settings and columns:** Change the general settings for the document library such as whether version control is enabled and add or remove columns.

Using document templates to create a new document

Every document library has a *default document template* used to create new documents. When you choose the New Document action, you create a new file quickly, using the default template. The value of this feature depends on how you expect to create new documents — in the application itself (such as Word or Excel) or in the document library. My guess is that you'll continue to create new documents in just the way you're already doing — and then simply save those documents to the library.

If you need a particular template, you can specify it when the library is created. You can also change the template for an existing document library by following these steps:

1. **Browse to the document library.**

2. **Click Modify settings and columns from the vertical navigation on the left.**

3. **Click Change general settings from the Customize page.**

4. **Type the URL of the new document template into the Template URL text box.**

The template must be stored in the Forms folder of the document library.

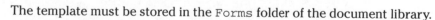

To control or not to control . . . what is the version?

By enabling version control in a document library, you tell the library to store each version of a file as it's checked in and out. Doing so creates a version history so you can easily revert to a previous version. Version information can also be viewed in Office applications.

Version control can be turned on or off for all the files in a document library, and you can enable it even after a document library is created.

I use version control on any document libraries for which I am the administrator. It saves an amazing amount of time and stress if a file is overwritten inadvertently (which is much more likely to happen if multiple people work on a file — exactly the kind of collaboration that SharePoint encourages). In my experience, most end users don't understand or use version-control features — but they're outrageously convenient for administrators.

Adding documents to a document library

When you've set up a document library for storing your company's communications templates, adding some template files would be the next logical thing. To add templates (or any kind of file) to your document library, follow these steps:

1. **Browse to the document library on your portal.**

2. **Click Upload Document on the toolbar.**

3. **Browse to the document you want to upload.**

4. **Clear the check mark next to Add a listing for this document.**

   You usually don't want to create a portal listing for individual files in a document library. That would get unmanageable quickly.

5. **Click Save and Close.**

   The file is uploaded to the document library, as shown in Figure 9-2.

You can put a check mark next to *Add a listing* to display a hyperlink to the document only if you place it on a portal. This option isn't displayed for document libraries stored on a site.

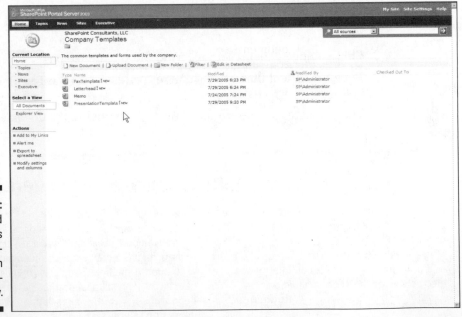

Figure 9-2:
Uploaded documents are displayed in the document library.

Custom properties

New SharePoint users always want to create a folder structure in document libraries. You can re-create all of your network file shares in a document library, but it's a waste of SharePoint's potential (and probably your time).

SharePoint is designed to overcome the limitations of the file folder. The biggest limitation is that nested file folders limit you to a single view of your files.

Imagine that you have a set of documents about sales information (and that the numbers are outstanding — it's more fun that way). Using a traditional file-folder structure, you can organize these files either by sales territory or by product line, as shown in Figure 9-3. You can't choose both.

Figure 9-3:
File-folder
structures
force you to
choose one
view only.

With SharePoint document libraries, you can define custom properties to emulate a file-folder structure. But why settle for that? You can change the view of the document library to match those custom properties. For example, you might create two custom properties specific to sales documents:

- ✔ Sales Territory
- ✔ Product Line

Then as you add documents to your document library, you would specify the sales territory and product line associated with each document.

"Custom properties" is just another name for *metadata* in SharePoint — "data about data" — the very thing needed for organizing data. (No wonder it's all the rage in software development.) To add a custom property, follow these steps:

1. **Browse to your document library.**

   Here I've created a new one called Sales Documents.

2. **Click Modify settings and columns.**

   The Customize screen appears.

3. **In the Columns section, click Add a new column.**

4. **Enter the column name.**

   For this example, I'm using "Sales Territory."

5. **Select the type of data to display in the column by choosing Choice from the list of data types.**

   A text box appears so you can enter the choices available for this column.

   The type of data stored in the column tells the computer how much memory to use, and how to display the information. Chapters 10, 11, and 13 show column data types in action.

6. **Scroll down and enter the choices.**

   For this example, I have three choices: Midwest, Northeast, and Southeast.

7. **Choose the option that displays the choices as radio buttons.**

8. **Click OK to create the column.**

   Figure 9-4 shows the Add Column screen.

9. **Repeat the preceding steps to add a column for Product Line with the choices of** Doors, Siding, **and** Windows.

   Now, when a document is added to the document library, the two columns that you added are displayed as properties so the user can select one or both of them — for example, the sales territory *and* the product line *for each document*. Figure 9-5 shows an example of a document being uploaded.

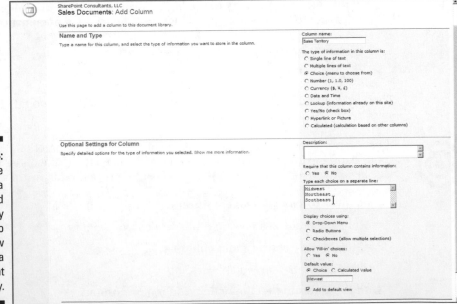

Figure 9-4:
Enter the name, data type, and display settings to add a new column to a document library.

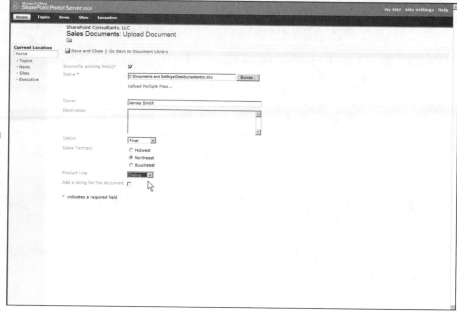

Figure 9-5:
Custom
properties
appear on-
screen
when a
document is
uploaded to
the docu-
ment library.

Custom properties are also displayed when a user uploads a document from an application such as Word or Excel.

Filtering out time-sensitive documents

When you want to store time-sensitive files in a document library, you also have to decide how long to keep them there. To deal with this scenario, you could create individual listings on your portal for the documents — and specify dates to start and end publishing each document. That makes sense for news and other time-sensitive information you want everyone to see. But that seems like overkill for other kinds of sensitive information that people may need to find right away — these, for example:

✔ Branding images that are only valid for the current year

✔ Promotional materials that expire

When a particular document has served its purpose, you want to make sure it's no longer visible, but maybe you don't want to archive it manually. (I can relate.) One easy way to accomplish this is to create two custom properties:

✔ **Expiration date:** Here's where you enter the date that the file should no longer be visible.

✔ **Can Expire?:** Here you set the Can Expire? property for the file to match its expiration date.

Sometimes custom properties don't apply

Think carefully about whether you want to require your users to fill in the custom properties. If you don't require them, many users ignore them — but if a required property doesn't apply to a particular document being uploaded, you have a potential hassle: The user gets stuck, doesn't know what to use, and (most likely) chooses the first choice just to move on. Result: garbage in your document libraries. To keep that mess from happening, give your users an out: Create a Not Applicable choice if you decide that a property is required.

The `Can Expire?` property comes in handy often. Here's how you set it:

1. **Browse to your document library.**

2. **Add a column called `Expiration Date` and set the data type to `date`.**

3. **Add a second column called `Can Expire?`. Set the data type to `calculated` and enter this formula:**

   ```
   =NOT(ISBLANK([Expiration Date]))
   ```

4. **Set the return type on the column to Yes/No.**

After you've created a column that tells whether the file can expire, put it to use with a view and a listing (or Web part) on the portal, like this:

1. **Create a custom view that filters on the `Expiration date` column.**

   Read the next section ("Get a new view") if you need the steps for creating a view.

2. **Set the filter to show all documents where:**

   - `Expiration date` is greater than `[Today]`.

   or

   - `Can Expire?` is equal to No.

   `[Today]` is a keyword that tells SharePoint to use today's date.

3. **Check the box next to Make this the default view in the Name section of the screen.**

4. **Add the filter to all the views.**

   Doing so ensures that readers see only unexpired documents.

5. **Add a listing to the portal, using the URL for a view that displays only active documents.**

6. **Add a Web part (using one of the custom views created in these steps) that filters out expired documents.**

The filter works for the custom view; documents marked as expired will still be listed when a user does a search.

Get a new view

The cool thing about adding custom properties is that you can use them to create custom views of your document library. You can use any column to filter, sort, or add subtotals.

To create a custom view that uses properties I added for sales documents in the preceding example, follow these steps:

1. **Browse to the document library.**

2. **Click Modify settings and columns.**

   The Customize page appears.

3. **In the Views section, click Create a new view.**

4. **On the Create View page, select Standard View.**

5. **Enter a name for the view and select the columns to display.**

6. **Scroll down to the Group By section. Click the plus sign (+) next to Group By to display the grouping options.**

7. **In the drop-down box for First group by the column, choose Sales Territory.**

   You can group by any column in the document library.

8. **In the drop-down box for Then group by the column, choose Product Line.**

9. **Click OK to save the view. Figure 9-6 shows the options selected to create the new view.**

If you get a hankering to view the documents in your library in a different way, add a property that allows you to create the view. For example, I created an additional view called By Product Line that grouped documents by product line and then by sales territory. Now I can view my sales documents both ways, as shown in Figure 9-7.

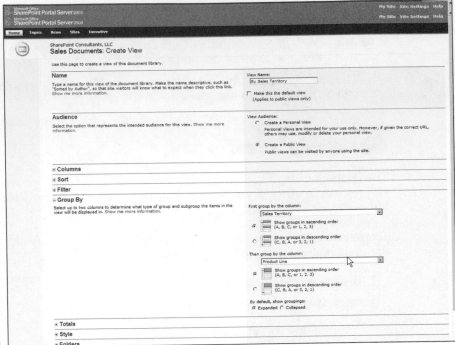

Figure 9-6:
Files in the document library can be grouped on any column.

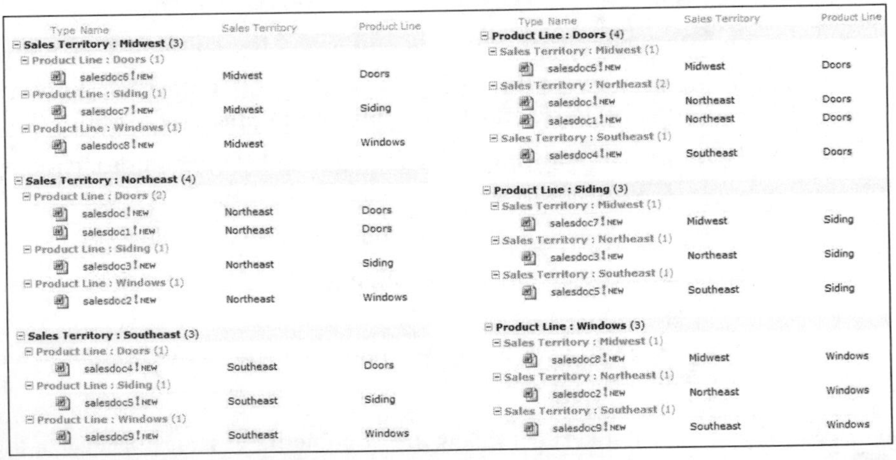

Figure 9-7:
Custom views allow you to see the same documents in many ways.

Creating custom views on the fly

Sometimes you want to create a view without going through all the trouble of creating a new view. You're in luck: You can create a custom view on the fly in only two steps:

1. **In your document library, click the Filter button on the toolbar.**

   Drop-down boxes appear under the columns.

2. **Click any drop-down box and select a value on which to filter.**

   In this case, I filtered on `Checked Out To`. A custom view — displaying just those documents checked out to the selected user — appeared.

You can also sort the list by clicking any of the column headings. Figure 9-8 shows the filtered and sorted view. The little arrow next to the `Modified` column indicates that the list is sorted on that column.

Filtered and sorted views can be saved in your Favorites or as a shortcut on your desktop. I'm going to e-mail the URL for this filtered view to ask this user to please check in these documents.

Using datasheet view for administration

Custom views and custom columns demand that you periodically review your document libraries. Otherwise they quickly deteriorate into a mess of files without any organization. (If you're thinking, *Hey, that sounds like a file share on* my *network,* you're not alone.)

One of the easiest ways to maintain a custom view is to browse to that view now and then to look for misclassified documents. Figure 9-9 shows a group of unclassified documents sitting at the top of the document library, begging for your attention.

Figure 9-8:
A custom view can be created on the fly with the Filter button.

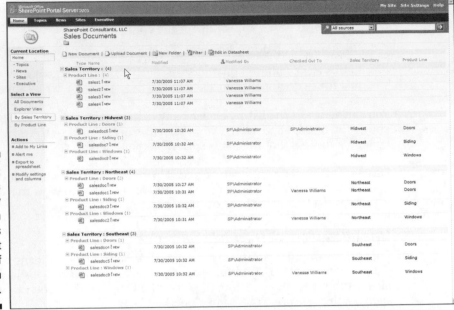

Figure 9-9:
Documents
with empty
custom
properties
show up at
the top of
the custom
view.

Use the Datasheet view to clean up these documents quickly, like this:

1. **Browse to your document library and click the custom view that groups documents by a certain property.**

   If you don't have a custom view, use the Filter button to view all documents that have a blank value for the custom property.

2. **Click Edit in Datasheet from the document library's toolbar.**

   The list of documents is displayed in a grid of columns and rows similar to a spreadsheet.

3. **Correct any missing or incorrect properties in the datasheet, as shown in Figure 9-10.**

4. **Click Show in Standard View to return to the custom view.**

Showing off your document libraries

What good is a document library if nobody knows it exists? Okay, there are some valid reasons *not* to share document libraries, but normally you'll provide some means of getting to them and viewing them, whether they're on your portal or on a site. This section shows several ways to do that.

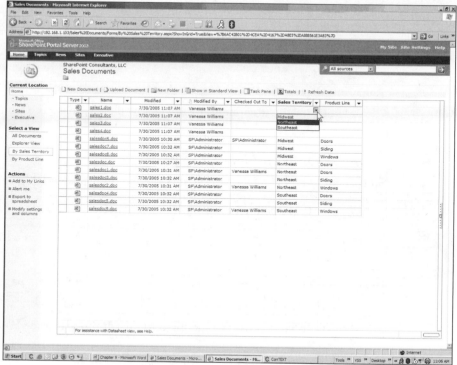

Figure 9-10:
Use the
datasheet
view to
correct
missing or
incorrect
document
properties.

Listing the document library on the portal

You can create a listing for each file in your document library — or add a listing for the whole document library to your portal. The best approach depends on how you want to lead your users to the content.

To add a listing for the document library to the portal, follow these steps:

1. **Browse to the document library in the portal.**

2. **Click Modify settings and columns from the vertical navigation on the left.**

3. **Click Select a portal area for this document library from the Customize page.**

   The Add Listing page appears with the URL for the document library already entered.

4. **Choose a location on the portal to display the listing:**

   • The default location is the portal's home page.

   • If you want to display the listing in a different location on the portal, click *Change location* in the Location section.

5. **Click OK to save the listing for the document library.**

   A listing for the document library is now displayed on the Home page of the portal.

Using the document library Web part

SharePoint provides cool reusable pieces of content called *Web parts*. Any time you create a new document library, SharePoint automatically creates a Web part for that document library.

Chapter 3 shows you the Web Part Gallery and explains how to add the MSNBC Weather Web part to your portal home page.

To add a Web part for a document library to your portal home page, follow these steps:

1. **Browse to your portal home page as an administrator or Web designer.**

2. **Click Edit Page from the Actions menu on the vertical navigation.**

3. **Click Modify Shared Page, and then choose Browse from the Add Web Parts menu.**

4. **In the Add Web Parts task pane, click Filter; then choose Libraries from the drop-down box, as shown in Figure 9-11.**

   In this case, I'm going to add the Company Templates library that I created earlier in the chapter.

5. **From the filtered list of libraries, choose a document library to add to your portal home page.**

6. **Drag and drop the Company Templates library to the middle-left zone of the portal home page.**

   The document library is now displayed on the portal home page, as shown in Figure 9-12.

You can modify the appearance and layout of the document library's Web parts, just as you can for any other Web part. You can also create a custom view for the document library — and make the Web part use that view. See the section "Get a new view" for more information about creating a new view.

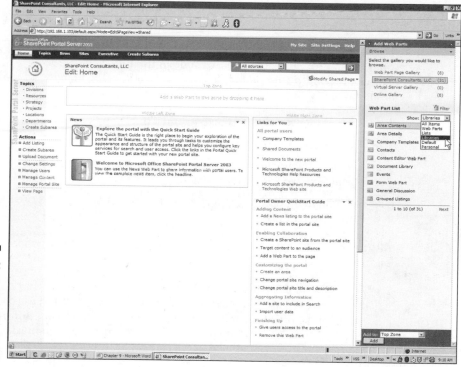

Figure 9-11:
Choose
Libraries
from the
filter drop-
down list.

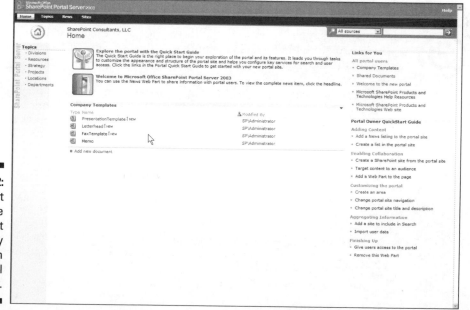

Figure 9-12:
A Web part
for the
document
library
appears on
the portal
home page.

Managing Logos and Branding Images

Logos and branding images can be tricky to manage. In SharePoint, you can boss them around by using either a document library or a picture library. The SharePoint *picture library* is designed for sharing images, so it offers some attractive advantages:

- ✔ Special views such as Filmstrip and Thumbnails help organize images.
- ✔ A compatible image editor makes images easy to modify.
- ✔ Special download and e-mail commands, made especially for images, streamline working with them.
- ✔ You can add custom properties and create custom views, just as you can for document libraries.

Although this is all cool, there are also some unfortunate drawbacks to using picture libraries:

- ✔ **There is no datasheet view.** You may say, "No big deal," but consider: When images are uploaded in bulk, you aren't prompted for custom properties. Although this is also the case with document libraries, there you can use the datasheet view to update properties en masse. Not so in a picture library. Gotcha! And the reason is . . .
- ✔ **You have to edit properties on each image file one at a time.** That makes it difficult (or at least time consuming) to create custom views.

I recommend using *document libraries* to manage files like logos and branding images. Heck, you can even dump those files into the same document library you use to store memo and fax templates. Just use custom properties to indicate that the logos and such are *images*.

If you decide to use picture libraries, you may want to use folders to organize your images. That way you can upload multiple photos without having to edit the properties individually for every photo. (Think of the savings in aspirin.)

Creating a picture library

Creating a picture library is similar to creating a document library. Follow these steps:

1. **Browse to the portal home page.**
2. **Click Manage Content.**

   The Documents and Lists page appears.

3. **Click Create.**
4. **Click Picture Library.**

5. **Give the picture library a name; then accept the defaults and click Create.**

Adding photos to the picture library

You can add photos one at a time or in a group. To add a single photo to the picture library, follow these steps:

1. **Click Add Picture from the toolbar.**

2. **Browse to the image file.**

3. **Enter any required properties.**

4. **Click Save and close.**

My experience is that files are often uploaded in bulk. (You probably have a bunch of files from, say, the company picnic — not just one or two.) These steps require Office 2003. To upload a batch of files, follow these steps:

1. **Click Add Picture from the toolbar.**

2. **Click Upload Multiple Files.**

    The Microsoft Office Picture Manager appears. If you do not see the Upload Multiple Files button, then Picture Manager is not installed on your computer. It can be installed from the Office 2003 disc.

3. **In Picture Manager, click Add Picture Shortcut.**

4. **Browse to the folder where your images are stored, and click Add.**

5. **Select the pictures you want to upload and click Upload and Close, as shown in Figure 9-13.**

You can also use the picture library's Explorer view to upload multiple files even if you don't have Office 2003. Just click on Explorer view and drag and drop your files onto the browser screen.

Picture Manager replaced Photo Editor in Office 2003. Photo Editor can be installed from the Office 2003 disc, but SharePoint uses Picture Manager to upload multiple files.

When files are uploaded in bulk, SharePoint doesn't use any of the properties that you enter for the files, even if the properties are flagged as required. Because there's no datasheet view in a picture library, the only way to update the properties is one file at a time.

If you need a tool for serious image management, take a look at the image-management solution for SharePoint from Scene7 (at www.scene7.com).

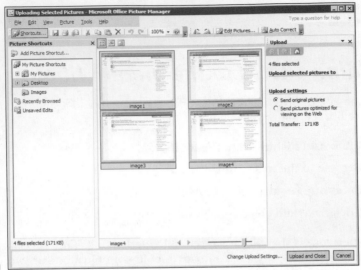

Figure 9-13:
Use Picture
Manager to
upload a
group of
image files.

Using picture library features

A picture library has several built-in features for managing images. Click the check box next to each image you want, and then select one of these buttons from the toolbar:

✔ **Edit Pictures:** Opens the selected image files in Microsoft Office Picture Manager. Picture Manager enables you to adjust the picture size and other attributes such as brightness and color. Figure 9-13 shows the Picture Manager.

✔ **Download:** Opens a page that enables you to select download options for the selected files. Figure 9-14 shows the Download Pictures screen.

✔ **Send To:** Enables you to send the selected images to any Office application.

Using the picture library's views

The picture library provides some special viewing features that might almost make you forget that you can't mass-update your file properties. There are three views:

✔ All Pictures
✔ Selected Pictures
✔ Explorer

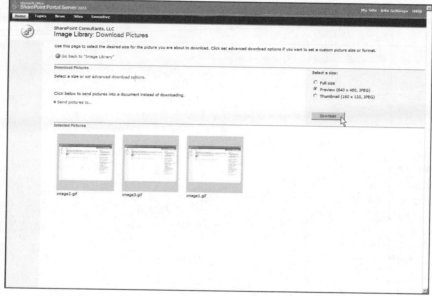

Figure 9-14:
Download
multiple
images by
using the
Download
feature.

Alone, these views are nothing special — but wait, there's more. Each view in a picture library inherits three *subviews*:

- **Details:** Displays each file's properties (or lack thereof)
- **Thumbnails:** Displays a thumbnail view of each image along with the file's name
- **Filmstrip:** Displays a filmstrip view of five thumbnails, along with an exploded view of each selected image. A navigational arrow enables you to advance the filmstrip, as shown in Figure 9-15.

The Selected Pictures view enables you to create custom views on the fly: Simply place a check mark next to the images you want to display.

SharePoint also provides a Slide Show view that enables you to advance through your images in a slide show.

You can also create custom views in picture libraries. Handy.

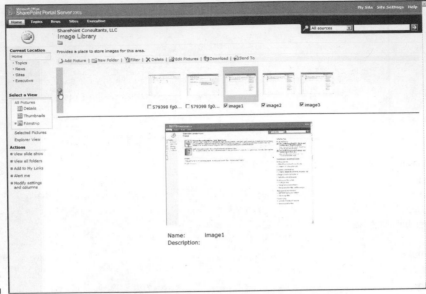

Figure 9-15:
The filmstrip
view can be
advanced
with the
navigational
arrow.

Creating a mini picture library

By combining the flexibility of the Selected Pictures view with the sleekness of the slide-show view, you can work around the lack of image properties to create custom views.

When you use the Selected Pictures view, all the images checked are displayed. SharePoint builds a URL like this:

```
http://<portal>/Image%20Library/Forms/Selected.aspx?View=
        {B86C0FD4-7A0E-4834-BE18-FBA711B483D9}&
        FilterName=ID&FilterMultiValue=3;4;10;11
```

Here's a closer look at the last part of the URL, which pertains to filtering:

```
&FilterName=ID&FilterMultiValue=3;4;10;11
```

This tells SharePoint to filter on the ID field for the values 3, 4, 10, and 11. The numbers at the end of the URL are unique identifiers for each image file that was checked.

The URL for a slide show looks like this:

```
http://<portal>/Image%20Library/Forms/slideshow.aspx?
         ViewStyle=slide show
```

This URL, however, displays a slide show of *all files in the library.* To limit the slide show to just the selected files, append the filtering part of the Selected Pictures URL to the slide URL — like this:

```
http://<portal>/Image%20Library/Forms/slideshow.aspx?
         ViewStyle=slideshow&FilterName=ID&Filter
         MultiValue=3;4;10;11
```

This URL will display a slide show of just those four image files.

Okay, that's the underpinning. To create an actual slide show by using this technique, follow these steps:

1. **Upload your files to the image library.**

   Because properties aren't helpful in image libraries, use folders to group the common images.

2. **Place a check mark next to every file you want to include in your slide show.**

   The files can be in separate folders in the image library. Click the check mark at the top of the library to select all displayed images.

3. **Click the Selected Pictures view.**

4. **Copy the last part of the URL, starting with &FilterName.**

   Be sure to get all the ID numbers at the end of the URL.

5. **Click View slide show from the Actions menu on the vertical navigation bar.**

6. **On the slide show, right-click the page and then click Properties.**

   Be sure to click the white part of the page, not the image file itself.

7. **Highlight the URL for the slide show, right-click, and then click Copy, as shown in Figure 9-16.**

8. **Append the &FilterName part of the URL to the URL you copied for the slide show.**

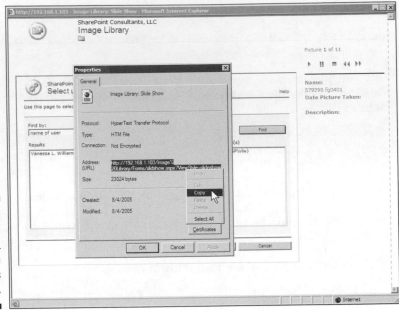

Figure 9-16:
Get the slide
show's URL
from the
page's
properties.

To get the URL from which you can download the filtered list of pictures,
click the <u>Download pictures</u> link while you're in Selected Pictures view.

To display the filtered slide show, follow these steps:

 1. **Create a Web-part page.**

    A *Web-part page* is a Web part used to display (you guessed it) Web
    parts. To create a Web-part page, follow these steps:

    a. Click Manage Content on the portal home page.

    b. Click Create on the Documents and Lists page.

    c. Scroll down to the Web Pages section and click Web Part Page.

 2. **Add the Page Viewer Web part to the new Web-part page and set the
    hyperlink to the filtered slide show.**

    See Chapter 3 for more information about adding Web parts to a page.

 3. **Add a Content Editor Web part.**

 4. **In the Source Editor for the Content Editor Web part, type the HTML
    shown in Figure 9-17.**

    The HTML creates a hyperlink to the Download Pictures page. Be sure to
    grab the URL for this page while in the Selected Pictures view.

 5. **Create a listing for the Web-part page on the portal or site.**

You can also create customized slide shows with the Slide Show Wizard, which can be downloaded from Microsoft's Web site. The Slide Show Wizard is part of the Windows XP Power Toys. It creates a Web-based slide show from a list of images you provide.

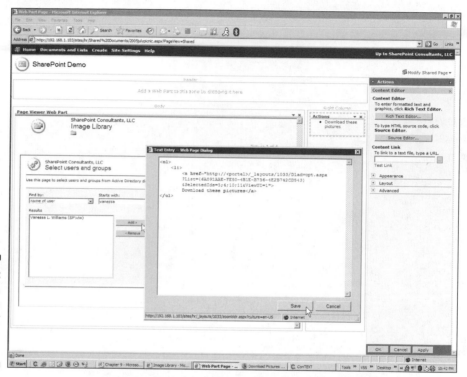

Figure 9-17:
Create a
custom
hyperlink for
your slide
show.

Part V

Power to the People: Engaging Employees with SharePoint

The 5th Wave   By Rich Tennant

"We have no problem funding your web site, Frank. Of all the chicken farmers operating web sites, yours has the most impressive cluck-through rate."

In this part . . .

1 show you some SharePoint features you can use to create self-service sites for human resources and marketing. You get a look at the role of self-service sites and how they can be implemented in SharePoint.

With the self-service site for human resources, you find out how to display upcoming anniversaries and birthdays. You can make announcements about new hires and post job openings.

The self-service site for marketing demonstrates using the document and image libraries for managing digital assets. I also show you how to link lists and Web parts together to create a product gallery.

Chapter 10

Managing Employee Relations

- -

- -

Human resources is *the* perfect SharePoint application. The content from HR screams *collaboration*. Example uses of SharePoint for HR include

- ✔ Document libraries for company policies
- ✔ Announcements to tell people about events
- ✔ Web parts for sharing information about upcoming birthdays and new hires

SharePoint can also be used to create a self-service site to manage

- ✔ Job postings
- ✔ New hires
- ✔ Benefits administration

But Human Resources is also a department. It has a private face that requires collaboration and document storage.

Two Faces Have 1

Because Human Resources provides so many opportunities for SharePoint, it's easy to overlook the two faces of Human Resources:

- ✔ The public, or service side, of HR
- ✔ The private side, or HR as a department

As a department, Human Resources has all the same needs as other departments. It needs a place to store items such as these:

- Department contacts
- Tasks, events, and issues
- Document and image files
- Custom lists

Those requirements scream SharePoint team site. However, they also have a great deal of public content that must be shared with the entire company (or maybe even multiple companies).

See Chapter 8 for in-depth coverage of SharePoint team sites.

There are several options for accommodating both these private and public views:

- Create two separate sites: one for the department and another for self-service.
- Create a single site for the department and use document libraries and lists on the portal itself.
- Create a single site for the department and create a portal area for self-service.
- Use a single site for both views and manage permissions on the public/private content.

Using a single site keeps all HR's content together in one place, but it requires them to diligently manage the permissions. I am not a fan of storing content on the portal itself, because I think it's harder to organize and manage.

I prefer to create two separate sites because it minimizes the risk of departmental content making its way into the public view. You can take it one step farther and not even list the department HR site in the site directory. Because there's a public and private site, only the public site has to be listed on the portal. The HR staff can access the departmental HR site from a URL.

Creating the departmental site

To create the departmental site, follow these steps:

1. **Browse to the portal.**
2. **Click Sites from the horizontal primary navigation.**
3. **Click Create Site from the Actions toolbar on the vertical navigation.**

4. **Give the site a name, description, and URL. Click Create.**

   Make the URL something that people won't guess, such as

   ```
   http://<portal name>/sites/depthr
   ```

   The Add Link to Site screen appears.

5. **Clear the check mark next to List This Site in the Site Directory, and then clear the check mark next to Include in Search Results. Click OK.**

   The Template Selection screen appears.

6. **Choose Team Site and click OK.**

   You now have a site that has a one-way connection to the portal. Users can get to the portal from the site, but they can't get from the portal to the site.

Creating the self-service site

To create the self-service site, walk through the same steps for creating the department site. When you get to Step 5 where the Add Link to Site screen appears, don't clear the check marks. This will list the site in the site directory. The rest of this chapter describes how to add content to the self-service site.

For more information about your options for displaying content from the self-service HR site on the portal, see Chapter 6.

Spreading Good News

HR has a lot of announcements to make. I never have to look farther than my Inbox to know who just got a promotion or who just had a baby. I'll show you a couple of ways to handle this content.

Birthdays and anniversaries

In a perfect world, the birthdate and service date data that's stored in your HR information system or your payroll system would magically display this week's birthdays or anniversaries on your self-service site. To be honest, that's easily doable in SharePoint. However, it requires some coding. Because this isn't a book about coding, I'm going to show you how do it without coding — all it takes is two actions:

✔ Get the birthdate and anniversary data from your HR or payroll system.

✔ Create a custom list in SharePoint to save this data.

Importing data

I'm going to assume that you have a spreadsheet that lists your employees' names and their birthdates and in-service dates. Take that list and import it into a custom list on the self-service site:

1. **Browse to the self-service site you created for HR.**

2. **Click Create from the horizontal primary navigation bar.**

   The Create Page screen appears.

3. **Click Import Spreadsheet from the Custom Lists section.**

   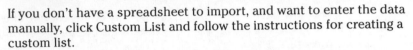

   If you don't have a spreadsheet to import, and want to enter the data manually, click Custom List and follow the instructions for creating a custom list.

4. **Enter a name and description, and then browse to your spreadsheet and click Import.**

   You can only import the spreadsheet if you're using Office 2003.

5. **Select the range of cells to import from the Import window in Excel, as shown in Figure 10-1.**

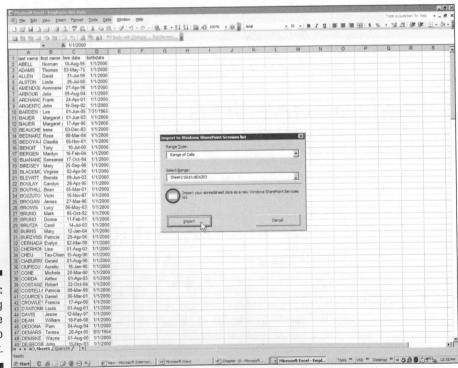

Figure 10-1:
Selecting the range of cells to import.

The data from the spreadsheet is imported as a custom list in SharePoint. The column headings in Excel become the columns in the custom list.

Cleansing the data

You could cleanse the data in Excel or in SharePoint — but given the subject of this book, I show you how to do it in (surprise!) SharePoint.

What do I mean by "cleanse the data?" The data that comes from other systems isn't usually in the exact format you want. For example, I want to display the employee name in the format *First Name Last Name*, as in John Smith. The data I got from my payroll system listed last names in uppercase in one field and first names in another field. I have to clean all that up.

SharePoint provides many functions for manipulating text. If you're familiar with the text functions in Excel, you should have no problems in SharePoint.

To create a column that displays the employee name in the format *First Name Last Name*, follow these steps:

1. **In the custom list where you imported the spreadsheet, click Modify settings and columns.**

2. **Click Add a new column.**

3. **In the Add Column screen, enter the name** Employee **for the column name.**

4. **Choose the data type of Calculated.**

   That's because this column will combine the values in the last name and first name columns in the custom list.

5. **Type this formula into the formula box:**

   ```
   =PROPER(TRIM([first name])) & " " & PROPER(TRIM([last name]))
   ```

   Where [*first name*] and [*last name*] are the column names representing (well, yeah) the employee's first and last name, respectively.

6. **Click OK to save the column.**

7. **Go back to the custom list to check the columns.**

   You should now have a column named Employee that lists the employees' names in the format *First Name Last Name*, as shown in Figure 10-2.

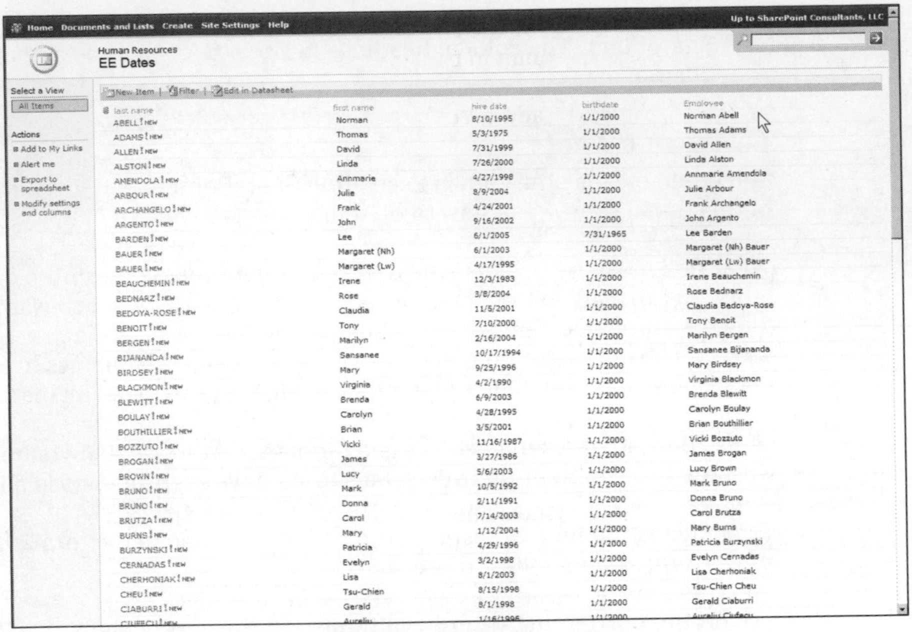

Figure 10-2:
Calculating
an
Employee
column
based on
the First
Name and
Last Name
columns.

Getting upcoming birthdays and anniversaries

Before you can display the upcoming birthdays and anniversaries, you have to convert those dates to the current year. Follow these steps to get that done:

1. **Add a new column to the custom list called** Current Birthday.

2. **Set the data type to calculated.**

3. **Enter this formula:**

   `=DATEVALUE(MONTH(`*`birthdate`*`) & "/" & DAY(`*`birthdate`*`))`

   Where *birthdate* is the name of the Birthdate column.

4. **Set the return type for the data as Date and Time.**

5. **Click OK to create the column.**

Create another column called `Bday - 14` with a data type of `calculated`. Enter this formula and set the return type to date and time:

`=[Current Birthday]-14`

Repeat these steps for the hire date. Substitute the `hire date` column for the `birthdate` column in the formula.

Use this formula to add a `Years of Service` column:

```
=DATEDIF([hire date], [Current Anniversary], "Y")
```

This formula calculates the difference between the value in the hire `date` column and the `current anniversary` column. It returns the number of years between the two dates, so set the return type as number.

You could use the same formula to add a column for the employee's age, but I don't think it would be appreciated.

Creating the upcoming birthdays and anniversaries view

You now have all the pieces you need to create a custom view for displaying the upcoming birthdays and anniversaries. To create the view, follow these steps:

1. **Click Modify settings and columns in the custom list.**
2. **Click Create a new view from the Views section of the Customize page.**
3. **Click Standard View.**

   The Create View page appears.
4. **Name the view** Birthdays.
5. **Clear all check marks in the Columns section except for `Employee` and `Current Birthday`.**
6. **Sort by `Current Birthday`.**
7. **Enter these filters in the Filters section, as shown in Figure 10-3:**
   - `Bday - 14` is less than or equal to `[Today]`
   - AND
   - `Current Birthday` is greater than or equal to `[Today]`
8. **Click OK to save the view.**

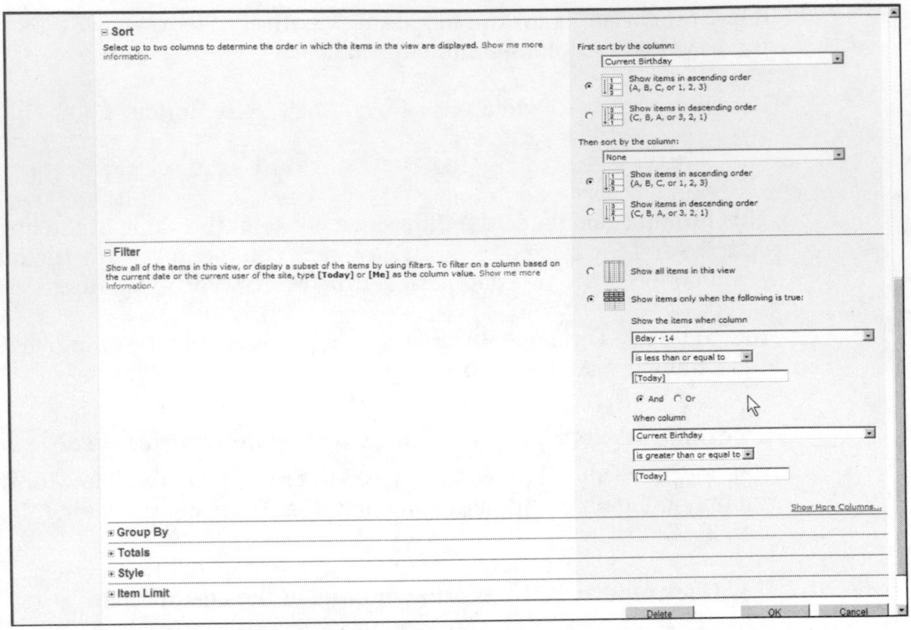

Figure 10-3:
Filter inputs.

Repeat these steps to create a view for upcoming anniversaries. If you've been following along, then you have these columns for your anniversary views:

- **Current Anniversary:** A calculated column that displays the employee's anniversary date in the current year, using the following formula and a return type of date and time:

```
=DATEVALUE(MONTH([hire date])&"/"&DAY([hire date]))
```

- **Ann – 14:** A calculated column used for showing the upcoming anniversaries. Use this formula with a return type of date and time:

```
=[Current Anniversary]-14
```

- **Years of Service:** Yet another calculated column. This one shows (you guessed it) an employee's tenure. Use this formula and a return type of number:

```
=DATEDIF([hire date],[Current Anniversary],"Y")
```

To create views for people celebrating one-, five-, and ten-year anniversaries, follow these steps:

1. Add a calculated column called `YearBreak` with this formula:

```
=IF([Years of Service]=1,1,IF([Years of
        Service]=5,5,IF([Years of Service]=10,10,0)))
```

2. **Create a view grouped by the `YearBreak` column. Filter records where `YearBreak` isn't equal to zero.**

To create a grouped view sorted by a range — in this case, `[Years of Service]` — follow these steps:

1. **Add a calculated column called `YearRange` with this formula:**

```
=IF([Years of Service]=1,"(d) Celebrating one year",
IF(AND([Years of Service]>1,[Years of
     Service]<=5),"(c) Celebrating two to five
     years",
IF(AND([Years of Service]>5,[Years of
     Service]<=10),"(b) Celebrating six to ten
     years",
IF([Years of Service]>10,"(a) Celebrating more than
     ten years",[Years of Service]))))
```

2. **Create a view with these properties:**

   - Sorted by years of service, in descending order

   - Values filtered on `YearRange` aren't equal to zero

   - Grouped by `YearRange` and collapsed

   - `Item Limit` equal to 1000 (or whatever number it takes to get all your collapsed groups onto one page)

New hires and new babies

HR sends out announcements about new hires, new babies, new executives, new policies, and company picnics. (Not necessarily in that order, but you get the idea.)

To create a common repository to store these announcements, follow these steps:

1. **Click Create on the primary navigation bar of the self-service HR site.**

2. **Click Announcements from the Lists section.**

3. **Enter a name and description and click Create.**

4. **Add a custom column called `Type` to designate whether the announcement is for a new hire or a new policy.**

   Doing so enables you to create a custom view that shows just that type or grouping, arranged by type.

The `Announcements` list type includes an `Expires` column by default.

Making contact with HR

I never know whom to call when I have questions about payroll and human resources. Don't get me wrong. I have access to the employee directory. But that doesn't tell me who to call for what — I have to guess.

When you're deciding how to list contact information for human resources, there are a few options:

- ✔ List the basic contact information for the department such as main switchboard number, mailing addresses, and department manager.
- ✔ List the individual employees and their contact information.
- ✔ List the services provided by the department and the contacts for each.

In this section, I show you how do all three.

Providing basic contact information for the department

Use a Content Editor Web part to display basic contact information about the department. In the self-service human resources site, follow these steps:

1. **Click Modify Shared Page in the upper-right corner.**
2. **Choose Browse from the Add Web Parts menu.**
3. **Drag and drop the Content Editor Web Part to the top of the right zone.**
4. **Click the open the Tool pane's hyperlink inside the Content Editor Web part.**
5. **Click Rich Text Editor and enter the contact information for your HR department.**
6. **Click Save to save the information.**

You can use the Source Editor button when you want to type in some HTML. (HyperText Markup Language, which is used to construct and customize Web pages.)

The self-service portal has summary contact information on its home page, as shown in Figure 10-4.

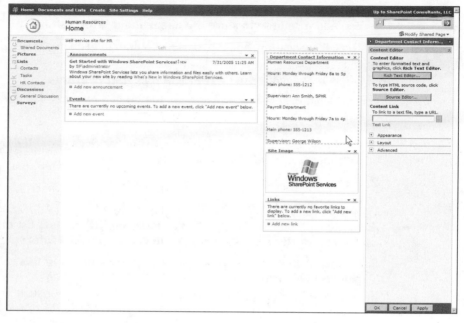

Figure 10-4:
Use the
Content
Editor Web
part to add
free-form
contact
information.

Sharing a list of contacts

SharePoint provides a template for managing contacts. To create a list of contacts, follow these steps:

1. **Click Create on the horizontal primary navigation bar of the HR self-service site.**

2. **In the Lists section, click Contacts.**

3. **Enter a name and description for the contacts. Click Create.**

4. **Add your departmental contacts for human resources and payroll to the list.**

   You can add contacts in three ways:

   • Click New Item

   • Click Edit in Datasheet view

   • Click Import Contacts to bring contacts in from Outlook

You can paste rows of contacts into the Datasheet view.

TIP

5. **If you plan to keep contacts for human resources and payroll in this list, add a column to store the department information.**

    To ease navigation, add a hyperlink column to each contact's user profile.

Providing a supercharged list of services and contacts

To create a list of services provided by the human resources department, follow these steps:

1. **Create a custom list and enter the list of services provided by HR such as benefits administration and job postings.**

2. **Add a new column called Primary Contact.**

3. **Select the data type Lookup.**

4. **In the Optional Settings section, choose the HR contact list that you created earlier from the drop-down list labeled Get information from.**

5. **Choose Full Name from the drop-down list labeled In this column, as shown in Figure 10-5.**

6. **Click OK to save the column.**

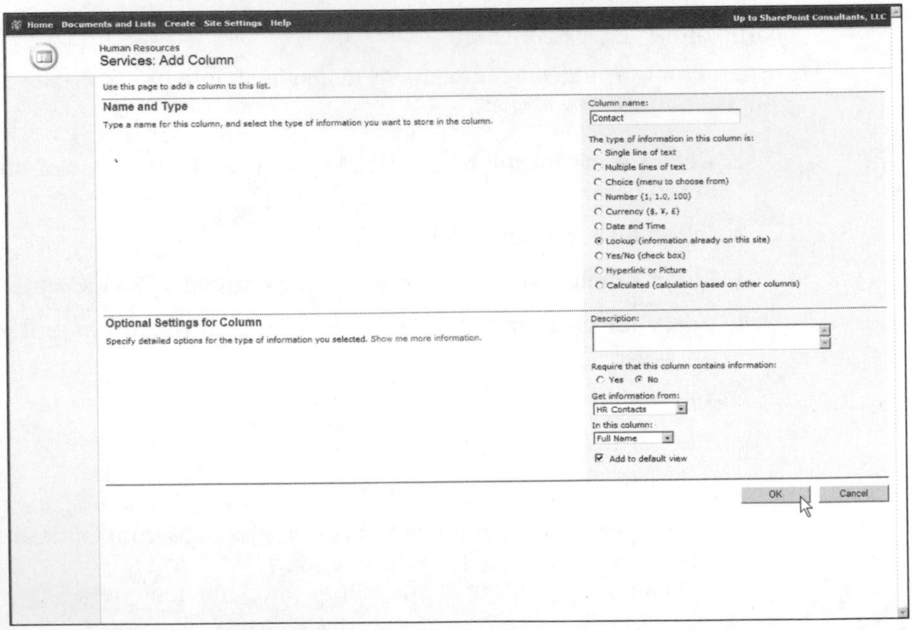

Figure 10-5:
Create a lookup column that links to data in another list.

Associate a primary contact with each service in your list. You can also create a backup-contact column in the event the primary contact is unavailable. Users can click the primary contact next to the service and get that person's contact information.

Use views to group services by type or primary contact.

Self-Service with a Smile

The Human Resources Department provides many services to a company and its employees. Unless your company is mature, these services are probably provided with a hodgepodge of paper forms, e-mail, and good old-fashioned telephone calls. SharePoint can provide self-service access to information just about everybody in the company wants to know, such as

- Company policies
- Benefits and compensation
- Paperwork for new hires
- Job postings
- Suggestions

At your service

SharePoint includes self-service capabilities that can provide highly personalized employee information from HR, while at the same time involving employees actively in the life of the company. This section describes ways to make company policies accessible, introduce new hires, and post job descriptions, as well as process suggestions and surveys. Now, *that's* service.

Company policies

There are several choices for managing company policies.

- **Easy to implement, but low impact:** Store your policy manual in PDF format on the HR self-service site. Using version control would ensure that readers see only the latest version.

- **Middle of the road:** Save your policy manual pages as Web pages in Word and upload them to your site. Use the page viewer Web part to display the policy manual Web pages on Web-parts pages.

> ✔ **Over the top:** Create a document library that stores the final Word files of your policies. Create a custom list that includes every policy along with its pertinent properties (such as to whom it applies and who issued it). Store a hyperlink to the actual policy document with every representative listing.

Always keep a PDF version of your policy manual available for easy printing.

New hires

New hires are the lifeblood of a business, but the paperwork they cause can be a nightmare. I suggest you create a kit to manage the process:

> ✔ Create a custom list for managing fill-in forms.
>
> ✔ Add a column called `Kit Type`. Use this column to store whether the document is for new hires, change of status, or another process.
>
> ✔ Attach an electronic version of the new hire form to an entry in the custom list that describes the form (or create a column to store a hyperlink to the electronic version).
>
> ✔ Create a view that filters where the kit type equals new hire.
>
> ✔ Add a list Web part to your site and use the new hire view.

You have several options for fill-in forms:

> ✔ Use fill-in PDF or Word forms if you expect people will want to print their forms and route them manually.
>
> ✔ Create a custom list and have users enter their information directly into it.
>
> ✔ Use InfoPath to create a form and publish it in a form library.

The last two options keep the information in an electronic format. They also allow you to create alerts to e-mail an HR employee when a new hire form is completed.

Generating alerts is a useful way to monitor a list's activities without actually checking the list periodically. When you create an alert, SharePoint sends you an e-mail when the list is added, modified, or deleted.

See Chapter 12 for more information on InfoPath. The following section shows an example of using alerts.

You can use these suggestions to manage forms related to most HR services, such as benefits administration and job descriptions.

Get a job

Custom lists and alerts make the tasks of managing job postings so much easier. To manage job postings, follow these steps:

- ✔ Create an announcements list.
- ✔ Add columns for department, hiring manager, pay grade, or any other pertinent information.
- ✔ Put the job description in the body, attach a Word document describing the job, or use a lookup column that links to a job-description list.
- ✔ Create custom views to help HR manage the list.

Your employees can create individual alerts that will e-mail them any time changes are made to the job-postings list. To create an alert, follow these steps:

1. **Browse to the job-postings list.**
2. **Click Alert me from the Action menu on vertical navigation.**
3. **Choose the type and frequency of the alert, as shown in Figure 10-6.**
4. **Click OK to create the alert.**

Figure 10-6:
Choose the type and frequency when creating an e-mail alert.

If you want employees to submit résumés to one central place when they apply for a job posting, four steps do that job:

1. **Create a document library to store the résumés.**

2. **Add columns for the employee's name, department, and supervisor.**

3. **Add a lookup column that links to a job posting in the job-posting list.**

4. **Instruct employees to upload their résumés to the document library, enter their names, departments, supervisors, and click the drop-down list for the job posting for which they are applying.**

You could also use a custom list and ask employees to attach their résumés to their individual list entries. Normally, however, a list won't let you require an attachment; some employees might make their entries and forget to upload their résumés.

To supercharge your résumé document library, add a `Status` column that HR updates to indicate the résumé has been reviewed. Employees with résumés stored there could create alerts to notify them when their particular items change. Figure 10-7 shows how to add an alert to an individual item.

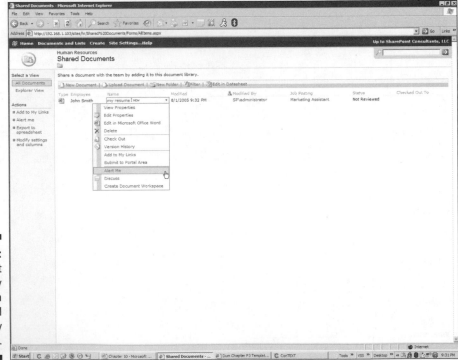

Figure 10-7:
Add an alert to notify you when an individual entry changes.

Penny for your thoughts

Use an issues list to create an electronic suggestion box:

- ✔ Create an issues list.
- ✔ Add columns to categorize the suggestions.
- ✔ Create views that filter the suggestions by category.
- ✔ Have the parties responsible for each category post a resolution to each suggestion, updating its status.

To allow people to cast votes for suggestions, follow these general steps:

1. **Create a custom list.**
2. **Add a column that links to the suggestions list.**
3. **Create a view that groups by suggestion and provides a count subtotal.**

Using this view, employees can cast their votes for a suggestion by adding a new entry to the custom list and selecting one of the suggestions from the drop-down list. As employees add entries to the list, the grouped subtotals increment when a suggestion is chosen.

Employees should know that their votes will not be anonymous.

Surveys

SharePoint can help you poll employees on (for example) where they want the company picnic. A survey works like any other list; to create one, follow these steps:

1. **Click Create from the primary navigation bar on the HR self-service site.**
2. **In the Surveys section, click Survey.**

   The New Survey screen appears.
3. **Enter a name and description for the survey.**
4. **Indicate whether employees' names are visible in the survey results and whether to allow multiple responses. Click Next.**
5. **Enter your question and possible answers to the questions.**
6. **To add another question, click Next Question. Otherwise click Finish.**

   When the employee clicks Respond to Survey on the survey's default view, the form shown in Figure 10-8 appears. When the forms are all filled in and submitted, you can browse to the survey to view results.

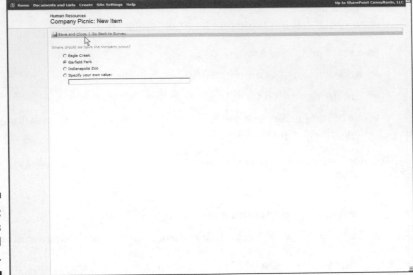

Figure 10-8:
Use surveys
to poll
employees.

Charting the organization

Organizational charts are great visual tools for displaying an organization's formal power and reporting structures. Unfortunately, many companies don't have the tools to properly update organizational charts. Worse yet, updated organizational charts often aren't shared throughout the organization.

If your company is using a third-party tool to generate organizational charts, see whether you can save your chart as a Web page. If so, you can upload it to SharePoint and use the Page Viewer Web part to display it.

Another option is to use the Organization Chart Wizard in Visio. If you have no other means of generating organization charts, I think you should buy Visio just for this wizard alone.

Here's how the wizard works, play by play:

1. **Create a spreadsheet with these columns:**

   - Employee

   - Reporting Manager

   - Title

   - Department

   - Hyperlink

2. **Enter the reporting manager, title, and department for each employee.**

3. **In the `Hyperlink` column, enter the URL for each employee's personal site.**

The URL for the personal site is in the following format:

```
http://<portalname>/MySite/Public.aspx?accountname=<username>
```

I build the URL dynamically from the employee's name.

4. **Use the Visio Organization Chart Wizard to import the spreadsheet.**

5. **Save the organization chart as a Web page in Visio.**

6. **Upload the Web page and its content files to SharePoint.**

7. **Create a listing on SharePoint for the organization chart Web page or use the Page Viewer Web part on a Web-parts page.**

Ask your IT staff to export the employee and reporting information from Active Directory.

To use the Organizational Chart Wizard in Visio, follow these steps:

1. **In Visio, choose File⇨New⇨Organization Chart⇨Organization Chart Wizard.**

2. **In the wizard, choose the option to create the organization chart from information already stored in a file or database. Click Next.**

3. **Choose Excel as your file source. Click Next.**

4. **Browse to your Excel file and click Next.**

5. **Map the Excel columns for `Employee` and `Reporting Manager` to the wizard's `Name` and `Reports to` columns respectively, and then click Next.**

6. **Choose the fields from your spreadsheet to display, and then click Next.**

   I like to display `Employee`, `Title`, and `Department`.

7. **Add the `Hyperlink` column as a custom property field, and then click Next.**

   You can allow the wizards to insert automatic page breaks or do that manually. Cut to the chase and let the wizards do it. . . .

8. **Click Next until the Finish button is available, and then click Finish to build the chart.**

Visio provides many tools for manipulating the chart to make it visually appealing. When you're satisfied with the chart's appearance, you can upload it like this:

1. **In Visio, choose Save As Web Page from the File Menu.**

2. **Browse to the document library in your SharePoint self-service HR site.**

3. **Choose Upload Document.**

4. **Click Upload Multiple Files.**

An Explorer view appears.

5. **Browse to the HTML file for your organization chart and place a check mark next to it.**

6. **Click Save and Close.**

A dialog box nags you to be *sure* you want to upload multiple files.

7. **Click OK.**

The HTML file for your organizational chart is uploaded to the document library, along with its supporting files. To view the organizational chart, click the file in your document library.

You must upload all the supporting files for a Visio Web page. If you have broken links in your organizational chart, then all your supporting files didn't get uploaded. Fortunately, there's an easy fix: Because Visio places all those files in the single file folder where you saved the organizational chart, you can just upload that whole file folder to fix any broken links.

Linking it all together

Most of the examples shown in this chapter relate to information about employees. It seems redundant to keep uploading the same employee names every single time you want to add a piece of data. And beware: Redundant data can lead to inconsistencies in your site. To eliminate this redundancy, you have some possible approaches:

- ✔ Create lists for your master data. They might include some standard business categories:

  - Employees
  - Departments
  - Jobs

- ✔ In lists where you want to reference this master data, create a lookup column that links to the master list.

Make sure the master record exists *before* you paste or import data into lists that reference the master record. Otherwise you get a mess.

Chapter 11 goes into greater detail on how to create Web parts that link data from one list to another.

Because many people are familiar with Microsoft Access, I advise people to think of SharePoint in similar terms, imagining lists as tables and SharePoint list views as forms or reports in Access. When you design lists and views in SharePoint, think about how you would do it in a database tool such as Access.

Chapter 11

Mixing Up Your Marketing Mix

- -

- -

*E*ven if you have a marketing information system, your company may be hard pressed to keep track of all your marketing materials and share information with relevant people. In this chapter, I show how you can use SharePoint for collaboration inside and outside your marketing department.

Internal Uses

SharePoint is one step better than a million spreadsheets, but it can't replace a full-blown marketing information or marketing automation system. However, you can use SharePoint as an important part of information sharing in your marketing department. Within a marketing department, you can use SharePoint to

✔ Share product brochures and presentations with others in the company

✔ Manage digital assets such as media for advertisements

✔ Gather information about competitors

You can use SharePoint's custom list feature to drive information about your company's marketing mix in SharePoint.

A company's *marketing mix* is made up of the four Ps:

✔ Place (or distribution)

✔ Product

✔ Promotion

✔ Price

Building the marketing site

Before you can add any content for marketing to SharePoint, you need a place to store the content. To create a site for marketing, follow these steps:

1. **Browse to your portal.**

2. **Click Sites on the primary horizontal navigation bar.**

3. **Click Create Site from the Actions menu on the left vertical navigation bar.**

4. **Give the site a title and URL.**

5. **Click Create.**

   The Add Link to Site page appears.

6. **Enter a title and description for the site directory.**

7. **Place a check mark in the box next to Spotlight Site.**

   Checking Spotlight Site lists the marketing site in a special section of the site directory.

8. **Click Change Location to add a link to the marketing site on the portal.**

   I added mine to Home⇨Topics⇨Departments. You can add a link to any page on your portal where you expect people to look to find marketing's site.

9. **Click OK to create the listing in the site directory.**

   The Template Selection page appears.

10. **Select Team Site.**

11. **Click OK.**

You now have a marketing site that's listed in the site directory. If you choose a location on the portal in Step 8, then the site is also listed on the portal in the location you specify. (See Chapter 8 for more information about team sites.)

Going to the library

Document and image libraries are the quickest wins when starting up any departmental site. Two simple uses for these libraries for marketing are

- ✔ Sharing product brochures and sales presentations in a document library
- ✔ Storing digital assets (such as the art for a marketing campaign) in a picture library

Check out Chapter 9 for an overview of SharePoint libraries.

Sharing brochures and presentations

Using a document library to store product brochures and sales presentations can reduce the costs that come with producing and distributing these items. To create a document library, follow these steps:

1. **Click Create on the primary horizontal navigation bar on the marketing site.**

2. **Choose Document Library from the Create page.**

3. **On the New Document Library page, enter the name** Marketing Brochures and Presentations.

4. **Accept the default to display the library on the quick launch bar.**

5. **Select the Yes radio button to enable version control.**

   Enabling version control allows you to store all the versions of a document as the document is developed. This is helpful if you ever need to revert to a previous version of the document.

6. **Click Create to create the document library.**

   You now have a generic document library for storing marketing brochures and presentations.

To customize the document library for marketing brochures and presentations, you can take one of two approaches:

✔ **Add custom properties that perform these two tasks:**

   • Specify the document type (for example, a brochure or presentation)

   • Associate a region, sales territory, product, or customer with the document

   See Chapter 9 for more about creating custom properties.

✔ **Create views that group items or filter on the custom properties.** Chapter 9 also shows you how to create views.

If you want to use lookup columns in your document library for product, customer, or another relevant value, first create a custom list to store that information. For example, two quick steps add a product drop-down list to your document library:

1. **Create a custom list to store products.**

2. **Create a lookup column in the document library that displays values from the products custom list.**

When you add a new sales brochure or presentation to the document library, you can select a product from the drop-down list to designate that the sales brochure or presentation is about that product.

There is sometimes a tendency to upload everything in a PDF format, especially brochures. Okay, the PDF format works well when you want to print, but it doesn't always look good on the screen, and it means extra work: You may need to maintain

- ✔ PDFs for printing
- ✔ Other file formats (such as Word documents) for on-screen viewing

Managing digital assets

Managing a marketing department's many digital assets in a picture library ensures that everyone uses the same version of the asset. The picture library also protects assets and reduces the risk of errors that result from people using the wrong versions of digital assets.

To use SharePoint to manage digital assets, you need a combination of SharePoint's features, including the:

- ✔ **Picture library:** To store images
- ✔ **Document library:** To store audio, video, and other files
- ✔ **Custom list:** For a consolidated view of your digital assets regardless of whether the asset is stored in the document or picture library

Chapter 9 covers some limitations of picture libraries; after considering them, you may decide not to use a picture library. On the up side, however, a picture library can give you thumbnail and filmstrip views, along with special features for downloading and sending images to other applications.

To create a picture library, follow these steps:

1. **Click Create on the primary navigation bar on the marketing site.**

2. **Click Picture Library on the Create page.**

3. **Select the radio button next to** No **in the Navigation section.**

   This selection keeps the library from being displayed on the Quick Launch Bar in the SharePoint site.

4. **Name the library** Digital Asset Images.

5. **Enable versioning.**

   For more about versioning and how to enable it, see Chapter 8.

6. **Click Create.**

When you have your new picture library in place, create an additional document library, following the same steps used to create the document library for storing product brochures and sales presentations (in the section called

"Sharing brochures and presentations"). Call this new document library **Digital Asset Files**. A list of those assets is the next order of business.

To create a custom list that you can use as a tool to manage the digital-asset files stored in the picture and document libraries you create in the preceding steps, follow these steps:

1. **Click Create on the primary horizontal navigation bar on the marketing site.**

2. **Click Custom List.**

3. **Name the list** Digital Assets List.

4. **Click Create.**

   The new list is created.

5. **Add the following custom properties to the list:**

   - **Document type:** A column of type Choice with the choices of logo, photograph, audio, or video

   - **URL:** A column of type Hyperlink, specified to format the URL as a hyperlink

   - **Status:** A column of type Choice with status values that show whether the asset is still valid for use

   Figure 11-1 shows an example of what the final custom list looks like using these custom properties.

You can also add these custom properties to your document library instead of creating a separate custom list. However, using a custom list lets you consolidate artifacts from a document and picture library, and create multiple entries for a single artifact. For example, you can add entries to the custom list for all the images and video files for a single product even though these files are stored in different libraries.

Figure 11-1:
Use a custom list to display digital assets stored in picture and document libraries.

Title	Document Type	URL	Status
ABC Promotion	Photograph	View Image	Active
XYZ Event	Photograph	View Image	Active
ZZZ Promotion	Audio	Listen	Active
2005 Sales Conference	Video	View Video	Active
D Commercial	Advertisement	View Advert	Active
Product 1 NEW	Photograph	Front Image	Active
Product 1 NEW	Photograph	Side Image	Active

To manage your digital assets, follow these steps:

1. **Upload your image files to the picture library.**

2. **Upload your audio, video, and other files to the document library.**

3. **In the custom list, create an entry for each digital asset.**

4. **Specify the asset's type such as logo or video, using the Document Type column.**

5. **Paste the URL that links to the digital asset.**

   This URL should take a site visitor to the digital asset being catalogued.

6. **Enter a status indicating whether the asset is active.**

7. **Create views in the custom list to group or filter by document type and status.**

Figure 11-2 shows an example of adding a digital asset to the custom list. In this example, a lookup column is used to select a product from the Product drop-down list. You can add lookup columns to your custom digital assets list to associate your digital assets with elements from your marketing mix.

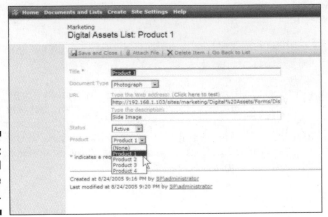

Figure 11-2:
Add a digital
asset to the
custom list.

Keeping an eye on the competition

As any marketer knows, you have to keep your eyes on your competition. You not only need to watch your competitors, you have to keep an eye on elements in your external environment, such as:

✔ Your industry

✔ Technology

> ✔ Laws
>
> ✔ Politics

That takes a lot of eyes! It's easy to overlook something. Instead of relying on employees to remember to look at a competitor's Web site periodically or check changes in tariffs, use SharePoint to make your monitoring processes part of your employees' everyday routines:

> ✔ Incorporate searches of your competitors' Web sites in your internal marketing site.
>
> ✔ Display news headlines from government agencies, industry associations, or news media sources, such as Associated Press, right on your marketing site.

As your employees access SharePoint on a daily basis to check tasks and upload documents, they see these features.

Crawling the competition

SharePoint has an indexing feature that lets you crawl other Web sites. For example, you can tell SharePoint to index your competitor's job openings page so that you can monitor it for personnel changes. Or, you can have SharePoint search their product pages for new product announcements. Unfortunately, configuring and maintaining the indexing and search features of SharePoint is very resource-intensive — both in terms of hardware and the time spent tweaking the configuration. It might not be worth it in your enterprise.

Have you ever wondered how a search engine such as Google knows what Web pages to show you when you search the Web? Search engines use software to *crawl* Web sites — that is, to follow all the hyperlinks on a particular site. The search engine then analyzes the content on the Web pages and builds an index (similar to the index in the back of this book) that it uses to reference the Web pages.

If you see the value in using search and indexing to monitor your competition and external environment but don't have the resources to invest in SharePoint's native features, you have alternatives. One very simple approach is to use Google's search features on your SharePoint site. Instead of using your own server resources to index content, why not use Google's?

And Google doesn't mind. Heck, they even tell you how to do it. They provide a tool called Google Free. You can use Google Free to search another company's Web site from within your SharePoint site. To get the code, follow these steps:

1. Browse to `www.google.com/searchcode.html`.

2. **Read the terms of service (yeah, right!) and click Get the Free Search code button.**

3. **Scroll down to the option for Google Free Web Search with Site Search.**

4. **Copy the code in the box.**

5. **Paste the code into a Notepad file.**

6. **Replace every instance of YOUR DOMAIN NAME with the site that you want to search.**

    In this case, I'm going to use `www.marketingpower.com`, the site of the American Marketing Association.

7. **Save the file with an HTML extension in a document library on your marketing site.**

See the FAQ on the Google Free page for tips on how to customize the look and feel of your search results, including opening the search results in a new Web page.

To add the Google Free search to your site, follow these steps:

1. **Click Modify Shared Web in the upper right-hand corner of your marketing Web site.**

2. **Click Add Web Parts⇨Browse.**

3. **Add the Page Viewer Web part to the page.**

4. **Click the <u>Open the Tool Pane</u> hyperlink in the Web part.**

5. **Type or paste in the hyperlink to the Google Free search page you create in the preceding steps.**

6. **Click OK.**

You now have limited your Google search to a single Web site, as you can see in Figure 11-3. Every time your employees go to your marketing site in SharePoint, they can conduct a search of the American Marketing Association's Web site. Not only is this convenient for your employees, but it reinforces to them that your organization values the AMA, and it leverages your AMA subscription if you have one.

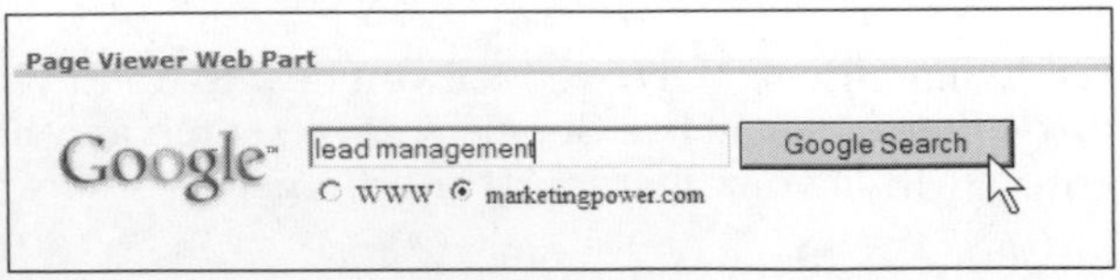

Figure 11-3:
Use Google
Free to
create a
custom
search
feature.

Page Viewer Web Part

Google™ | lead management | Google Search
○ WWW ● marketingpower.com

Hungry for news feeds

Back in the good old days, if you wanted to see the latest updates for a Web site, you had to go visit the site daily. Nowadays, some really cool technology lets Web designers create *news feeds* — automatic updates for Web viewing — of their content. Other Web designers can put these news feeds on their own Web sites, where the news-feed display updates every time the original site changes.

The technology behind news feeds is called RSS. There is some debate as to what RSS actually stands for. From what I've seen, most people have settled on Really Simple Syndication. RSS is a technology that has been around for a long time, but it only recently has found fame. (For a detailed description of RSS, see the sidebar, "What the heck is RSS, anyway?" later in this chapter.)

Web sites big and small offer RSS feeds of their content. To determine whether a site offers RSS feeds, look for either an RSS or XML logo, like the logos in Figure 11-4.

Figure 11-4:
The RSS or XML logo indicates the site has an RSS news feed.

Users of the Mozilla Firefox browser can also look for the little orange icon in the lower right-hand corner of the screen, as you can see in Figure 11-5. When you see this icon, you know that the site has RSS feeds.

Figure 11-5:
Firefox has built-in functionality for RSS news feeds.

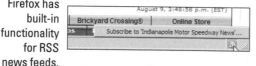

You can use Firefox to grab RSS feeds much more easily than browsing around a site looking for little RSS and XML logos. If a site has feeds, you'll see the little orange icon in the corner of the screen. I use it all the time. You can download Firefox for free at www.getfirefox.com.

What the heck is RSS, anyway?

An *RSS file* is a text file that encapsulates information in special markup tags. You can use RSS to publish — that is, *syndicate* — Web-site content. You can use RSS to display links to news headlines or newly added entries to a Web log (blog). Check out this example of a news item in RSS format:

```
<item>
<title>Stewart Fulfills Dream
   by Winning Allstate 400 at
   The Brickyard</title>
```

```
<link>http://www.indianapolis
   motorspeedway.com/news/
   story.php?story_id=5216
   </link>
<description />
</item>
```

If your Web browser doesn't have a built-in RSS viewer, you need to get a viewer that can transform the information from its RSS format into another format, such as HTML.

Instead of just listing hyperlinks to other Web Sites on your SharePoint site, you can list RSS news feeds that update on their own. Look for RSS news feeds on the Web sites of your

- ✔ Competitors
- ✔ Suppliers
- ✔ Partners
- ✔ Trade associations

When you find the RSS or XML logo, click it and grab the URL of the page that appears. If you're using Firefox, you can subscribe to the feed and grab the URL from the bookmark that Firefox creates. Figure 11-6 shows you an RSS file and its content displayed in an HTML viewer.

SharePoint doesn't include a Web part for displaying RSS news feeds. Although this is obviously a major oversight on Microsoft's part, many third parties have created Web-part RSS viewers. To find one of these viewers, just Google for "SharePoint RSS viewer". I like to use the viewer at George Tsiokos's Web site, `http://george.tsiokos.com/projects/wssrss`.

To use the tool on George's site, follow these steps:

1. **Paste the URL for the RSS news feed into the Enter feed URL text box.**

2. **Specify your desired properties for the feed, such as the number of items that you want displayed.**

3. **Click Get wss-rss.dwp.**

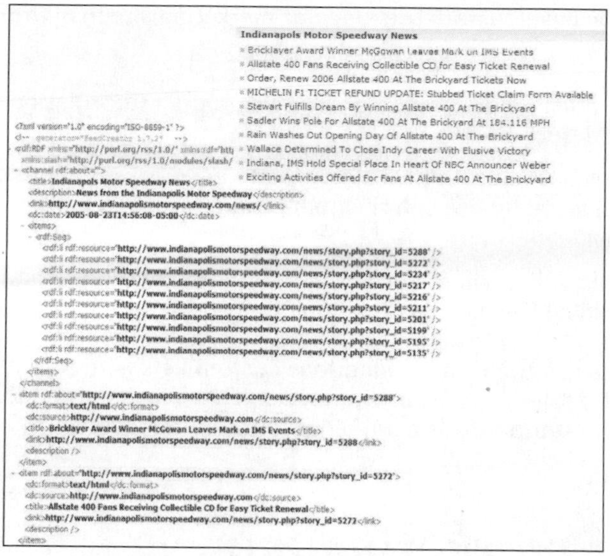

Figure 11-6:
You have
to use a
viewer to
transform
RSS
content.

George's Web site generates a Web-part file that you can download to your computer and import to your site. To import the file, follow these steps:

1. **Browse to your marketing site on SharePoint.**

2. **Click Modify Shared Page in the upper left-hand corner of the screen.**

3. **Click Add Web Parts⇨Import.**

4. **Browse to the Web-part file that you download in the preceding example from George's Web site.**

5. **Click Upload.**

   The Web part appears below the Upload button.

6. **Drag and drop the Web part to a zone on the page.**

George's Web site includes instructions for creating your own tool for generating Web parts for viewing RSS news feeds. George rocks — and so does RSS!

See Chapter 6 for more about using RSS feeds in SharePoint.

Getting Everyone on the Same Page

In the following sections, I show you how to share information about your company's marketing mix with your enterprise. These examples assume that you have custom lists on your marketing site in SharePoint for your:

- ✔ **Products:** A list where you enter all your product information such as name and description.

  Put the product name in the title property in your product list. This allows you to easily use your custom product list as a lookup column in another list.

- ✔ **Promotions:** A list where you enter information about upcoming promotions, including the dates of the promotion and what media you are using.

The point of the products and promotions custom lists is to provide support data you can use to educate your employees. These lists don't need to be held to the same standards as a full-blown information system.

Sharing your marketing mix

In large organizations or organizations with a diverse product mix, employees can have a hard time knowing useful details about products. From my own personal experience, I never know when or what promotions are going on. In today's world of relationship management, every person in your company has an opportunity to be an ambassador, but it's hard for your employees to be ambassadors when they're clueless about your products.

Here are some ideas for using SharePoint to share information about your company's marketing mix:

- ✔ Create a product gallery by using a Web-parts page.
- ✔ Share news about new products and promotions by using a scrolling banner.
- ✔ Emphasize brands by using them to navigate to SharePoint content.
- ✔ Engage your enterprise in lead management, using SharePoint's list templates.

Creating a product gallery

Use a product gallery to highlight the products your company sells and provide information about those products that may be useful to your employees.

You don't have to list every product you sell. You may choose to highlight three or four products each month. You create a product gallery using

- ✔ A list of products
- ✔ A document library of product images
- ✔ A Web-part page that displays the products and its images

To associate product images with a product from your product list, follow these steps:

1. **Add a custom lookup property to the document library.**

   The lookup property stores the link to the product.

2. **Choose the products list from the** Get information from **drop-down list.**

3. **Choose the Title column.**

   Adding the lookup property to the image in the document library lets you associate multiple images with a single product (for example, images of a product's front, back, and side views).

4. **Go through the images library and associate the products with each image in the library, as Figure 11-7 shows you.**

You may want to use a document library rather than a picture library to store the product images. You can't create connections between Web parts with picture libraries. One more reason to consider not using a picture library.

Figure 11-7:
Associate
the digital
asset with
its product.

	Type	Name	Modified	Modified By	Checked Out To	URL	Product
		a.jpg	8/23/2005 08:28 PM	SP\administrator			Product 1
		advert1.wma	8/9/2005 09:03 PM	SP\administrator			Product 2
		advert2.avi	8/9/2005 09:03 PM	SP\administrator			Product 1
		advert3.avi	8/9/2005 09:03 PM	SP\administrator			Product 3
		b.jpg	8/23/2005 08:28 PM	SP\administrator			Product 2
		c.jpg	8/23/2005 08:28 PM	SP\administrator			Product 3
		d.jpg	8/23/2005 08:28 PM	SP\administrator			Product 1
		pr1.wma	8/9/2005 09:03 PM	SP\administrator			Product 2
		pr2.wma	8/8/2005 10:10 PM	SP\administrator			Product 3
							Product 4
		promo1.avi	8/9/2005 09:03 PM	SP\administrator		URL	Product 4

Home   Documents and Lists   Create   Site Settings   Help

Marketing
Digital Assets

Repository for non-image digital assets.

Select a View
All Documents
Explorer View

Actions
- Add to My Links
- Alert me
- Export to spreadsheet
- Modify settings and columns

New Document | Upload Document | New Folder | Show in Standard View | Task Pane | Totals | Refresh Data

To build the products gallery, follow these steps:

1. **Browse to the marketing site.**

2. **Click Create on the primary horizontal toolbar.**

3. **In the Web Pages section, click Web Part Page.**

4. **Give the page the name Product Gallery.**

5. **Choose a layout template and a document library to store the Web-part page, as shown in Figure 11-8.**

6. **Click Create.**

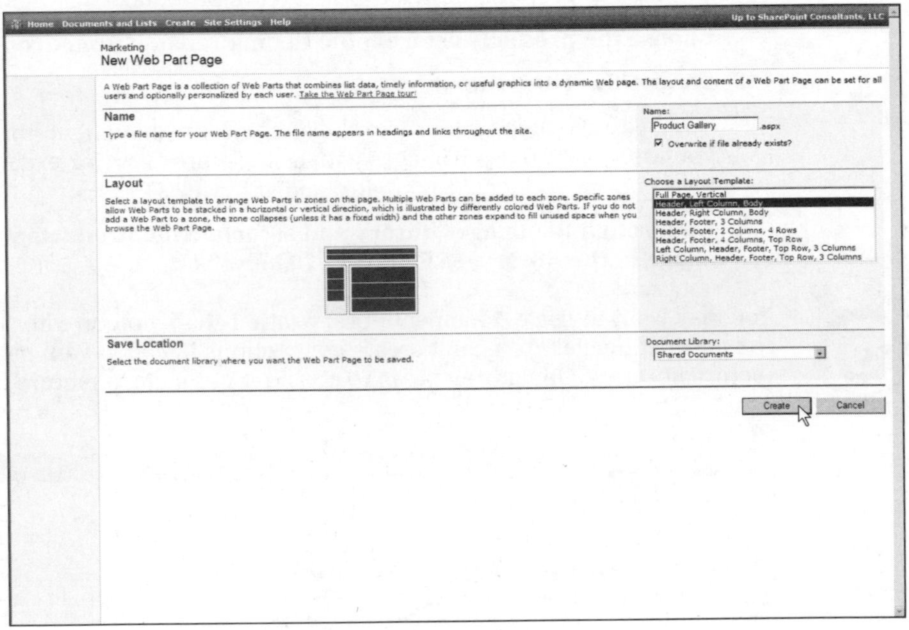

Figure 11-8:
Create a
Web-part
page to
display the
product
gallery.

On the Product Gallery page that you create by using the preceding list, follow these steps to add Web parts for the products list and document library where product images are stored:

1. **Add the product list Web part to the Web-part page.**

2. **Add the Web part for the document library with the product images to the Web-part page.**

3. **Click the drop-down menu on the product list Web part.**

4. **Choose Connections⟶Provide Row To.**

5. **Select the document library, as you can see in Figure 11-9.**

6. **In the Edit Connection dialog box, choose the Title column to apply the filter.**

7. **Click Next.**

8. **Choose Product (or the name of the lookup column that you create in your document library, as the first example in this section describes) as the column to link to the Products list.**

9. **Click Finish.**

   Radio buttons appear next to the products listed in the products list Web part that allow you to select a product that you want to display images for in the document library Web part.

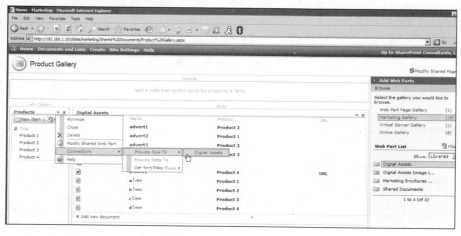

Figure 11-9:
Connect
two Web
parts by
using the
Connections
Menu
option.

You can only make a connection between visible columns. Create a new view to add columns you need to link Web parts together.

Select a radio button next to a product to filter the images and other digital assets for that product, as Figure 11-10 shows you.

Figure 11-10:
Clicking the
radio button
filters the
connected
Web part.

Figure 11-11 shows an alternative layout of a product gallery. This gallery uses the digital asset custom list that you find out how to create in the section "Managing digital assets," earlier in this chapter.

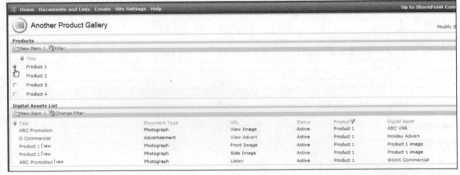

Figure 11-11:
A product
gallery
example
that uses
two custom
lists.

Instead of storing the images separately from the products list, you can embed your product images in the products list.

By storing the image with the product, you have everything related to that product all in one place. Separating the image from the product requires more overhead, but it creates a slicker and more flexible gallery.

To store an image with a product, follow these steps:

1. **Add a custom property to the product list called Product Image.**

2. **Set the data type to** Hyperlink or Picture.

3. **Choose to format the column as a picture.**

You now have a product list that looks like Figure 11-12.

You can also add your product images as attachments to the product in the product list. To add an attachment, click the Attach File button when you add a new product or edit an existing product in the custom products list. After you attach your file, you can click Attach File again to attach another file.

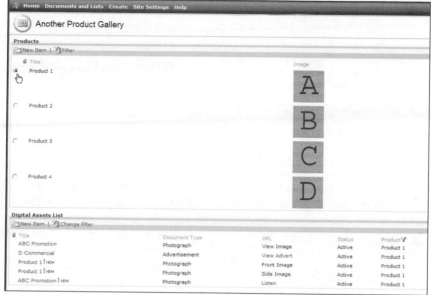

Figure 11-12:
A custom
list can also
store a
product
image.

Highlighting products and promotions

When your company decides to promote a product, do you also consider how to promote the promotion within your company? Nothing is more embarrassing than when customers call to inquire about new products, specials, or promotions and your employees have no idea what they're talking about.

In the following examples, I show three ways you can highlight product promotions on your site and your portal to keep your employees in the loop.

Chapter 6 shows more examples of displaying content from your sites, such as marketing and human resources, on your SharePoint portal.

To highlight announcements about products, promotions, or other marketing news on your portal, follow these steps:

1. **Browse to your portal home page.**
2. **Click Manage Content in the Action list.**

   The Documents and Lists page appears.
3. **Click Portal Listings.**
4. **Click the Grouping and Ordering view from the list of views on the left of the screen.**
5. **Click the Add Group button.**

6. **Add a Marketing group and click OK.**

7. **Click the Add Listing button to add a new marketing related listing.**

   The Add Listing page appears.

8. **In the Group section, in the drop-down list choose the group that you create in step 6.**

9. **Click OK to create the listing.**

   Add the Grouped Listings Web part to your portal home page to display the grouped listings. Click Manage Grouping and Ordering to change the order of the groups.

You can also create a scrolling banner that features hyperlinks and pictures of product or promotion information that you have stored on your site. This is not a feature of SharePoint, but it demonstrates how you can use existing technologies used for building Web sites to display content on SharePoint.

To create the banner, follow these steps:

1. **Open Notepad.**

2. **Enter the following code in the Notepad file:**

```
<html>
<head>
<script language="JavaScript">
i = 0;
imagepath =
        "http://<portal>/sites/marketing/<library>/";
productpath =
        "http://<portal>/sites/marketing/Lists/<list
        name>/DispForm.aspx?ID=";

pics = new Array("b.jpg", "c.jpg", "d.jpg", "a.jpg");
urls = new Array( "2", "3", "4", "1");
urlnames = new Array ("Product 2", "Product 3",
        "Product 4", "Product 1");

function rotateBanner(){
    document.getElementById('pic').src = imagepath +
        pics[i];

        document.getElementById('url').innerHTML=urlna
        mes[i];
    document.getElementById('url').href = productpath
        + urls[i];

    if (i < pics.length - 1) {
        i = i + 1;
    }else{
```

```
        i = 0;
    }
    setTimeout("rotateBanner();",5000);
}
</script>
</head>
<body onLoad="rotateBanner();">
<img id="pic" border="0"
        src="http://<portal>/sites/marketing/<library>
        /a.jpg"><br>
<a id="url"
        href="http://<portal>/sites/marketing/Lists/<l
        ist name>/DispForm.aspx?ID=1">Product 1</a>
</body>
</html>
```

3. **Type in the paths to where you have your product images are stored, and to the list that displays your stored product images:**

   a. In the `imagepath` line, put the URL to your document library where product images are stored.

   b. In the `productpath` line, substitute your portal's server name in the `<portal>` tag and the name of the custom products list in the `<list name>` tag.

   The `productpath` is used to create a hyperlink that a user can click when a product is displayed in the scrolling banner. It's the URL to a product in your custom products list except no product ID is listed after the equal (=) sign. No product ID is listed because the product ID is substituted, using the values in the `urls` line.

   c. In the `pics` and `urls` lines, substitute your image names and product IDs from your custom product list.

   d. In the `urlnames` line, substitute the product names you want displayed in the scrolling banner.

   e. In the img tag line that starts with `<img id="pic"`, substitute the URL to the image of the first product you display in the scrolling banner.

   f. In the line that starts with `<a id="url"`, substitute the URL for the hyperlink that displays the product-list entry for the image specified in the preceding step.

   To get the URLs you need for this example, click an image file in your document library. The URL you see in the address bar of your browser should look similar to the one in the `imagepath` line. For the product URL, browse to your custom product list and click one of the products in the list. Use the URL you see in your browser's address bar in the `productpath` line.

4. Save the file with an HTML extension.

5. Upload it to a library on the site.

6. Add a page viewer Web part to the front page of the marketing site (or the home page of the portal, if you want).

7. Type or paste the URL to the HTML page that you upload in Step 5 to your site library.

You can download the image files used in this example and see a working version of the scrolling banner at www.sharepointgrrl.com.

You now have a rotating banner of images with hyperlinked titles. See an example of the rotating banner in Figure 11-13. If a viewer clicks on one of those titles, it takes that viewer to the page that describes that particular product. You can easily substitute promotions or even brands in this example — just substitute the hyperlinks for the URLs to the images in the document library and the entries in the custom list.

Make sure that all users have at least reader permission to the locations where you have the images and products stored.

You can also effectively communicate promotions by adding a calendar view of your promotions to your marketing site. Follow these steps:

1. Create an events list to store your promotions information.

2. Add a custom lookup property to associate the promotions with a product, if you want.

3. Add custom properties for the start and finish date for the promotion.

4. Create a calendar view that uses the start and finish date for the promotion.

5. Add the calendar view to the site home page.

You can only use a list's calendar view Web part on the site where the list is stored. You can't display a list Web part from a site on a portal — and vice versa — but Chapter 6 shows you how to get around this limitation.

Looking at the other Ps

The earlier sections of this chapter cover products and promotions. You may also want to include information about price and place. But unless you have some need to educate your employees about prices, you probably don't want to share your price lists with the whole company.

However, if your company still uses Excel and Word documents to create price lists, then you may benefit from either storing those documents in a library or creating a custom list. The nice thing about using a custom list is that you can have the marketing assistant update the list, and then everyone works off the same copy.

I offer the same advice about place that I do about price. If you want a list of distributors, create a contact list. Add any custom properties that you need for territories or sales reps to suit your business needs.

If you decide to add content for price and place, remember that you can link that content to your custom products list, using a custom lookup property.

Navigating with brands

Your company spends a lot of resources on brand management. Capitalize on your branding investment with SharePoint. Here are three ways to put your brand to good use in your portal:

- ✔ **Brand your portal:** See Chapter 7 to get the lowdown on how to brand your portal.

- ✔ **Use brands on the primary navigation bar:** Chapter 3 gives you some examples of how to display the names of your brands across the top of your portal.

- ✔ **Use brands on the secondary navigation bar:** Use Chapter 3 to see how to add your brands to the Topics page so they appear in the secondary navigation bar on your portal's Home page.

Figure 11-13 shows you an example of primary and secondary navigating with brands. You can have a single portal page for all brands or a page for each brand. You can even have an entire site with its own document libraries and lists dedicated to a single brand. Go with whatever works best for your organization.

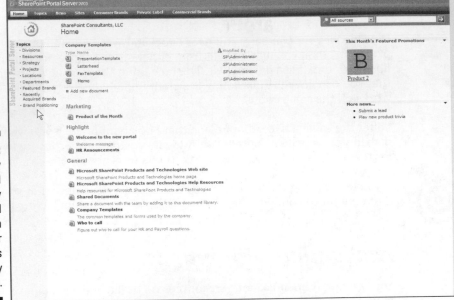

Figure 11-13:
Use primary
and
secondary
portal
navigation
to keep your
brands
constantly
visible.

Taking the lead with your leads

Languishing leads are worthless to your organization. Make your leads actionable with SharePoint. Use SharePoint to capture, distribute, score, and (most important) act on your leads:

- ✔ **Capture:** Create a task list for capturing leads and put a link to the task list in a prominent place on your portal.

- ✔ **Distribute:** Add a custom property to your task list for routing leads with the choices New, Routed, Scored, and Pending. Set the default value to New. Create custom views that filter or group by the routing property. After a new lead is reviewed, update the lead's status to Routed. Assign someone the task of viewing all leads with Routed status. It's that person's job to score the leads.

- ✔ **Score:** Add a custom property called Scoring. The scoring property allows you to score your leads in a way that's meaningful in your organization. Have the scoring person update the score and update the status of the lead to show that the lead is scored.

- ✔ **Act:** Have people respond to the scored leads accordingly. You need to mark any lead that has a problem or can't be scored as Pending.

SharePoint and CRM

The buzz in business right now is relationship management, especially customer relationship management (or CRM). Microsoft even has its own product dedicated just to CRM, which they gave the very original name of Microsoft CRM. And Microsoft isn't the only software company with its eye on customer relationship management.

Looking at the capabilities of SharePoint, you may be tempted to wonder whether you can use

SharePoint for customer relationship management. Although a SharePoint-based CRM solution works better than spreadsheets or nothing at all, it doesn't even come close to the capabilities of a true CRM system. Before you jump to the conclusion that you can use SharePoint for CRM, take time to evaluate using SharePoint as a CRM system, as you would any other system.

You can use whatever statuses you want to suit your organization. By changing the status, the lead moves through the process. The lead stops moving, however, if your people don't take ownership of each status.

To really dress up lead management, you can

✔ Create custom views for each step in lead management. Use a Web part to display each custom view. Display all the Web parts on a single Web-part page to create a dashboard effect.

✔ Automate the status column by using a calculated status. For example, if the lead has a value in the Scoring column, then a calculated status could update itself to Scored.

✔ Use alerts to subscribe to individual leads in the list. Have a list manager receive alerts every time a change is made to the lead list.

Tooting your own horn

As you brainstorm content ideas, don't forget to toot your horn a little. Use announcements, custom lists, and even plain old HTML to share information about

✔ Top deals that recently closed

✔ Top 25 customers

✔ Results of customer-satisfaction surveys

Marketing Campaigns

Just when you think you have plenty of ideas for using SharePoint with marketing, Microsoft releases two site templates for SharePoint geared specifically to marketing:

- ✔ Marketing campaigns
- ✔ New products

You can download the Microsoft templates for marketing at www.microsoft. com/technet/prodtechnol/sppt/wssapps/default.mspx.

You can find 30 templates for various aspects of business available for download at this site.

Follow the instructions on Microsoft's site to download the template that you want. Microsoft recommends that you install the template on your server, but you don't have to. You can simply download and execute the template on your local machine, if you want. This is helpful if you don't have access to the server.

To install the template, follow these steps:

1. **Browse to a site where you want to use the template.**

2. **Click Site Settings.**

3. **In the Administration section, click Go to Site Administration.**

4. **Click Manage Site Template Gallery in the Site Collection Galleries section.**

5. **Click Upload Template, as you can see in Figure 11-14.**

6. **Browse to the location on your server or local machine where you installed the template file.**

7. **Upload the template file to the template gallery.**

Figure 11-14:
Upload the Microsoft templates to the site gallery in your marketing site.

	Home Documents and Lists Create Site Settings Help
	Marketing **Site Template Gallery**

Make a template available for use in Web site creation by adding it to this gallery. The templates in this gallery are available to this site shown.

Select a View
- Default View
- All Templates

⬆ Upload Template | ▼ Filter

Actions
- ⊞ Add to My Links
- ⊞ Alert me
- ⊞ Export to spreadsheet
- ⊞ Modify settings and columns

Name	Edit	Title
MarketingCommunicationsCampaignSite_Basic		Marketing Communications Campaign Site - Basic
MarketingCommunicationsCampaignSite_Custom		Marketing Communications Campaign Site_Custom
NewProductDevelopment_Basic		New Product Development - Basic
NewProductDevelopment_Custom		New Product Development - Custom

8. **Click Create on the primary navigation bar.**

9. **Scroll down and choose Sites and Workspaces from the Web Pages section.**

10. **Enter a title and URL for the site.**

11. **Click Create.**

12. **On the Template Selection page, choose the template that you uploaded in Step 7, as Figure 11-15 shows you.**

    SharePoint creates a site, using the marketing campaign template.

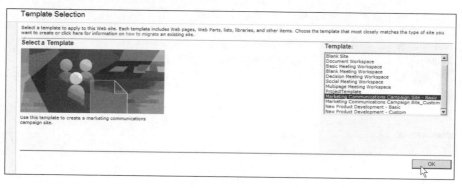

Figure 11-15: Select the marketing campaign template from the list of available templates.

You can see the campaign template in Figure 11-16. This template includes these elements:

- ✓ **Document libraries:** For storing market research, marketing plans, budgets, and marketing collateral. You can just as easily combine all this content into one library and use a property to identify the type of documents that you're storing.

- ✓ **A task list and event calendar:** For staying on top of campaign-related duties.

- ✓ **A list of contacts:** Shows the people responsible for moving the campaign process along.

- ✓ **A threaded discussion:** For having asynchronous online discussions about issues related to campaign details.

To use the campaign site, you may want to install the basic site and get a feel for how it works. Then either install the blank site or just get ideas to use in your existing site. (For more about blank sites, see Chapter 8.)

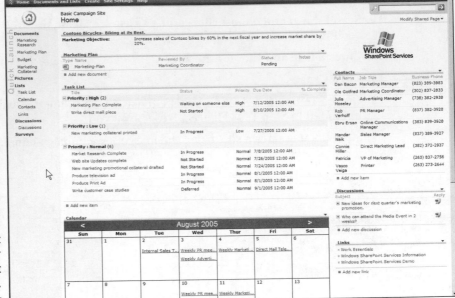

Figure 11-16:
Use the marketing campaign template to jump-start your SharePoint usage.

Part VI
Throw Away the Spreadsheets

The 5th Wave   By Rich Tennant

"We're much better prepared for this upgrade than before. We're giving users additional training, better manuals, and a morphine drip."

In this part . . .

I show you how to use SharePoint to manage business processes. You'll see how to use a form library and InfoPath to create a process for managing expense reports. I'll show you how to build a help-desk application using the Issues list. You'll use Web parts pages to make dashboards for managing each of these processes.

Chapter 12

Expense Report

Say that your company uses paper expense reports. Our make-believe business process for expense reports goes something like this:

✔ Our business professional, Tom, travels to a large customer and closes a huge deal.

✔ After being on the road and away from his family for the whole week, Tom must categorize and log his business receipts into a paper Expense Report form to request reimbursement.

✔ After searching high and low for a copy of the Expense Report form, Tom enlists the help of a co-worker. With two business professionals unable to find the form, they reluctantly ask an administrative assistant who harrumphs and gets them the form.

✔ Tom forwards the completed form and all of its source receipts to his immediate supervisor for approval. There it sits on Tom's boss's desk for another week, buried amid dozens of other paper forms. Meanwhile, Tom is off to close another deal.

✔ Mary, who is a clerk in accounts payable, receives Tom's report via interoffice mail. Because Mary has so many paper forms to process, she has a lot of rules about how she expects to receive those forms. Paperclips, no staples. Expense report folded in half, print side out, with receipts, in ascending date order, on the inside. You get the idea.

✔ Tom's boss doesn't make many business trips, so he doesn't know Mary's rules — and violates every one of them. Tom's report doesn't meet Mary's standards, so she puts it in her "needs staple-pulling" stack.

✔ Finally, at the end of the week, Mary pulls out Tom's report, only to find that the report is missing a receipt. She throws it into her problem pile.

✔ Meanwhile, Tom gets his credit-card bill and remembers that he still doesn't have his expense check. He phones Accounts Payable, only to find they have no record of his expense report. Panicked, he phones his boss and asks if his boss thought to make a copy of Tom's report. Of course, his boss didn't, but he assures Tom that he'll be reimbursed.

✔ The next day, Mary phones Tom to ask about the missing receipt. She can't explain why someone in accounts payable told Tom that they never received his expense report. After all, it's been sitting on her desk all this time. Relieved, Tom tells Mary to short-pay the item with the missing receipt. He tells her he'll resubmit it when he gets back in town.

✔ Mary enters the expense report in the AP system, a full three weeks after Tom submitted his request.

✔ When the checks are run the following Tuesday, the accounting manager notices that the amount of Tom's check is higher than most of the other expense checks for that week. She asks Mary to pull the documentation.

✔ Noticing several expensive dinners, the accounting manager decides to phone Tom's boss to remind him that the company has a limit on dining expenses.

✔ In the meantime, Tom phones to inquire about the whereabouts of his expense check. Mary checks the system and tells Tom that the check was cut yesterday. He should have it today or tomorrow.

✔ A week later, Tom's boss returns the accounting manager's call, and the accounting manager agrees to release the check.

I wonder if SharePoint can offer a better solution for managing expense reports . . . ?

Building a Better Expense Report

SharePoint's form library can store forms for everything from expense reports to supplies ordering. SharePoint uses a special kind of form that's based on XML.

XML is an acronym for extensible markup language. Like HTML, the markup language that you use to create Web pages, XML uses opening and closing tags with attributes — like this:

```
<tag attribute=value></tag>
```

Although HTML has a predefined set of tags and attributes such as `<body background=yellow>`, XML lets you define your own tags and attributes.

This flexibility makes XML the perfect language for describing the kind of data you have in an expense report.

You don't need to understand anything about XML to use forms in SharePoint. You can use Microsoft Office InfoPath, which is part of Microsoft Office 2003, to create XML forms. Like other Office tools, InfoPath plays nice with SharePoint. Using InfoPath, you can

✔ Create and modify XML-based forms

✔ Publish XML forms to a SharePoint form library

✔ Display list data from a source such as a SharePoint list in an XML form

✔ Fill out XML forms that you can save in a SharePoint form library

Designing an InfoPath form

InfoPath comes with a number of form templates, including a few for expense reports. Rather than start from scratch, you can take an existing template and modify it — which is easier and faster.

To modify the existing expense-report template in InfoPath, follow these steps:

1. **Open InfoPath.**

   If you have a default installation, click Start⇨All Programs⇨Microsoft Office⇨Microsoft Office InfoPath 2003. Otherwise you find InfoPath wherever you chose to install Office 2003.

2. **In the Fill Out a Form dialog box, click Sample Forms in the Form categories section of the screen.**

   The Sample Forms gallery appears.

   If your screen looks different from Figure 12-1, it's probably because you're not using InfoPath with the latest service pack (which you can download from the Microsoft Web site).

3. **Click Expense Report (Domestic).**

   Be sure to single-click. If you double-click, you open the form.

4. **Click Design this Form from the list of Form tasks at the right of the screen, as shown in Figure 12-1.**

   The Expense Report opens in Design view. I show you how to modify this form in the next section.

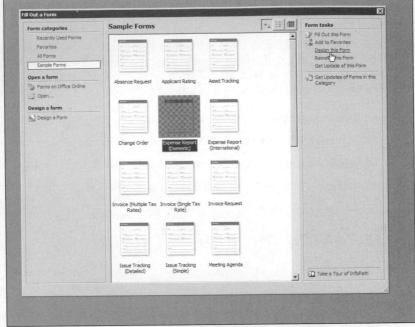

Figure 12-1:
You can
modify an
existing
form
template
more easily
than you
can start
from
scratch.

Modifying the base form

The Expense Report form that comes with InfoPath can get the job done. And with a few modifications, you can personalize the form to your organization:

✔ Provide a drop-down list of employee names from your Human Resources site.

✔ Provide a drop-down list of expense categories.

✔ Fill in the check-run period automatically (based on the form's completion date).

Making an employee roster

In the state that the Expense Report form comes in, the employee has to type in his or her name, department, manager, and contact information. You already have this information stored on the HR site, so it makes sense to provide it in the Expense Report form for the user to select.

In Chapter 10, you find out how to build the employee list by using a Human Resources team site. You need a list of employees like the one created in Chapter 10.

To create a drop-down list of employee names from the employee list on the HR site on the Expense Report form, follow these steps:

1. **With the Expense Report form in Design view, right-click the Name control in the Employee section of the form.**

   A menu appears.

2. **Choose Change To➪Drop-Down List Box from the menu, as you can see in Figure 12-2.**

   The Name control changes from a text box to a drop-down list box.

3. **Right-click the Name control.**

4. **Choose Drop-Down List Box Properties from the menu.**

   A dialog box appears. The dialog box has three sections: Binding, Validation and Rules, and List box entries.

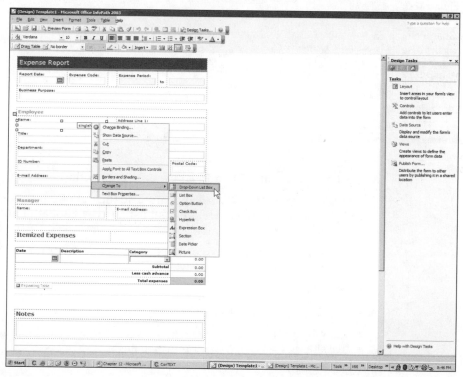

Figure 12-2:
Change the Name control from a text box to a drop-down list box.

5. **In the List box entries section of the dialog box, select the radio button next to the Lookup values in a data connection to a database, Web service, file, or SharePoint library or list radio button, as Figure 12-3 shows you.**

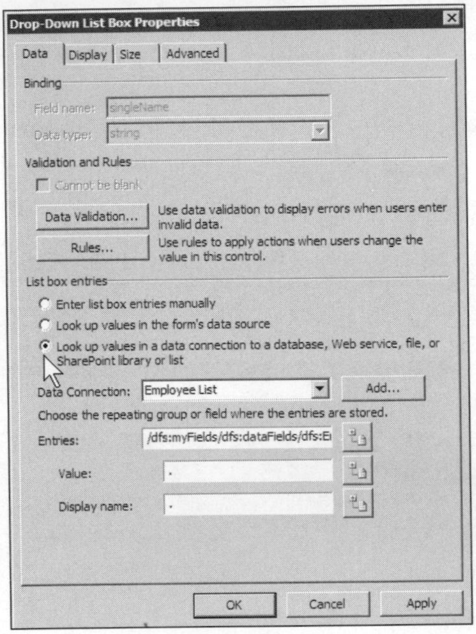

Figure 12-3:
Set
SharePoint
as the data
source for
the lookup
values in a
drop-down
list box.

6. **Click the Add button to add a new data connection.**

The Data Connection Wizard appears. Use the Data Connection Wizard to create a link between a SharePoint list and the InfoPath Expense Report form.

7. **In the Data Connection Wizard, select the radio button next to SharePoint library or list.**

8. **Click Next.**

9. **Enter the URL to the HR self-service site on SharePoint.**

If you haven't built the HR self-service site in Chapter 10, you need some other site that has a list of employee names.

10. **Click Next.**

InfoPath connects to the SharePoint site. A list of all list names and library names on the HR self-service site appears.

11. **Choose the Employee list, as Figure 12-4 shows you.**

12. **Click Next.**

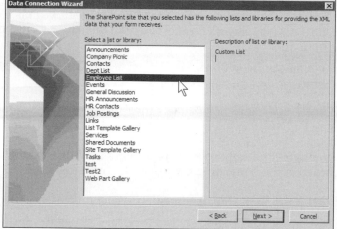

Figure 12-4:
All the lists
and libraries
available
on the
SharePoint
site appear.

A list of the fields available on the list appears.

13. **Choose fields for the employee's first name, last name, department, and role.**

    The Role field specifies whether the employee is a manager. (You use this field later to create a drop-down list of managers' names.)

    You can't choose calculated fields from a SharePoint list because they never appear.

14. **Click Next.**

15. **Give the connection a name.**

16. **Click Finish.**

    The Data Connection Wizard closes, and you're returned to the Drop-Down List Property box.

17. **Click the button next to the Entries text box.**

    The button has a picture of a plus (+) sign with a line connecting to a document.

18. **In the dialog box that appears, select a field from the Employee list to display in the drop-down box:**

    a. Expand the list of fields by clicking the plus (+) sign next to each folder until all folders are open.

    b. Click the employee's last name in the list of fields (as you can see in Figure 12-5).

    c. Click OK.

The Entries text box is filled in with a long string of text. This text tells InfoPath how to get to a list of employee's last names, using the list of employees on SharePoint to display in the Name drop-down box.

19. Click OK on the Drop-Down List Properties dialog box to close the dialog box.

You now have a drop-down box that lets the user select his or her name from a list of names; no need to have the user type in the name.

To set the value for the employee's department based on the employee's name (selected in the Name drop-down list), follow these steps:

1. Right-click the Department control.

The text boxes and drop-down lists used on a data-entry form are called *controls*.

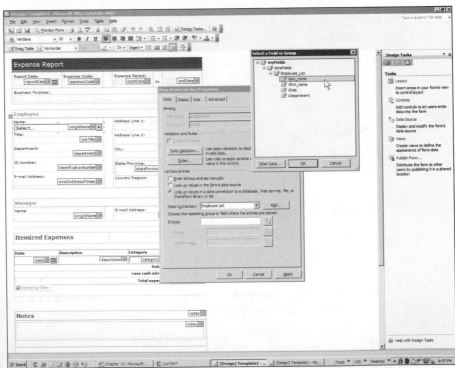

Figure 12-5:
Select a
data field
whose
value you
want
displayed in
the drop-
down box.

2. **Click Change To⇨Expression Box.**

   The Department control changes from a text box to an *expression box* — a control whose value is calculated by using a formula. Use an expression box to create a formula that sets the value of the employee's department according to the employee name selected in the Name drop-down list.

3. **Right-click the Department control.**

4. **Click Expression Box Properties from the menu.**

   A dialog box appears.

5. **On the General tab, click the Edit Formula button next to the Xpath text box, as you can see in Figure 12-6.**

   The Edit Formula button displays the math symbol `fx`. The Insert Formula dialog box appears.

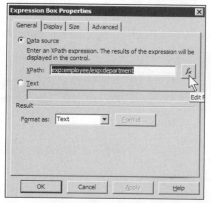

Figure 12-6:
Click the
Edit Formula
button to
change the
data source.

6. **Delete all the text in the formula box.**

7. **Click the Insert Field or Group button.**

8. **In the Select a Field or Group dialog box, click the Data Source drop-down list and select Employee List.**

9. **Expand the list of fields by clicking the plus (+) sign next to each of the folders until all the folders are open.**

10. **Click Department.**

    If you don't see a field for department on the list, then you probably didn't select the department field when you added the data connection. Go to Step 13 in the previous step list to add that field.

11. **Click the Filter Data button.**

    A dialog box appears.

12. **Click Add.**

    The Specify Filter Conditions dialog box appears.

13. **Follow these steps to create a filter for the Department field:**

    a. In the left drop-down list box, choose the employee's last name.

    b. In the far right drop-down list box, choose Select a Field or Group.

    c. Change the data source to Main (using the Data Source drop-down list) and then expand two folders: the employee folder, and the name folder inside the employee folder.

    d. Click the `singleName` field, as you can see in Figure 12-7.

14. **Click OK until you close all the dialog boxes.**

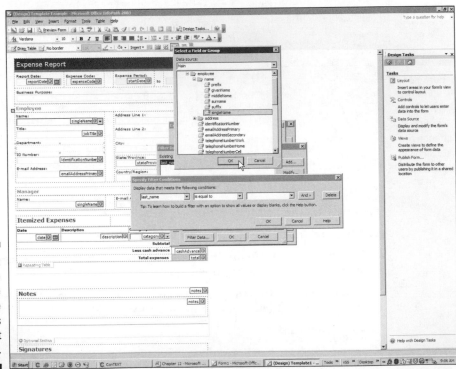

Figure 12-7:
Filter the data source so the employee's department appears.

The employee's department appears in the Department control, based on the employee name you select in the Name control.

To create a drop-down list of managers so the employee can select his or her manager, follow these steps:

1. **Right-click the Name control in the Manager section of the Expense Report form.**

2. **Click Change To⇨Drop-Down List Box from the menu.**

3. **Right-click the Name control in the Manager section again.**

4. **Click Drop-Down List Box Properties.**

   The properties dialog box appears.

5. **On the Data tab in the dialog box, select the radio button next to Look up values in a data connection to a database, Web service, file, or SharePoint library or list.**

6. **In the Data Connection drop-down box, choose the data source for the Employee list from the Data Connection drop-down list.**

   Use the same data source for the employee's Name control as the one created at the beginning of this chapter.

7. **Click the button next to the Entries text box.**

   The Select a Field or Group dialog box appears.

8. **Expand the myFields and dataFields folders in the dialog box.**

   Your custom list appears right below dataFields.

9. **Click the plus (+) sign next to the folder for your custom list to expand the list of fields in the list.**

   A list of fields appears, showing those available to use as the data source for the drop-down list.

10. **Click the field that displays the manager's name.**

    If you're using the employee list from Chapter 10, click the last_name field.

11. **Click the Filter Data button.**

    The Filter Data dialog box appears.

12. **Click the Add button in the Filter Data dialog box.**

    The Specify Filter Conditions dialog box appears.

13. In the left drop-down list, choose `Role`.

If your employee list in SharePoint doesn't include a role for the employee, you may want to add one to your list. Use the role to specify whether the person is an employee or manager. An alternative approach is to have one list for employees and another list for managers. It's easier, however, to have everyone in a single list and use role to filter the list.

14. In the right drop-down list, choose Type text.

The drop-down box converts to a text box with a flashing cursor, waiting for you to type text into it.

15. Type the word Manager (as you can see in Figure 12-8).

InfoPath adds double quotes after you click OK on the dialog box, so you enter the word — in this case, **Manager** — exactly as it appears in the SharePoint list.

The filtered value is case-sensitive. You have to type the value exactly as it appears in the SharePoint list.

16. Click OK on each of the dialog boxes to save your work.

Figure 12-8:
Create a
filter by
typing in a
value.

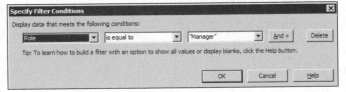

You now have a drop-down list of managers.

You could use an expression box rather than a drop-down list for the manager's name, similar to the previous example for setting the value of the department. You need a list on SharePoint where the employee is associated with the manager. For example, the list would include a record for an employee name and his or her manager's name. You set the filter on the manager's name where the employee name in the SharePoint list is equal to the employee's name on the Expense Report form.

Deciding where your money goes (or, at least, where you see it)

The Expense Report form provides a `Category` field with a drop-down list of categories. If you decide to change those categories down the road, you have to open the form in Design view; instead, use a SharePoint custom list to populate the list of categories. By using a SharePoint list, you can add new categories in SharePoint and eliminate the need to modify the Expense Report form.

To create a list to store the expense categories in SharePoint, follow these steps:

1. **In a SharePoint site, create a custom list called Expense Categories.**

   Chapter 10 shows you how to create a custom list.

2. **Add your company's expense categories to the custom list.**

   Use the instructions in Chapter 10 to import your categories into the custom list from Excel or see Chapter 10 for step-by-step instructions for adding data to a list.

You can add the general ledger account for each category to your Expense Categories custom list. Adding the general ledger account is valuable if you intend to import your Expense Report form into accounting software.

You add the expense categories to the Expense Report form in much the same way you add the employee list to the Name control (see "Making an employee roster" in this chapter). To add the expense categories to the Expense Report form in InfoPath, follow these steps:

1. **Right-click the Category control in the Itemized Expenses section of the Expense Reports form.**

2. **Click Drop-Down List Box Properties from the menu.**

3. **Select the radio button next to** Look up values in a data connection to a database, Web service, file, or SharePoint library or list **in the** List box entries **section of the dialog box.**

4. **Click the Add button to add a new data source.**

   The Data Connection Wizard appears.

5. **Walk through the steps of the Data Connection Wizard to add your custom expense categories.**

   Refer to the steps for adding the employee list (in the section "Making an employee roster") if you need more details.

6. **Click the button next to the Entries text box.**

7. **Expand the myFields and dataFields folders by clicking the plus (+) sign next to each folder.**

   Your expense category custom list appears right below dataFields.

8. **Click the folder for your expense category list.**

9. **Click OK.**

To save one value but display a different one, click the buttons next to the Value and Display Name fields in the Drop-Down List Properties dialog box. Choose a field to use from the list of fields displayed, as you can see in Figure 12-9.

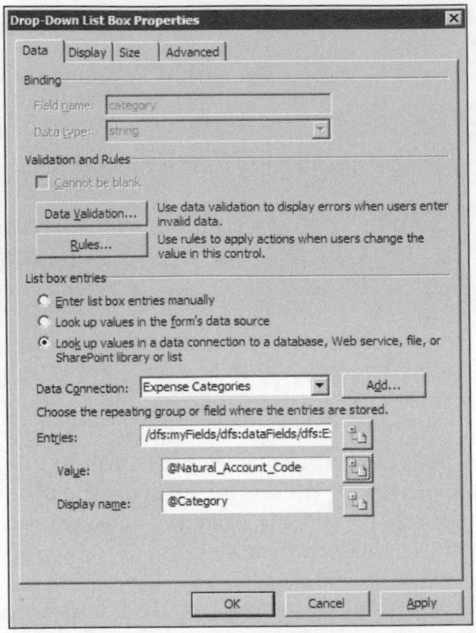

Figure 12-9:
Choose a
friendly
display
name but
save a
useful data
value.

Listing check runs

Before you publish the Expense Report form to SharePoint, you may want to customize this form in one more way. Suppose your accounting department has a schedule for doing check runs, similar to a payroll schedule. Accounts Payable prints a check when an employee submits an expense report. If you work with this setup, then you can easily calculate the expense period and display it on the expense report.

This basic outline gives you an idea of how to set up your expense report to use an expense-reporting period similar to a payroll period:

✔ Create a custom list in SharePoint to hold the check-run schedule.

Your check-run schedule lists the dates on which the expense period starts and ends, along with the date on which checks are run for expense reports submitted during that period.

 1. **Set the expense period values in the InfoPath Expense Report form based on the check run schedule.**

 2. **Display a dialog box in the Expense Report form, informing the user if a holiday falls in the expense period.**

 3. **Create a custom list called** Expense Periods **in SharePoint, specifying these values:**

 • Expense period start date

 • Expense period end date

- Check-run date

- A holiday flag to specify if a holiday falls in or near the expense period

    The term *flag* means a yes/no field. When the value of the field is set to yes, the record is considered "flagged."

- A Comments field

You can create this list in Excel first and then just import it to SharePoint. See Chapter 10 for more information about importing spreadsheets into SharePoint lists.

You set the expense periods in the InfoPath form very much like you do in the previous examples for setting the department and manager's values. Instead of populating a drop-down list, you set the default value of the expense period fields in the Expense Report form.

Before you can set the default values, you have to add a data source to the expense periods. The data source tells the Expense Report form where to get the values for the expense-period fields — in this case, your custom list in SharePoint where the expense periods are stored. To add the expense periods from SharePoint, follow these steps:

1. **Click the Tools menu from the menu bar at the top of the Expense Report form in InfoPath.**

2. **Choose Data Connections from the Tools menu.**

    The Data Connections window opens. It displays all the *data connections* (sources that InfoPath uses to get data) that exist for the form.

3. **Click the Add button.**

    The Data Connection Wizard starts.

4. **Select the radio button next to Receive Data.**

    You select the Submit Data radio button if you want to use your InfoPath form to send data to a data source, such as a database. The Receive Data button allows your InfoPath form to receive data from a data connection, such as a drop-down list displaying a list of values from a SharePoint list.

5. **Click Next.**

6. **Walk through the rest of the wizard and add your expense periods to the form.**

    If you need more details on completing the wizard, start at Step 7 in the instructions for adding the employee's name (in the "Making an employee roster" section of this chapter).

When the wizard prompts you to select data fields for use in the Expense Report form, check the holiday-flag column. (You use the holiday-flag column later to create a dialog box.)

7. **Click Close to close the data connection window.**

Now that you have the expense period data tied to the Expense Report form in InfoPath, use the following steps to set the default values for the expense period on the form:

1. **Right-click the starting text box for Expense Period on the Expense Report form.**

   Under the Expense Period label on the Expense Report form, there are two text boxes separated by the word "to". The text box on the right of the word "to" stores the starting value of the expense period; the text box on the left stores the ending value.

2. **Click Change To⇨Expression Box from the menu.**

3. **Right-click the starting expense period (changed to an expression box in Step 2), and click Expression Box Properties from the menu.**

   A dialog box appears.

4. **In the Data Source section, click the Edit Formula button next to the Value text box.**

   The Edit Formula button has the math symbol fx on it. After you click it, the Insert Formula dialog box appears. Delete any values in this dialog box before proceeding to the next step. Otherwise your formula winds up with errors in it.

5. **Click the Insert Field or Group button on the Insert Formula dialog box.**

6. **From the Select a Field or Group window, click the Data Source drop-down list, and then select the expense-period data source added in the previous set of steps.**

7. **Expand the data fields by clicking the plus (+) sign next to each of the folders.**

8. **Click the field for period start.**

   Use the field that stores the period-start value from your list of expense periods in SharePoint.

9. **Click the Filter Data button.**

   The Filter Data dialog box appears.

10. **Click Add on the Filter Data dialog box.**

    The Specify Filter Conditions dialog box appears. In Specify Filter Conditions, the left dialog box shows your expense period's Start field.

11. **Change the middle drop-down list to is less than or equal to.**

12. **In the right drop-down box, create a filter that sets the field on the left — the start of the expense period — to a value less than or equal to the date the Expense Report form was filled out:**

    a. Choose Select a Field or Group.

    b. Navigate to the main data source for the report by clicking Main in the Data Source drop-down list.

    c. Choose `reportDate`.

    d. Click OK.

13. **In Specify Filter Conditions, add another filter that sets the expense period's end date greater than or equal to the form's report date:**

    a. Click the And button.

    b. Change the left drop-down box so the Period End Field is chosen.

    c. Change the middle drop-down box to *is greater than or equal to*.

    d. In the right drop-down box, repeat Step 12 to add `reportDate`.

    Your filter conditions look like the image in Figure 12-10.

14. **Click OK on all the open dialog boxes to save your work.**

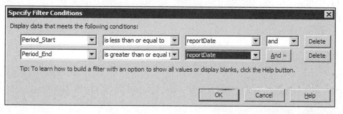

Figure 12-10: Set conditions for filtering the expense period data.

Boy, that list has a lot of steps! Thankfully, you can set the value for the end of the expense period value much more easily:

1. **Repeat Steps 1 and 2 in the previous set of steps.**

   Doing so changes the *Ending expense period* text box to an expression box.

2. **Right-click the expression box and click Expression Box Properties.**

   A dialog box appears.

3. **Click the Edit Formula button and specify the data source as the ending period on the Expense Report form.**

   Delete any values in the formula box before proceeding with the next step.

4. **Click the Insert Field or Group button.**

   5. **Navigate to the Period End value in the Expense Period data source.**

      Click the Data Source drop-down list to select the Expense Period data source. Expand the plus (+) sign next to each folder and click the `Period End` field.

   6. **Click the Filter Data button.**

   7. **Click Add to add a new filter.**

   8. **Set the left drop-down box to Period Start Date.**

   9. **In the right drop-down box, choose Select a Field or Group.**

  10. **Navigate to the `startDate` value in the main data source.**

      Click the Data Source drop-down list and choose Main from the list.

  11. **Click OK on all open dialog boxes to close them.**

To test your work, click the Preview Form button in InfoPath. If you wired everything correctly, then your expense-period dates update as you change the report date. (You can change the report date by clicking the little calendar button next to the Report Date field.)

When you look at the form in preview view, you see red dashes around the text box for the report date. When you get these red dashes, you have a validation error to fix. (A *validation error* occurs any time the data that is entered in a field is not the right kind of data. For example, entering text into a number field causes a validation error.)

To fix the report-date validation error, follow these steps:

   1. **Close the preview by clicking the Close Preview button.**

      You return to Design view.

   2. **Right-click the Report Date control, and then choose Data Picker Properties from the menu.**

   3. **Click the Data Validation button.**

   4. **Click the Remove button to remove the validation rule.**

      Preview your form again, and you no longer have those red dashes around the report date.

The Expense Report form in InfoPath is set up to calculate the expense-period dates (which you configure to use your custom expense-period list from SharePoint) to change as expense items are added to the Expense Report form. You want to remove that calculation; otherwise, your expense periods change as expense items are added to the Expense Report form.

To remove the calculation that occurs when expense items are added to the report, follow these steps:

1. **Click Tools⇨Programming⇨Microsoft Script Editor.**

   Use the Microsoft Script Editor to edit the programming for the InfoPath expense-reports form.

2. **In the document outline on the left of the script editor, double-click `msoxd__item::OnAfterChange`.**

   If you can't see the document outline, press Ctrl+Alt+T.

3. **In the code editor, find the third `If` statement, and then delete the following code from that statement:**

   ```
   || strChangedNode == 'exp:date'
   ```

4. **Place two forward slashes in front of the statement `calcDateRange`.**

   The statement turns green. See Figure 12-11 for an example of how you want the code to look.

5. **Close the script editor by clicking File⇨Exit.**

6. **Save your changes when prompted by the script editor.**

One side effect of modifying an existing InfoPath form is that you have to remove validation, formatting, and calculations that don't apply to the specific way you intend to use the form. While this is challenging (especially if you aren't used to poking around in a script editor), it's a heck of a lot easier than starting from scratch!

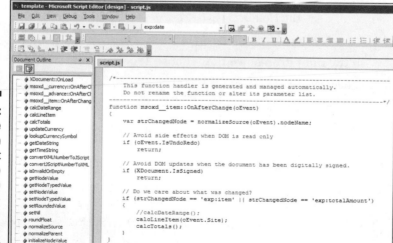

Figure 12-11: Modify the code in the script editor to remove the expense-period date calculation.

To really jazz up your form, add a dialog box that tells users when the expense period for the expense report falls near a holiday. You could use this to display a custom message that the checks won't be mailed on the usual date. To add the dialog box, follow these steps:

1. **Open the Properties dialog box for the expense-period start date on the form:**

   a. In the Data Source task pane, click the Data Source drop-down list and choose Main.

   If the Data Source task pane is not displayed, click View➪Task Pane from the menu in InfoPath.

   b. Right-click the `startDate` field in the Data Source task pane.

   c. Click Properties on the right-click menu.

   The Field or Group Properties dialog box appears.

2. **Click the Rules tab in the dialog box.**

3. **Click the Add button to add a rule.**

4. **Click the Set Condition button.**

5. **Navigate to the holiday-flag field in the Expense Periods data source:**

   a. In the left drop-down list of the Condition dialog box, click Select a Field or Group.

   The Select a Field or Group dialog box appears.

   b. Click the Data Source drop-down list and choose Expense Periods.

   c. Expand the folders by clicking the plus (+) sign next to each folder.

   d. Click the Holiday Flag field.

   e. Click OK to close the dialog box.

6. **In the right drop-down box, choose True.**

7. **Click OK.**

8. **Click the Add Action button.**

9. **Choose the Show a Dialog Box Message action from the Action drop-down list.**

10. **Enter text (such as** This is a holiday week) **that you want displayed in the dialog box.**

11. **Click OK.**

12. **Click OK on each of the open dialog boxes to save your work.**

Unfortunately, the rule that you create with the preceding list can't do the job that you want it to because you haven't made it specific enough. When building the rule, InfoPath never gave you the option to filter the data to look at the holiday flag for the selected expense period on the InfoPath Expense Report form. For the dialog box to display only when the report date falls within an expense period whose holiday flag equals `true`, you have to build the rule manually.

To get the holiday-flag filter, follow these steps:

1. **Add an expression box to the Expense Report form:**

   a. Click Insert⇨More Controls.

   b. Click expression box in the task pane on the right of the screen and drop the expression box onto the form.

   You may have to scroll down to see the expression box in the list of controls.

2. **In the Insert Expression Box dialog box, click the Edit Formula button.**

3. **Click the Insert Field or Group button.**

4. **Navigate to the holiday flag in the Expense Periods data source.**

   Refer to Step 5 in the preceding set of steps for detailed instructions.

5. **Click Filter Data.**

6. **Click Add.**

7. **In the left drop-down list, choose the period start field from the Expense Periods data source.**

8. **Set the right drop-down to `startDate` field in the Main data source.**

   Click Select a field or group from the drop-down list to get to the Main data source.

9. **Click OK until you return to the Insert Expression box.**

   The dialog boxes that you complete thus far build a long statement that now appears in the XPath field.

   Xpath is short for _XML path language._ For more information on Xpath, see the sidebar "XPath, help me find my way!" later in this chapter.

10. **Highlight the entire statement and press Ctrl+C to copy it.**

11. **Click Cancel on the Insert Expression dialog box to make the Insert Expression box go away.**

You now have a long statement that looks similar to this:

```
xdXDocument:GetDOM("Expense
        Periods")/dfs:myFields/dfs:dataFields/dfs:Expen
        se_Periods/@Holiday_Flag[../@Period_Start =
        xdXDocument:get-
        DOM()/exp:expenseReport/exp:startDate]
```

Your statement might look different if you named your list of expense periods — or your columns in the expense periods list different names. This statement says, in effect, *Get the value of the holiday flag from the record in the SharePoint list of expense periods, where the period-start value in the SharePoint expense periods list is equal to the* startDate *value on the Expense Report form.*

Now, add this long statement to your startDate rule:

1. **Open the rule from the startDate Properties dialog box.**

   Refer to Steps 1 and 2 in the previous steps (which added the rule to the startDate field). Click Set Condition on the Rules tab of the startDate Properties dialog box to open the Condition window.

2. **In the Condition window, click The expression in the left drop-down list.**

   You see a long statement that looks similar to this one:

   ```
   xdXDocument:GetDOM("Expense
             Periods")/dfs:myFields/dfs:dataFields/dfs:Expense_Periods/@Holid
             ay_Flag = string(true())
   ```

3. **To manually build the rule for the holiday flag:**

   a. Click in the text box and click the delete key to delete everything in the text box up to the equal sign.

   b. Replace "true()" with "-1" by typing it in the text box, as you can see in Figure 12-12.

   Fields with a yes/no or true/false value are called *Boolean*. Boolean values also appear as either *0 and 1* or *0 and any nonzero value*.

Figure 12-12: Delete everything in front of the equal sign.

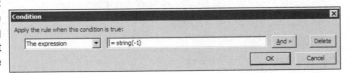

I have you replace true() with "-1" because -1 is a nonzero value that represents false in the holiday-flag field in the SharePoint expense-period list. To figure out what value you need to test for, use an expression box to display the field on your form.

XPath, help me find my way!

XPath is a part of the XML language standard. The XML standard includes many standards for manipulating XML — they usually start with the letter *X*, including XSLT and XSD. (Not to be confused with the popular television series, *The X-Files*.)

An XML file is a series of matching tags that enclose data. The tags are nested inside each other like this:

```
<item>
   <date>08/15/2005</date>
   <description>sharepoint
for dummies</description>
```

```
<amount>21.99</amount>
   <category>book</category>
   </item>
```

XPath is a language that lets you reach into an XML document and grab a set of tags and the data enclosed within.

You can find entire books with thousands of pages on each of these X-languages. Luckily for you, Microsoft created InfoPath, which builds all these X-language statements for you.

4. **Press Ctrl+V on your keyboard to paste the expression copied in Step 10 of the earlier steps into the expression box in front of the equal sign.**

   You now have an expression that looks like this:

   ```
   xdXDocument:GetDOM("Expense
           Periods")/dfs:myFields/dfs:dataFields/dfs:Expense_Periods/@Holid
           ay_Flag[../@Period_Start = xdXDocument:get-
           DOM()/exp:expenseReport/exp:startDate] = string(-1)
   ```

5. **Click OK to close all the open dialog boxes.**

6. **Preview the form by clicking Preview Form.**

As you change your report date, any expense periods with a holiday flag set to `true` display the dialog box you created in the rule. (Pretty cool, considering you don't have to write a single line of code.)

Publishing your brand-new form

Modifying the form, as you can read about in the section "Modifying the base form," earlier in this chapter, is the hardest part. After you have your form up to snuff, you're ready to publish it. To publish the form, follow these steps:

1. **With your form in Design view, choose File⇨Publish from the menu bar.**

    The Publishing Wizard starts.

2. **Click Next.**

3. **Select the radio button to publish your form in a SharePoint form library.**

4. **Click Next.**

5. **Accept the default value to create a new library.**

6. **Click Next.**

7. **Enter the URL for the site on which you want the form published.**

8. **Click Next.**

9. **Enter the name Expense Reports for the library in the Name text box.**

10. **Click Next.**

    Doing so calls up a list of columns to add to the form library.

11. **Click Add.**

12. **Choose the `startDate` field.**

13. **Change the column name to** Period Start **by typing into the column name text box (as you can see in Figure 12-13).**

14. **Click OK.**

15. **Click Finish.**

16. **Click Close.**

    You now have the form saved to a newly created form library in the SharePoint site you entered in Step 7.

You can add any field from the main data source as a column to the form library. If you want data displayed in your form library, add a field to your main data source. It can be populated in two ways:

- ✔ A user can enter values manually.

- ✔ You can populate it dynamically by setting the default value, using the examples in this chapter.

Figure 12-13:
Adding the
Period Start
column to
the form
library.

Managing Expense Reports

Before you just throw your Expense Report form out for people to use, think about how you plan to manage the entire expense-reports process.

In the following sections, I show you how to

- Enter data
- Create views of your data
- Create a routing and approval process
- Create a dashboard for viewing your expense-reporting process

Just the facts, ma'am

Entering data into an InfoPath form is pretty straightforward. If you can make it through the business of modifying the form (see "Modifying the base form," earlier in this chapter), entering data is a piece of cake.

To enter a new expense report, follow these steps:

1. **Browse to the Expense Reports form library on your SharePoint site.**

   You create this library in the previous set of examples.

2. **Click the Fill Out This Form button on the toolbar.**

   The expense report opens in InfoPath.

3. **Complete the form, as you can see in Figure 12-14.**

4. **Close the Expense Report form by clicking File⇨Close. Save the form to the form library when prompted by InfoPath.**

The client-side user must have InfoPath installed on his or her computer to open the Expense Report form.

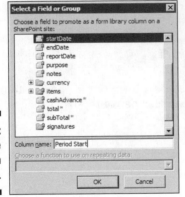

Figure 12-14:
Complete the form in InfoPath.

To design an existing form already published to a SharePoint form library, follow these steps:

1. **Open the form like you want to enter a new form following the steps shown previously.**

2. **On the Tools menu, choose Design this Form.**

Routing and approval with statuses

In Chapter 11, you find out how to specify status in such a way as to create a routing and approval process for managing leads. I do something very similar here for managing the expense-report process.

For this process, you create a custom property (called Status) in your expense-report form library in SharePoint, including these choice values:

- ✔ New
- ✔ Pending
- ✔ Approved
- ✔ Closed

You add columns to your form library is the same way you add columns to any library or list — namely, by following these steps:

1. **Browse to the form library.**

2. **Click Modify Settings and Columns.**

3. **Click Add a New Column.**

4. **Add the Status choice column and set the default value to New.**

   See Chapter 9 for an example of adding custom properties to a list.

I use a Choice column in the preceding list because it lets me set the default value of a new form and mass-update the status of a group of Expense Report forms in SharePoint. When a new Expense Report form is completed and saved to the form library, the Status column is automatically set to the value New. You can also add the Status field to the form itself, but then you must either manually update the status on each form or write a program to do it for you each time the status changes for the Expense Report form.

To create a routing and approval process for managing the expense-reports process, you have several general tasks to perform:

- ✔ Use views to filter or group on the statuses.
- ✔ Make someone take ownership of each status.
- ✔ Have an expediter create an alert to the list.
- ✔ Display the views on a Web-part page.

Viewing things in a whole new way

After you save a completed Expense Report form in the form library, the data appears in columns in the form library. The columns that you choose when you use the Publishing Wizard determine the data that appears.

The form library is like any other library: You can add custom properties and views, and you can export data to spreadsheets.

Use these views to manage your expense-report process:

- Filtered for each of the status values (New, Pending, Approved, and Closed)
- For expense reports over a certain amount, such as $500
- Grouped by employee name and status
- Grouped by period start date

Use the examples for displaying employee birthdates in Chapter 10 to display a two-week view of expense periods.

Putting expense reports up on the dashboard

You need one place to go for the administration of the expense reports process. Use Web parts and a Web-part page to create a *dashboard* effect — an on-screen one-stop shop that gives you access to information about a process.

Creating the Web-part page

To create the Expense Reports Web-part page for managing the expense-reports process, follow these steps:

1. **Click Create on the site primary navigation bar.**
2. **Scroll down to the bottom of the page, and then click Web Part Page.**
3. **Give the page a name.**
4. **Select a layout template.**

5. **Click Create.**

The new *Web-part page* (a special kind of Web page used to display Web parts) appears in Design view.

Adding Web parts

To add the Web parts for the Web-part page created in the preceding section, follow these steps:

1. **Click Filter next to Web Parts List in the Add Web Parts task pane.**

2. **Choose Lists from the Show drop–down list.**

3. **Drag and drop the Expense Periods list to the Web part page.**

   For more about how to create the Expense Periods list, see "Listing check runs," earlier in this chapter.

4. **Change the filter to Libraries on the Add Web Parts task pane.**

5. **Drag and drop the Expense Reports Forms library to the page four times — one for each status created in the section "Routing and approval with statuses."**

6. **For each Expense Reports form library added to the Web part page, do the following:**

   a. On the first Expense Reports Forms Library Web part, click the drop-down arrow in the Web parts title.

   b. Choose Modify Shared Web Part.

   c. Change the Selected View by clicking the drop-down list, and then select the view that's filtered by the status New.

   You create this view in this chapter's section called "Viewing things in a whole new way."

   d. Click OK for any warnings that appear about changing the view.

   e. Expand the Appearance options by clicking the plus (+) sign.

   f. Change the title of the Web part to New Expense Reports in the Title text box.

   g. Set the view for each Web part to reflect a different status value.

   After completing these steps, your page looks like the one in Figure 12-15.

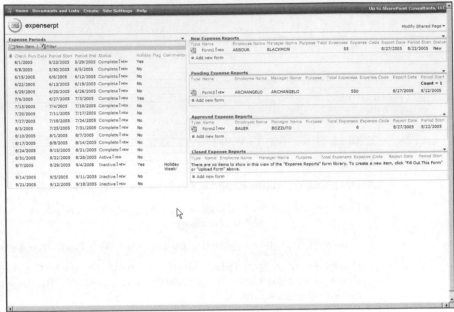

Figure 12-15:
Use a Web-
part page
to create a
dashboard
effect.

To link the Web parts together so you can view the Expense Report forms based on a chosen expense period, follow these steps:

1. **Click Modify Shared Page.**

2. **On each of the Expense Reports Form Library Web parts, click the drop-down arrow in the title of the Web part.**

3. **From the menu, choose Connections⇨Get Sort/Filter From⇨ Expense Periods.**

   This step tells the Expense Report Web part to only show the records that match the expense period selected in the Expense Periods Web part. It's possible to make a connection between the Web parts because the Expense Periods list is linked to the Expense Reports form (as described in the "Listing check runs" section).

4. **Repeat Steps 2 and 3 for each of the Web parts.**

5. **In the Edit Connection dialog box, choose the columns to use to create a connection between the Web parts:**

   a. Choose the `Period Start` column.

   b. Click Next.

   c. Choose the `Period Start` column again.

   d. Click Finish.

You now have a dashboard where you can filter the expense report views based on the period that you select in the Expense Periods Web part. You're ready to start using the dashboard to manage your expense-reporting process.

Finishing the dashboard

Follow these steps to finish the dashboard for managing the expense reports process:

1. **Click Modify Shared Page⇨Modify Shared Web Parts⇨Web Part Page Title Bar.**

2. **Enter a title, caption, and description for the page.**

   Figure 12-16 shows the final dashboard.

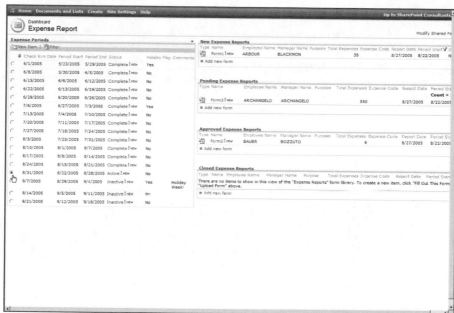

Figure 12-16: Click an expense period to filter the four expense-report views.

Making the Expense Report All Your Own

The hypothetical expense-reporting process that this chapter outlines probably doesn't duplicate your company's specific process for managing expense reports. Nevertheless, you can probably see the promise of using InfoPath with SharePoint. Here are some suggestions for moving forward with InfoPath and SharePoint:

✔ **Go custom:** An InfoPath form is just an XML file. If you have access to a programmer, then a custom solution featuring SharePoint, InfoPath, and the programming language of your choice can make beautiful processes together.

✔ **Go crazy:** Automate these paper-based processes by using InfoPath and SharePoint:

- Time sheets

- Supplies ordering

- Time-off requests

✔ **Go Microsoft:** As you can read about in Chapter 11, Microsoft has released many templates for SharePoint sites. These templates feature InfoPath forms:

- Human Resources Programs and Services

- Travel Requests

- Expense Reimbursement Requests

See the Microsoft Web site at www.microsoft.com/technet/prodtechnol/sppt/wssapps/default.mspx for more SharePoint site templates and instructions on how to install those templates.

Chapter 13

Technical Uses for SharePoint

In This Chapter

▶ Building a trouble-ticket solution

▶ Using your trouble-ticket solution

▶ Exploring new ways to use SharePoint

*M*ost businesses would never dream of operating their accounting or operations departments with pen and paper. Yet, many technical departments operate just that way. Their business processes for processing support requests or requests for new hardware or software are manual, and they usually can't repeat those processes easily.

Whether department managers believe it or not, the level of customer satisfaction often reflects how mature a department's process is (or isn't). Your customers know by the frequency with which their requests are misplaced or ignored. They know by how long it takes you to respond and whether the response answers the question that was asked in the first place. Professionalize your process by using SharePoint's out-of-the-box features to automate the support request process:

✔ Create work orders to track client requests

✔ Track the progress of a given work order over time

✔ Assign tasks to technicians and link their tasks to a work order

✔ Build a self-service dashboard for clients, managers, and technicians that makes the management of support requests visible

Building a Trouble-Ticket Solution

Help desks often use trouble-ticket software to manage incoming requests. When a request comes into the help desk, a work order is created. The work order stores all the basic facts of the request: who is making the request, what they are requesting, when they expect to have the work completed. The work order may generate tasks that are associated with the work order. SharePoint's issues and tasks list templates can help you build a trouble-ticket solution to track your incoming requests and their resolutions. The issues list can be used for the work orders and the tasks lists can be used for — you guessed it — tasks. These list templates have the same features as other SharePoint lists, including

- Custom properties
- Custom views
- Web parts for displaying list views

To start building your trouble-ticket solution, create a new site for storing the trouble-ticket lists or add those lists to an existing site. I suggest creating a site called Help Desk with the URL `http://<portal>/sites/helpdesk`.

Be sure to add your technicians to the help-desk site as site users.

Setting up support data

A trouble-ticket solution for a help desk requires some support data. Otherwise, you have to enter all your hardware and users' names into each work order manually every time you create a new work order. Save yourself some typing by storing information about your hardware and users in SharePoint lists and then creating drop-down lists in your work orders.

A work order requires custom lists to store at least the following data in the work order:

- **Hardware:** The hardware that your help desk receives requests about
- **Software:** The software applications that your help desk receives requests about
- **Users:** The people who call your help desk and make requests

You can enter all your hardware, software, and user data in spreadsheets and then import those spreadsheets into lists on your site. To import the data, follow these steps:

1. **Click Create on the primary navigation bar on your site.**
2. **Click Import Spreadsheet.**
3. **Follow the instructions to import the spreadsheet.**

You can find out more about importing spreadsheets in Chapter 10.

Got issues?

An issues list is a kind of SharePoint list, like a tasks list or a contacts list. Issues lists are special because they allow you to attach a resolution to an issue — just what you need to do to capture the resolution of a help-desk work order. You create issues lists like any other list in SharePoint. To create an issues list for work orders, follow these steps:

1. **In your SharePoint site, click Create on the primary navigation bar.**

2. **In the Lists section, click Issues.**

3. **Enter the name** Work Orders **in the Name text box.**

4. **Click Create.**

You now have an issues list for storing work orders. By default, issues lists include these columns with these generic choices:

- ✔ **Status:** Active, Resolved, Closed
- ✔ **Priority:** High, Normal, Low
- ✔ **Category:** Category 1, Category 2, Category 3

You can probably make sense of the default values that come with the status and priority columns. But you need to update the category values so you can assign your work orders to categories that have meaning to your business — unless you have a work order Category 1. To update the categories, follow these steps:

1. **Click Modify settings and columns in the issues list you created in the preceding steps.**

2. **On the Customize screen, click the Category column in the Columns section.**

3. **In the text box that lists the Category's choices, delete the default choices.**

4. **Enter new choices that have meaning for your business, such as these:**
   - Modify user account
   - Request hardware/software
   - Request report
   - Hardware failure

- Software failure
- Other

5. **Click OK.**

Now add the support data for hardware, software, and users to the Work Orders issues list. To add this data, follow these steps:

1. **Click Add a New Column on the Customize screen.**

2. **Give the column a name (Hardware, Software, or Users) in the Column name text box.**

3. **Select the radio button next to Lookup to set the type of data stored in the column.**

   The Customize screen updates; the Optional Settings section of the screen changes, allowing you to select the details for the lookup column.

4. **In the Get information from drop-down list, choose the appropriate column to use as the lookup value for the drop-down list — hardware, software, or users.**

   The screen refreshes so SharePoint can display the list of columns for the custom list you select in this step.

5. **Choose the column whose value you want displayed in the lookup column from the In this column drop-down list.**

6. **Click OK to save the column.**

Issues lists also provide an *Assigned to* property. This property lists all the users on the help-desk site and allows a manager to assign the issue to the lucky bloke selected from the drop-down list.

To assign issues to technicians who aren't users on the site, create a custom list to manage your technicians. For example, if your technicians are consultants who aren't site users, you can create a custom list to store their contact information and use that list to assign the technicians to work orders.

Getting on task

Make your issues list actionable by giving it its very own task list. After all, issues often generate follow-up tasks. If a technician closes the work order before he or she completes the task, the technician often forgets the task altogether. Or the technician may have to solve the issue with a workaround because he or she just doesn't have the time to research solutions.

Examples of tasks that issues can generate include these:

✔ Reboot server on the weekend

✔ Move code to production

✔ Download latest service pack

✔ Install software patch

✔ Find out whether you want to upgrade hardware or software

To keep the tasks on the radar, follow these steps to create a task list:

1. **Click Create on the primary navigation bar for the site.**

2. **In the Lists section, click Tasks.**

3. **Give the task list a name.**

4. **Click Create.**

If you want to keep your issues and tasks linked together, follow these steps to add a lookup column that displays your issues in the task list:

1. **Click Modify Settings and Columns in your Tasks list that you create in the preceding steps.**

2. **Click Add a New Column in the Columns section.**

3. **Give the column the name** Issues.

4. **Set the data type for the column as Lookup.**

5. **Choose the Work Orders issues list from the Get Information From drop-down list.**

6. **Choose Title from the In This Column drop-down list.**

7. **Click OK to create the column.**

You now have a lookup column in your tasks list that displays the title field from your Work Order issues list. Use this lookup column to tie an issue to a task when you create the task.

Bringing it all together

You probably want to display your work orders and tasks together on a single page so it's easy to see which tasks go with which work orders. You can either

- ✔ Add the tasks and work orders Web parts to an existing page in a self-service site.

- ✔ Create a dashboard to display the entire work order process, using a Web-part page.

To build a trouble-tickets solution dashboard like the dashboard in Figure 13-1, follow these steps:

1. **Create a Web-part page.**

   See Chapter 12 for the specific steps that create a dashboard with a Web-part page.

2. **Add Web parts for the work orders, help-desk tasks, hardware, and software lists that you create in this chapter.**

   Chapter 12 shows you how to add Web parts to a Web-parts page.

3. **Create a connection between the Web parts for the help-desk tasks and work orders lists that allows you to display the list of tasks associated with a selected work order:**

   a. Click the drop-down arrow on the title bar for the tasks Web part.

   b. Click Connections⇨Get Sort/Filter From to display a list of available Web parts that can be used to sort or filter the tasks Web part.

   If you don't see the Connections menu on the tasks Web part, click Modify Shared Page⇨Design this Page in the upper-right corner of the page to put the Web-part page in design view.

   c. Click the work orders Web part from the Connections menu.

   The Edit Connections dialog box appears.

   d. Choose the column `Title` from the Column drop-down list and click Next.

   e. Choose the lookup column Issues from the Column drop-down list and click Finish.

   The `Issues` column is the lookup column you create in your tasks list in the preceding steps. If the `Issues` column isn't listed in the Column drop-down list, then add the `Issues` column to the Web-part view.

   Only the columns displayed on-screen can be selected to create a connection between Web parts.

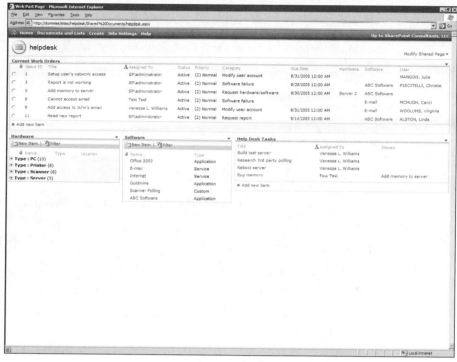

Figure 13-1:
Use a Web-
part page to
create a
dashboard
for the
trouble-
ticket
solution.

For more details on how to build a dashboard, check out Chapter 12.

Putting the Trouble-Ticket Solution to Work

With your issues and tasks on the same page, technicians now have some capabilities they can use very easily:

- ✔ Add or modify issues
- ✔ Create links between issues
- ✔ Add or modify tasks
- ✔ Resolve open issues

And, using our good old friend Microsoft Access, technicians can even synchronize their SharePoint tasks with their Outlook tasks so they can see their help-desk tasks in Outlook.

Working with your issues

Entering data into the issues and tasks lists is very similar to entering data in other SharePoint lists. Issues, however, let you make multiple entries — such as the actions being taken to resolve the issue — against a single issue. You can track the progress of an issue over time by having technicians edit an existing issue.

Entering a new issue

To enter a new issue, using the help-desk dashboard you create in the preceding steps, follow these steps:

1. **Click the Add New Item link in the Work Orders Web part.**

2. **Give the new issue a title.**

3. **Assign the issue to a technician.**

4. **Assign a category to the issue.**

5. **Give the issue a priority and enter a comment describing the request.**

6. **Complete the work order with this information:**

   • Due date

   • Related hardware or software

   • The user who made the request

   You add the lookup columns for hardware, software, and users in the preceding section ("Got issues?").

7. **Click the Save and Close button.**

Editing an existing issue

When you edit an existing issue, SharePoint presents you with a blank data entry form. Instead of editing the original entry, you actually add a new entry that SharePoint ties to the original entry. This approach gives you a very helpful way to track the progress of an issue because you can see all the entries made for an issue over a period of time.

To edit an existing issue, follow these steps:

1. **Click the issue's title and choose Edit Item from the drop-down menu, as shown in Figure 13-2.**

   The form to edit the item appears.

2. **Enter new information related to a step in resolving the issue, or resolve the issue.**

3. **Click the Save and Close button.**

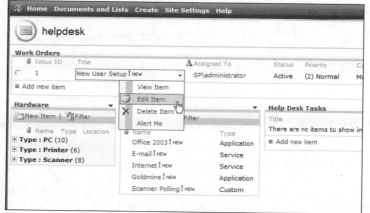

Figure 13-2:
Choose Edit Item from an issue's title drop-down menu to edit the issue.

To view all the entries made for an issue — an issue's history — click the hyperlinked title for the issue in the Work Orders Web part. Any entries for that issue appear when you click the title, as you can see in Figure 13-3.

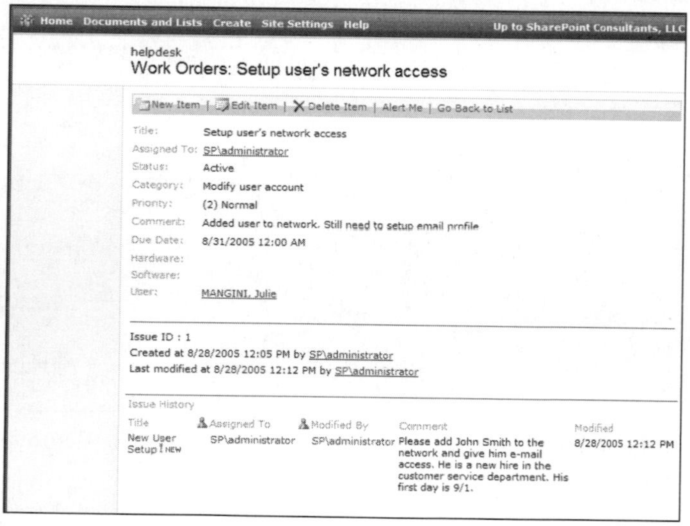

Figure 13-3:
When you click on an issue, the issue's history is displayed at the bottom of the screen.

Linking two issues

One issue can often create a new issue, especially with a recurring problem. You can link an issue to another issue in the same list.

To link two issues, follow these steps:

1. **Get the Issue ID for the issue to which you want to link.**

   The Issue ID is displayed in the Work Orders Web part.

2. **Create a new issue (or edit an existing one).**

3. **Enter the Issue ID for the linking issue in the Add Related Issue field in the issue's data entry screen.**

You can add more than one related issue by repeating the preceding steps with the appropriate Issue ID.

Each issue shows all the other issues that it's related to in the Related Issues section of the screen, as you can see in Figure 13-4.

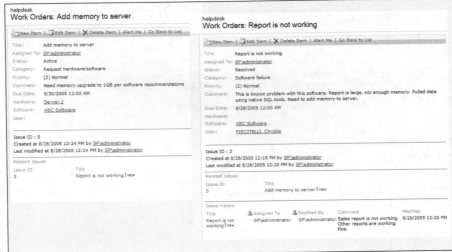

Figure 13-4:
The Related Issues section shows the issues that are related

 TIP

Remove related issues by editing an issue and clicking the Remove hyperlink for the related issue.

Entering a task

Say that you have a work order to upgrade the memory in a server. Before you can upgrade the memory, however, you have to actually buy the memory. Create a task to buy memory and assign that task to the person who buys memory:

1. **In the Help-desk dashboard, click Add New Items in the Help Desk Tasks Web part.**

   A new task entry form appears.

2. **Enter a title for the task.**

3. **Assign the task to the technician responsible for buying hardware.**

4. **Enter a due date.**

5. **Select the issue that's related to the task from the Issues drop-down list, as Figure 13-5 shows you.**

6. **Click the Save and Close button.**

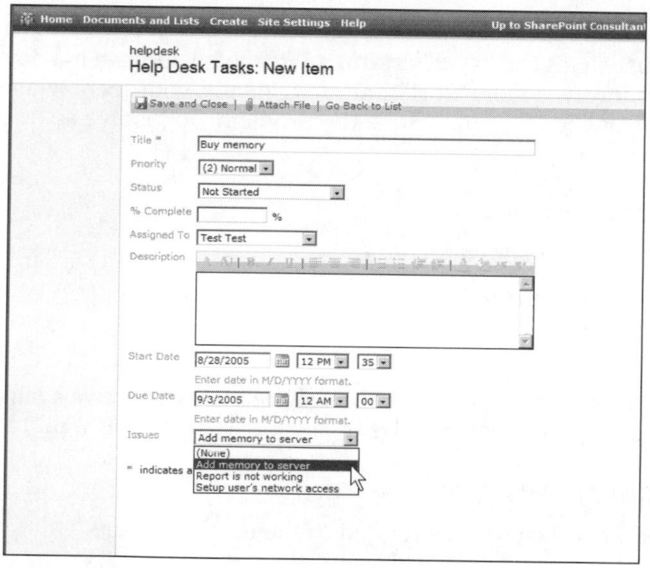

Figure 13-5:
Select an
issue to link
to the new
task.

You now have linked a task to an issue. To view all the tasks for a given issue, select the radio button next to the work order on the dashboard. The list of help-desk tasks is filtered so that only the tasks relevant to the issue are displayed, as you can see in Figure 13-6.

The Work Order Web part filters the Task Web part because you create a connection between the two Web parts. You can find out more about making this connection in the section "Bringing it all together," earlier in this chapter.

Figure 13-6:
Select the
radio button
next to a
work order
to display
a list of
associated
tasks.

Resolving open issues

You can't just change an issue's status to Resolved and call it a day. Resolving open issues involves more work than that. Ideally, your technician records the steps he or she takes to resolve the problem. To resolve an open issue, follow these steps:

1. **Edit the open issue.**

2. **Enter any relevant comments.**

3. **Change the status to Resolved.**

4. **Save the issue.**

TIP

You can edit a resolved issue and change the status to active again. Before you go back through a resolved issue, decide whether you want to

✔ Reopen resolved issues

✔ Create a new issue that's related to the resolved issue

Viewing your tasks in Outlook

Unfortunately, you can't link tasks in Outlook the way that you can link contacts. However, you can get around this obvious oversight on Microsoft's part in a few ways. In this section, I show you a workaround with Microsoft Access and Outlook.

To find out more about linking contacts in Outlook, see Chapter 8.

The basic process for importing SharePoint tasks into Outlook is

1. **Link to the SharePoint task list in Access.**

2. **Create a copy of the task list.**

3. **Import the copy into Outlook.**

   Of course, the devil's always in the details.

Anyone with even just a novice's know-how in Access can import tasks into Outlook with Access. You can get started by doing the preparatory work in Access:

1. **Open Microsoft Access 2003.**

2. **Create a new database.**

3. **On the File menu, choose Get External Data⇨Link Tables.**

4. **In the Link window, create a link to the SharePoint tasks list:**

   a. Click the drop-down list for Files of Type.

   b. Choose Windows SharePoint Services from the drop-down list, as Figure 13-7 shows you.

   c. Click the Link button.

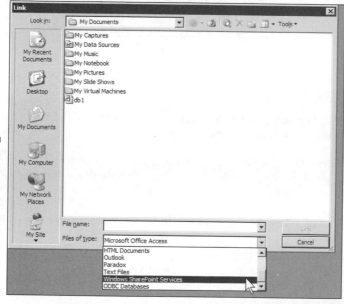

Figure 13-7:
Choose
Windows
SharePoint
Services
from the
drop-down
list to create
a link.

The Link to Windows SharePoint Services Wizard starts.

5. **Type or paste in the URL to your SharePoint help-desk site.**

6. **Click Next.**

7. **Choose your task list (as Figure 13-8 shows you).**

8. **Click Next.**

9. **Choose the All Tasks view and click Next.**

10. **Keep clicking Next until you reach the end of the wizard.**

11. **Click Finish to create the link between the SharePoint tasks list and Access.**

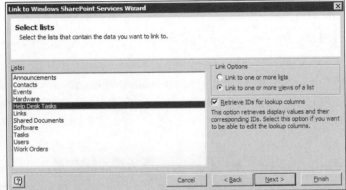

Figure 13-8:
Choose the
Help-Desk
Tasks list
from the list
of lists.

You now have a table of your SharePoint tasks linked in Access. You can add, modify, and delete records in your linked table.

If you're like me, your wheels are spinning with all the ways that you can use Access to display and modify SharePoint lists.

Unfortunately, Outlook doesn't let you upload a linked table. So you need to make a copy of the data in the linked table. Follow these steps to get yourself a copy of your table data:

1. **In Access, click the Tasks table that you link to in the preceding example.**

2. **From the menu, choose Insert⇨Query.**

   The New Query dialog box appears.

3. **Click Design View.**

4. **Click OK.**

5. **Double-click these columns to add them to the output grid:**

   • Title

   • Assigned To

- Status

- Priority

- Due Date

- % Complete

- Description

If you don't see all these columns, the column isn't visible in the SharePoint view. Either add the column to the All Tasks view in the SharePoint tasks list or skip it for now.

6. **In the output grid, enter the ID number for the technician whose tasks you want to copy in the criteria field for the Assigned To column, as Figure 13-9 shows you.**

   Filter the `Assigned To` column so you see only the tasks you've imported into Outlook.

   You can get the technician's ID number from the `UserInfo` table, which was imported into Access with your tasks list.

7. **On the Query menu, choose Make-Table Query.**

8. **Name the query MyTasks.**

9. **Click OK.**

10. **From the Query menu, choose Run.**

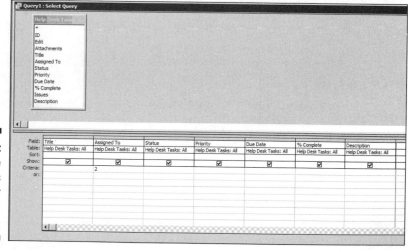

Figure 13-9: Enter the technician's ID number in the criteria field.

The tasks are added to a new table called MyTasks.

To import the tasks to Outlook, follow these steps:

1. **Click your Tasks folder in Outlook.**

2. **Choose File⇨Import and Export from the menu.**

   The Import and Export Wizard starts.

3. **Highlight Import from Another Program or File.**

4. **Click Next.**

   The Import a File wizard starts.

5. **Select the file type of Microsoft Access.**

6. **Click Next.**

7. **Browse to the location of your database.**

8. **Click Next.**

9. **Choose the destination folder as your tasks folder.**

10. **Place a check mark next to Import "MyTasks" into folder: Tasks.**

    The Map Custom Fields dialog box appears. If the dialog box doesn't appear, click the Map Custom Fields button. The Map Custom Fields dialog box allows you to map the fields from the MyTasks table in Access to the Tasks folder in Outlook.

11. **Create mappings by dragging the fields on the left to the fields on right.**

    Create these mappings:

    - `Title = Subject`
    - `Description = Notes`

12. **Click OK.**

13. **Click Finish to import the tasks from the Access MyTasks table to your Outlook tasks folder.**

    Your tasks are imported, as you can see in Figure 13-10.

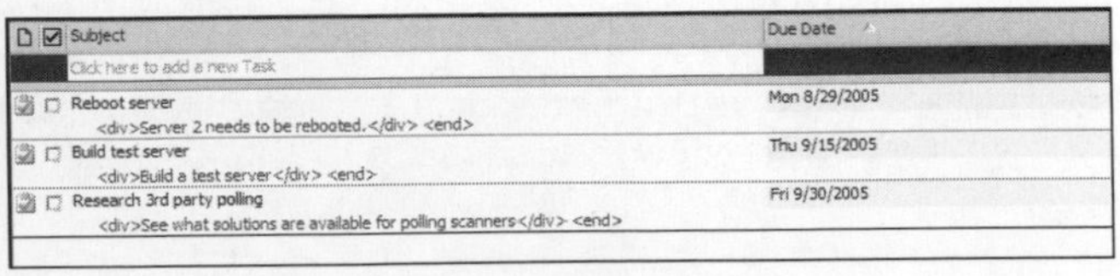

Figure 13-10:
You import the SharePoint tasks into the Outlook tasks list.

This one-way solution is very manual, but you can easily automate it. Although this solution doesn't work for a large enterprise, you can easily put it to work in a small-to-medium shop. Even though it's beyond the scope of this book, someone with intermediate Access experience can automate this approach and even make it a two-way synchronization.

Taking the Next Steps

A technical department can extend the trouble-ticket solution in this chapter to fit its needs. The following sections give you a few ideas.

Creating a self-service help desk

You can build a self-service help desk that lets both the *requesters* (users who need help) and the technicians delivering support to (you guessed it) help themselves to some help.

To give a help desk the capabilities that make it self-service (from a requester's standpoint) requires making some adjustments in your setup:

- Place a hyperlink on the portal or other accessible location that takes the user to the new form entry.

- Don't make the requester complete more than the title and the description. If you make him or her categorize or prioritize, chances are they won't categorize it the way you would.

- Create a dashboard view that allows the requester to easily check the status of any outstanding work order.

- Show users how to create alerts to their requests. SharePoint can use the alert to send the requester an e-mail any time their request is updated. See Chapter 10 for an example of creating an alert.

If you really want to get an A+ in customer service, start a new work order form when a requester phones in for support. E-mail a link to that work order to the requester, asking him or her to confirm the details of the request.

SharePoint allows users to create personal views of pages in the portal and on sites. By using a personal view of the help desk, the technician can lay out the page in a way that suits his or her needs. For example, the technician can add a filter to the Work Order view that shows only that technician's assigned work orders.

To create a self-service dashboard from the technician's perspective, follow these steps:

1. **Browse to the help-desk dashboard in SharePoint.**

2. **Click Modify My Page⇨Personal View.**

   If you don't see Modify My Page, click Modify Shared Page⇨Personal View.

   A personal view of the help-desk page appears. A user must belong to the Contributor site group or higher to use personal views. (See Chapter 4 for a discussion of site groups.)

3. **Click Modify My Page⇨Design this Page to customize the page's layout.**

The URL for the personal view of a page ends with ?PageView=Personal while a shared view ends with ?PageView=Shared. You can add hyperlinks to the shared and personal views of a page to that page so that users can easily switch back and forth.

From a management perspective, SharePoint provides a few built-in features to help manage issues. The following sections tell you about some of these features.

Viewing reports

SharePoint provides a special reporting function with the issues list template that lets you monitor the status of your issues.

To use this feature, follow these steps:

1. **Browse to your help desk's list of Work Orders and Issues.**

2. **Click View Reports in the Actions list.**

View Reports provides pivot-table reports of the following data. It presents issues

- ✔ By category
- ✔ By person
- ✔ Created over a range if dates
- ✔ For a date range

Each of these reports provides additional filters. Use these reports to see what's going on with your help desk.

E-mailing technicians

The issues list template comes with the ability to notify a technician via e-mail when someone assigns him or her an issue.

To turn on e-mail notification for technicians, follow these steps:

1. **Browse to your Issues list.**

2. **Click Modify Settings and Columns.**

3. **Click Change General Settings.**

4. **In the E-mail Notification section, turn on e-mail notification.**

5. **Click OK.**

   SharePoint notifies your technicians when an issue is assigned owner-ship or is changed.

Archiving issues

You may want to implement a policy of archiving resolved issues after they reach a certain age. Unfortunately, SharePoint doesn't provide an archival feature. You can, however, export your issues to a spreadsheet or Access table for offline viewing and reporting. The next section shows you how to create a view that displays all the issues in an issues list, including an issue's history. You need a view with all an issue's history if you want to have an accurate archive.

Displaying details on your dashboard

The dashboard configuration that you can read about in section "Bringing it all together," earlier in this chapter, displays just the most recent entry for an issue. But an issue may have several entries that track its progress over time. You can easily add all the history for an issue to the dashboard.

To add an issue's history to the dashboard, follow these steps:

1. **Create a new view in the Work Orders Issues list.**

   Make sure you have the view's filter set to Show All Items. By default, views in the issues list template only show items where the Current field is equal to yes.

2. **Add a second Work Orders List Web part to the dashboard.**

3. **Set the view for this Web part to the unfiltered view that you create in Step 1.**

4. **Create a connection between the two Work Order Web parts where the second Web part is filtered by the Issue ID of the first Web part.**

Now you can view all the history for a given work order, as you can see in Figure 13-11.

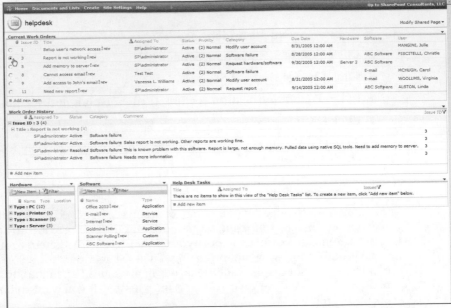

Figure 13-11:
Display
work-order
history by
using a
second
Work
Orders List
Web part.

Getting creative

This chapter shows you just the tip of the iceberg. In many ways, you're limited only by your creativity. What you can do out of the box in SharePoint is similar to what you can do out of the box with a product like Microsoft Access. See the sidebar "How I use SharePoint," later in this chapter, for more ideas for using SharePoint.

You may want to try some of these ideas:

- ✔ Build an inventory management system for your hardware.
- ✔ Track technicians' schedules and expertise.
- ✔ Track software licenses.
- ✔ Track software bugs by using an issues list.
- ✔ Use a Visio flowchart diagram to document your processes. Hyperlink documentation or list entry forms to steps in the flowchart.

How I use SharePoint

As part of my job, I develop and support custom software. I use SharePoint to help me manage my projects better:

✔ I use tasks and issues in ways very similar to what I describe throughout this chapter.

✔ I have a list of projects linked to my task list. I create the project as a master list and the tasks as the *work-breakdown structure* (which is just a fancy way of saying all the stuff that I have to do for that project).

✔ I use a document library for storing all the artifacts related to solving work order issues and developing software. Documents are linked to the issue, task, or project to which they're tied.

✔ I have a custom list of applications and the objects that application uses. *Objects* include all the reports and units of code that make the software work.

✔ I link the `Objects` list to the `Issues` list, thereby allowing me to trace work orders to the objects that those work orders affect. This setup allows me to view all the work orders that lead to code changes.

I'm working on a Visio flowchart that documents the software development life cycle where each step in the process is actionable. Every time I turn around, I think of some new way to use SharePoint that makes me more productive!

Quite a pair of Microsoft templates

In August of 2005, Microsoft released a number of SharePoint site templates designed to help people jump-start their use of SharePoint. Microsoft created two very cool templates for Information Services/Information Technology folks:

✔ Help Desk
✔ IT Developer Team Site

Like this book, these templates can fuel your ideas for developing SharePoint sites for your technical teams.

You can download the templates from the following Web site:

```
www.microsoft.com/technet/prodtechnol/sppt/wssapps/default
            .mspx
```

The Help Desk template includes the following features:

✔ An issues list that's based on a task list template
✔ A list of help-desk contacts
✔ A knowledge base to store information about solving problems

Their knowledge base is a document library with custom properties that allows the library to capture a description and source. You can also link the knowledge base to your hardware and software lists.

The IT Developer Team Site template is more developed (no pun intended) than the Help Desk template. It has these features:

✔ A custom list for storing information about reusable code

✔ A list for storing a list of technical experts

✔ A directory of development tools

✔ Lists of recommended reading and resources

✔ Lists of applications and projects

The IT Developer template gives you a lot of good ideas for collaboration among developers on a team. And, hey, isn't sharing the whole idea behind SharePoint?

Part VII
Maintenance

The 5th Wave   By Rich Tennant

"I'm ordering our new PC. Do you want it left-brain or right-brain-oriented?"

In this part . . .

1'll show you how to monitor the health of your SharePoint installation. You'll learn about managing disk space and analyzing usage data. No SharePoint book is complete without a discussion of your backup-and-recovery options. In this part I discuss your options and offer advice on formulating a strategy.

Chapter 14

Monitoring SharePoint

In This Chapter

▶ Getting feedback from your portal

▶ Setting limits on your users

▶ Keeping sites tidy with monitoring tools

*J*ust like you need to change your car's oil regularly, you need to give your SharePoint portal regular maintenance. Maintaining a SharePoint portal involves

✔ Monitoring the site's usage

✔ Managing database and disk space

✔ Locking down unruly sites

✔ Configuring sites so that they delete automatically after periods of inactivity

And you don't even get your hands dirty!

Watching the Store

Every time someone clicks on your portal, a lot of information about that click transmits to your SharePoint server. By enabling site usage monitoring in SharePoint, you can see

✔ Who's accessing your site

✔ What kinds of browsers they use

✔ What they click (and what they don't)

SharePoint disables site-usage monitoring by default. Enabling site-usage monitoring is a two-step process; you have SharePoint

- **Capture the usage data:** The usage data that tells you who's accessing your site doesn't get collected unless you turn on the feature to capture the data in SharePoint.

- **Process the usage data:** After you've started capturing the data, you have to tell SharePoint to process it for viewing.

Capturing the usage data

Unless you explicitly tell SharePoint to save the data each time a user clicks on your portal, that data disappears forever. Many companies save terabytes worth of usage data from their public Web sites. Although that amount of data saving is probably overkill for your portal, periodically reviewing your usage data can tell you a lot about user habits.

To start capturing usage data in SharePoint, follow these steps:

1. **Open SharePoint Central Administration:**

   a. **From the portal's home page, click Site Settings.**

   b. **Click Go to SharePoint Portal Server Central Administration.**

   You can also access SharePoint Portal Server Central Administration by clicking Start➪All Programs➪SharePoint Portal Server➪SharePoint Central Administration on the local server.

2. **In the Component Configuration section at the bottom of the Central Administration page, click Configure Usage Analysis Processing.**

3. **Put a check mark next to Enable Logging.**

4. **Click OK to accept the defaults for file location and the number of log files you want SharePoint to create, as you can see in Figure 14-1.**

Microsoft recommends setting the number of log files to one to three times the number of database servers in your configuration.

Processing the usage data

Collecting data doesn't have much point unless you do something with it. Telling SharePoint to process the usage data lets you view built-in usage reports that tell you how your sites are used.

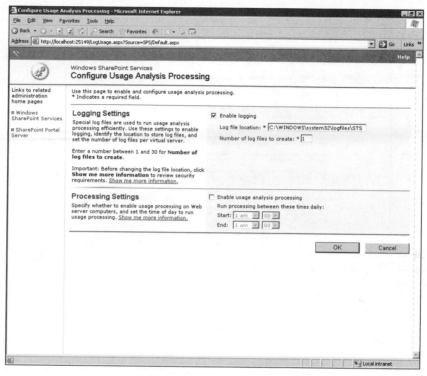

Figure 14-1:
Enable
logging of
usage data.

You enable processing usage data on the same screen that you enable capturing the usage data. To process usage data, follow these steps:

1. **Browse to the Configure Usage Analysis Processing screen, as the preceding section describes.**

2. **Under Processing Settings, place a check mark next to Enable Usage Analysis Processing.**

3. **Specify a start and end time for the processing job in the Start and End drop-down boxes.**

   Specify a time window during non-peak usage periods so the server is not taxed with processing usage data rather than users' requests for files.

   The job doesn't start at the beginning of the time window. Rather, the job runs anytime during that processing window. You can't control the job's exact start time.

4. **Click OK, as you can see in Figure 14-2.**

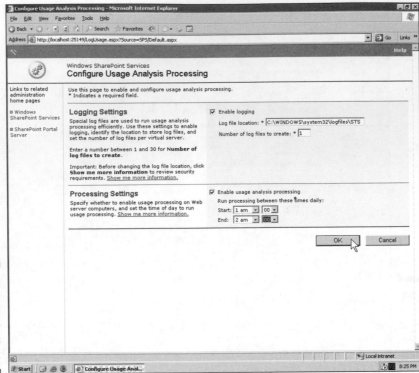

Figure 14-2:
Enable
processing
of the usage
analysis
data.

Processing the usage data takes a lot of resources, especially memory and disk space. Although the built-in reports work better than nothing, third-party software for processing Web site usage data gives you so much more information. You may decide to capture the usage data in SharePoint and then use third-party software to process and analyze the results.

Analyzing the usage data

SharePoint makes a log entry each time a user clicks on your portal. Usage reports summarize and format these log entries. Use usage reports to tell you

- ✔ Number of hits per page
- ✔ Number of unique users
- ✔ Browser and operating system information for each user
- ✔ Referring domains and URLs
- ✔ Unused Web sites
- ✔ Popular sites

By reviewing your usage reports on a regular basis, you can

✔ Manage resources effectively

✔ Make sure that users see important content

You can access usage reports for 31 days in your SharePoint site. SharePoint doesn't delete the log files used to create the usage reports.

You can view the usage reports in either of two time frames:

✔ **Daily:** Displays daily activity in a cross-tab report

✔ **Monthly:** Displays a summary of all activity

SharePoint creates five usage reports for each time frame. These reports are

✔ **Browser:** Displays the kind of browser with which the user viewed the site

✔ **OS:** Displays the user's operating system

✔ **Page:** Displays the pages that the user hits

✔ **Referrer URL:** Displays the Web page that brought the user to the site

✔ **User:** Displays activity such as page hits by the user

To view usage reports, you have to browse to a special page on each site in your portal, following these steps:

1. **From the portal home page, click Sites in the horizontal navigation bar.**

2. **Click a site that you want to view site usage data for in your site directory, as Figure 14-3 shows you.**

   To view all sites in your directory, click All Items under Select a View. Chapters 2 and 3 walk you through using and modifying the site directory.

3. **Click Site Settings in the horizontal navigation bar, as Figure 14-4 shows you.**

4. **On the Site Settings screen, click Go to Site Administration.**

   You go to the Top-level Site Administration page.

5. **In the Site Administration page, scroll down to the Management and Statistics section and click View Site Usage Data.**

6. **The Site Usage Report opens, as you can see in Figure 14-5.**

   You can get additional reports by changing the drop-down options in the Select Report drop-down list on the report.

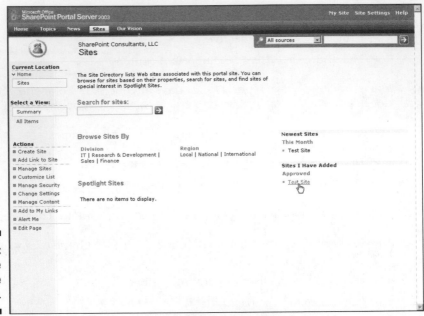

Figure 14-3:
Select a site
in the site
directory.

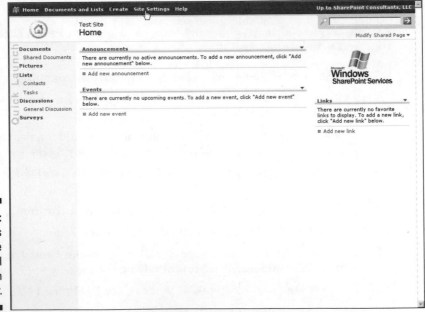

Figure 14-4:
Site Settings
in the
horizontal
navigation
bar.

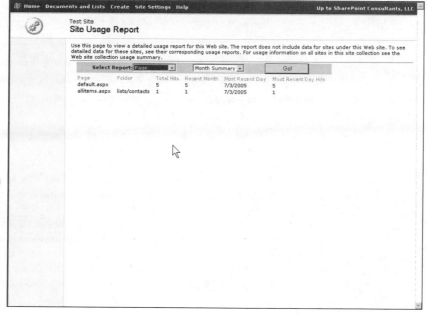

Figure 14-5:
The Site
Usage
Report
shows how
the site is
used.

You can access usage data 24 hours after that data is processed. If your Site Usage Report isn't available, make sure you have completed the steps above to capture and process data and then wait 24 hours to see your report.

You access usage analysis for the portal and its pages — Home, News, Sites, Topics — differently than you do for team sites. For more information about the differences between sites and portal pages, see Chapter 2.

To access usage analysis reports for portal pages, follow these steps:

1. **Browse to a portal page, such as Sites from the portal home page.**

2. **Change the URL from**

```
http://dummies/SiteDirectory/Lists/Sites/Summary.aspx
```

   to

```
http://dummies/SiteDirectory/_layouts/1033/usageDetails.aspx
```

   You can access the usage report for any portal page by appending `_layouts/1033/usageDetails.aspx` to the page's URL.

You need to have the SharePoint Timer service running to make the processing job start. Otherwise your Site Usage Reports aren't available.

If you have more than a few sites on your portal, viewing the log files can seem to take forever. Here are a few strategies for managing the analysis of usage data:

✔ **Automate analysis:** Write a program that parses the log files into a database where you can query them later.

✔ **Centralize analysis:** Create a single page on your portal with hyperlinks to all your sites' usage reporting pages.

✔ **Decentralize analysis:** Make each site administrator responsible for reviewing his or her site's usage logs.

Parse is a technical term for taking data in one format, a text file, for example, and formatting the data to fit in another format, such as a database or Excel file.

You can find a code example on the Microsoft Web site for parsing log files by using C++. Unless you have some previous programming knowledge, you may want to stick with an easier tool, like Excel or Access. If you plan on doing some serious data crunching, then hire a programmer to build a custom tool. Or consider buying a third-party tool that does the parsing and data crunching for you.

Setting Quotas and Locks

Unless your company has unlimited resources, you need to manage your sites' disk space usage. You can take either of two approaches to managing disk space. The right strategy depends on how you expect to use your portal:

✔ **Proactive:** Specify in advance how much disk space you want to give to each site.

You may want to use this strategy if you anticipate having large storage requirements based on the quantity and kind of files being stored. If you expect to use document versioning in your libraries, you'll also want to take a proactive approach.

✔ **Reactive:** Wait until you run out of disk space before you think about how much space you want a given site to use.

You can use this strategy if you have plenty of disk storage and a small amount of sites — presumably you have enough disk storage that you won't run out of disk space. Nevertheless, I suggest you monitor your disk usage periodically.

Size matters

You manage disk space by setting an upper limit (a *quota*) on how much disk space the site can use. SharePoint allows you to create quota templates that you can apply to groups of sites.

Defining quota templates

With a quota template, you specify

> ✔ **Disk space quota:** The upper limit on disk space usage
>
> ✔ **A warning limit:** Notifies anyone who accesses the site that the site is near its disk space quota

To calculate a quota template, decide

> ✔ How you think users want to use the site
>
> ✔ The types and quantities of files that users will save and the average file size

See the sidebar "Guesstimating File Sizes," later in this chapter, for common files types and file sizes.

Here are some example quota templates:

> ✔ **Team sites:** These sites can get very large, so set your limits from 60 MB to 100 MB.
>
> ✔ **Meeting and workspace sites:** Because Word documents make up most of these sites, you can set the quota lower, to around 30 MB to 45 MB.
>
> ✔ **Personal sites:** SharePoint already defines a personal-site quota by default as 100 MB. It sends a warning message at 80 MB. You may want to set your site quotas lower for personal sites — say, 20 to 30MB — depending on how you expect personal sites to be used.

You can increase, decrease, or even completely remove the quota for individual sites. I show you how to manage quotas for an individual site in the section "Applying quota templates".

SharePoint uses quota templates at the server or server-farm (a group of SharePoint servers) level. To define a quota template, follow these steps:

1. **Browse to the Central Administration page for Windows SharePoint Services.**

2. **In the Component Configuration section, click Manage Quotas and Locks.**

3. **In the Manage Quotas and Locks page, click Manage Quota Templates.**

4. **Select the radio button for Create a New Quota Template.**

   You start with the template [new blank template], as you can see in Figure 14-6.

5. **Enter a name for your template in the** New template name **text box.**

6. **In the on-screen text boxes, enter the maximum storage size (in megabytes) and when to send the warning e-mail.**

7. **Click OK to save your quota template.**

SharePoint saves your quota template and presents you with the same Manage Quota Templates screen so that you can edit or add additional templates.

Applying quota templates

Applying quotas to sites depends on whether the site is a

✔ Virtual server

✔ Top-level site

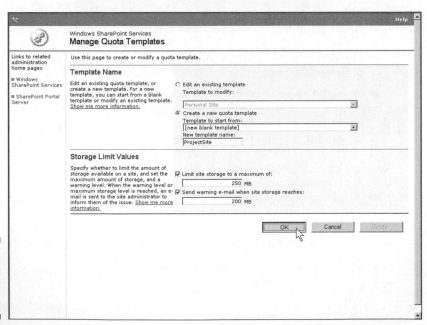

Figure 14-6:
Creating a
new quota
template.

Setting the quota template for a virtual server sets the default quota template for all sites in that virtual server. To set a default quota template for a virtual server, follow these steps:

1. **In Windows SharePoint Services central administration, click Configure Virtual Server Settings.**

2. **Select the virtual server that you want to manage.**

   My virtual server is `http://dummies`, as you can see in Figure 14-7.

3. **In the Virtual Server Settings page, select Virtual Server General Settings in the Virtual Server Management section.**

4. **Click the drop-down list in the Default Quota Template section.**

5. **Choose a quota template from the Select quota template drop-down list, as Figure 14-8 shows you.**

   The storage limit shown on-screen updates to match the storage limit that you set for the quota template. (The preceding section, "Defining quota templates," shows how to create quota templates.)

6. **Click OK to save the default quota template.**

SharePoint applies the virtual server's default quota template to all new sites you create on that server. Existing sites keep their existing quotas.

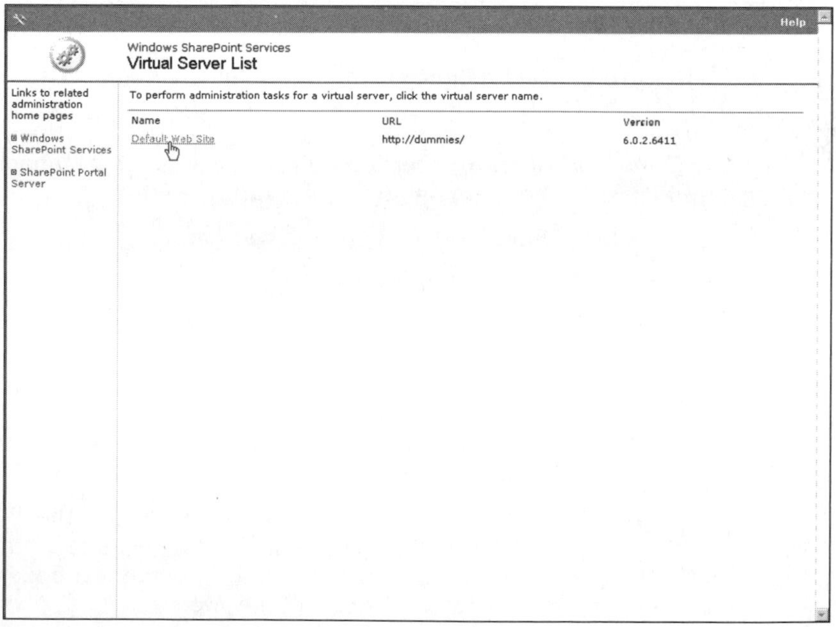

Figure 14-7: Selecting a virtual server to manage.

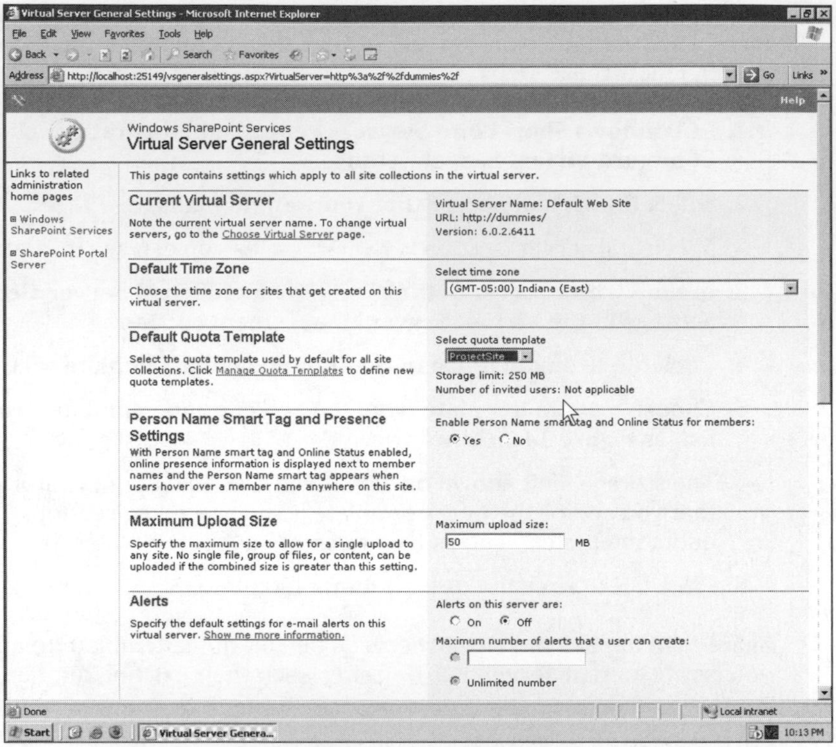

Figure 14-8:
Setting the
default
quota
template
for all sites
in a virtual
server.

You can override quota templates for any site in SharePoint. To specify a quota template for a specific site, follow these steps:

1. **In Windows SharePoint central administration, click Manage Quotas and Locks in the Component Configuration section.**

2. **Click Manage Site Collection Quotas and Locks.**

3. **Enter the URL for the top-level site.**

   The URLs are typically in the format `http://server_name/sites/site_name`.

4. **Click View Data, as Figure 14-9 shows you.**

5. **In the Site Quota Information section, select the quota template that you want to apply to this site, as Figure 14-10 shows you.**

   You can override the quota template values by clicking the check marks in the Site Quota Information section and typing the site storage maximum in the text box. Do not enter any values in the text boxes if you don't want any limit set on the size of the site.

6. **Click OK to save your site with the new quota template.**

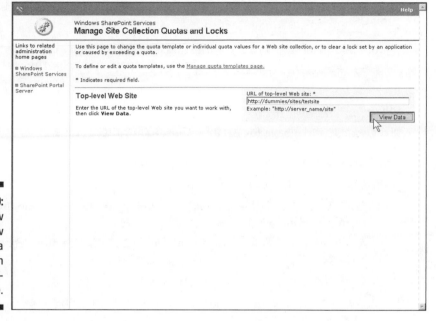

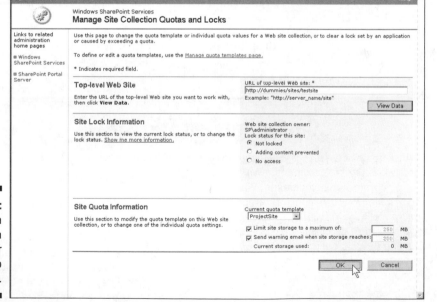

To set a quota for a portal, enter the portal URL rather than a site collection URL.

Quota templates apply to the entire site collection. They're specified for the top-level site. Any subsites roll into the disk space usage for the entire site collection.

Viewing site disk usage

To view site disk usage for existing sites, follow these steps:

1. **Browse to the site and click Site Settings.**

2. **Click Go to Site Administration.**

3. **Click View Site Collection Usage Summary in the Site Collection Administration section.**

    A summary of the disk space usage appears in the section labeled Storage.

4. **Click the Storage Space Allocation link.**

    You can also access Storage Space Allocation from the Site Administration page.

    In the Storage Space Allocation page, a graphical representation of disk space usage appears, along with the disk usage by folder, as you can see in Figure 14-11.

Click the Show Only drop-down list to view disk usage for specific documents and lists.

Guesstimating File Sizes

Setting disk quotas means you have to look into your crystal ball to see how people will use a site. In a corporate environment, you can expect a lot of Word documents and Excel spreadsheets. Also prepare for the digital photos from the company picnic and the owner's son's music collection. Use these file size estimates to determine your disk-usage requirements:

✔ **Office files (like Word and Excel):** Small (1KB to 2MB)

✔ **Graphics files:** Medium (100KB to 2MB)

✔ **PDF files:** Medium (100KB to 2MB)

✔ **Sound files:** Large (1MB to 5MB)

✔ **Video files:** Very large (5MB to 10MB)

You can play with the upper limits on these file types. A user can quickly eat up many gigabytes of disk space with graphics, sound, and video files. If you plan to enable version control, then you can multiply a file's size by the number of versions you expect a user to save.

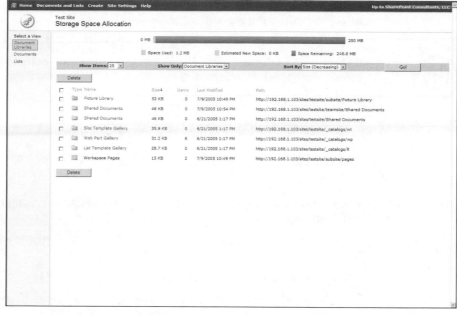

Figure 14-11:
Viewing detailed disk usage for a top-level site.

Under lock and key

After a site exceeds its quota, it's automatically locked. The administrator can also lock sites manually.

When a user accesses a locked site, the error he or she gets depends on whether the site lock is

✔ **Automatic:** Users see a disk-full error.

✔ **Manual:** Users receive an access-denied error.

Avoid locking sites accidentally — that's what happens if you set the quota lower than the actual disk space a site already uses.

You can both lock and unlock a site by using the same screen. To configure how your site locks and unlocks, follow these steps:

1. **Browse to Windows SharePoint Services central administration.**

2. **In the Component Configuration section, click Manage Quotas and Locks.**

3. **On the Manage Quotas and Locks screen, click Manage Site Collection Quotas and Locks.**

4. **Enter the URL for the top-level site that you want to lock or unlock, using the following format:**

```
http://server_name/sites/site_name
```

If you aren't a whiz at typing URLs, browse to the site, copy the URL, and paste it into the URL text box.

5. **Click View Data.**

In the Site Lock Information section, you can see the site lock status. When the site's locked, you receive an error message when you try to access the site. The message that you receive depends on the type of lock and how you access the site:

✔ If you're not allowed to add content, the messages tell you so in several different ways.

- **Application access:** If you're using Microsoft Word, for example: You get a cryptic message with no explanation:

```
Word did not save the document
```

- **Browser access:** You get this message

```
Additions to this Web site have been blocked. Please contact the
           administrator to resolve this problem.
```

- **Web-folder access:** You get this message:

```
Cannot copy <file>: Not enough quota is available to process this command.
```

✔ If you're denied access to what's in the folder, here's what you get:

- **Application access:** You can browse to the folder, but you can't access content.

- **Browser access:** You get the error message

```
Access to this Web site has been blocked.
```

- **Web-folder access:** You can browse to the Web folder, but the folder is empty. Attempts to copy files to the Web folder meet with an `Access Denied` message.

If users call the help desk to complain about cryptic access-denied errors, check the site's locks and quotas.

If you want to make a site view-only, use the Site Lock Information section on the Manage Site Collection Quotas and Locks page. It's simple:

1. **Lock the site to prevent anyone from adding new content.**

2. **Put a custom message on the site, informing users that the site is inactive.**

Keeping an Eye on Your Sites with Monitoring Tools

SharePoint monitoring and maintenance occurs at the portal or site level. To access portal maintenance features, follow these steps:

1. **From the portal home page, click Site Settings in the upper right-hand corner.**

2. **In the General Settings section, click Go to SharePoint Portal Server Central Administration.**

   Here you find configuration settings for the portal, as you can see in Figure 14-12.

3. **From SharePoint Portal Server central administration, click Windows SharePoint Services in the left navigation bar.**

   From here, you can configure top-level sites.

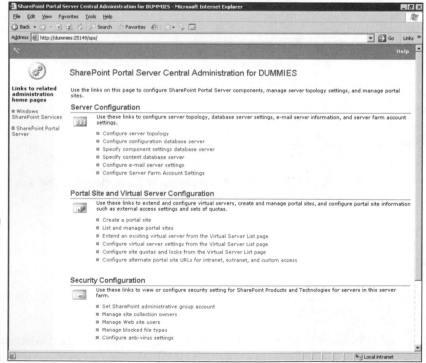

Figure 14-12: Viewing SharePoint Portal Server central administration.

You can do some administration at the top level or at individual-site level. To administer a site, follow these steps:

1. **Browse to the site that you want to administer.**

2. **Click Site Settings in the horizontal navigation bar, as Figure 14-13 shows you.**

3. **Click Go to Site Administration.**

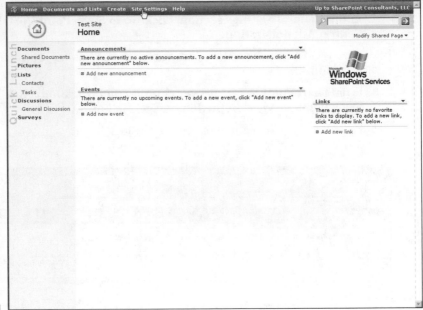

Figure 14-13:
View site settings for a top-level site.

The portal home page has site-administration options that you can access through Site Settings.

Setting a site's self-destruct

You can configure sites to delete automatically after a period of inactivity. This automatic deletion is an example of portal-level administration. To configure a site to delete automatically, follow these steps:

1. **Browse to Windows SharePoint Services central administration.**

2. **Click Configure Virtual Server Settings.**

3. **Click the portal that you want to administer.**

4. **In the Virtual Server Settings screen, click Configure site collection use confirmation and deletion.**

5. **Specify whether to send e-mail notification to site owners.**

6. **Specify whether to automatically delete the site.**

You remove content _permanently_ when you delete a site. You can restore the content from backup, but only if you have a good backup available. (See Chapter 15 to get the skinny on good backups.)

7. **Click OK to save, as Figure 14-14 shows you.**

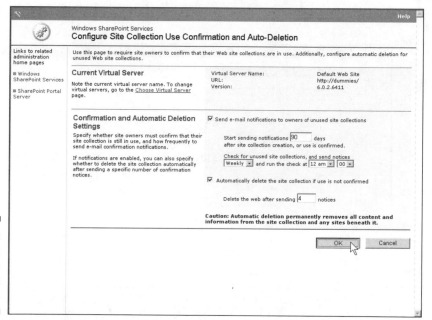

Figure 14-14:
Configuring
automatic
site
deletion.

Managing Web discussions

Web discussions are site-level administration items. SharePoint stores Web discussions separately from the documents that they discuss. Your users participate in Web discussions by clicking the Discuss button on the Internet Explorer toolbar. Unfortunately, you can't delete a Web discussion simply by deleting the document that it discusses.

To delete a Web discussion, follow these steps:

1. **Browse to the site that has the Web discussion that you want to delete.**

2. **Click Site Settings.**

3. **In Site Administration, click Manage Web Discussions in the Management and Statistics section.**

   A list of Web discussions saved from the site appears.

4. **Place a check mark next to the discussions that you want to delete.**

5. **Click Delete, as Figure 14-15 shows you.**

Managing Web discussions works best if you assign local site administrators to monitor and maintain the Web discussions for their individual sites.

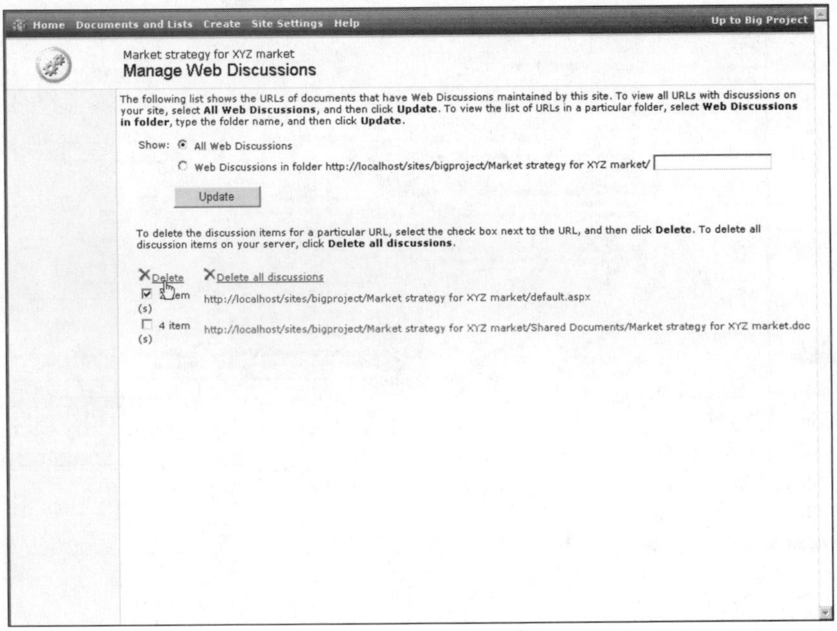

| Home | Documents and Lists | Create | Site Settings | Help | | Up to Big Project |

Market strategy for XYZ market
Manage Web Discussions

The following list shows the URLs of documents that have Web Discussions maintained by this site. To view all URLs with discussions on your site, select **All Web Discussions**, and then click **Update**. To view the list of URLs in a particular folder, select **Web Discussions in folder**, type the folder name, and then click **Update**.

Show: ⦿ All Web Discussions

○ Web Discussions in folder http://localhost/sites/bigproject/Market strategy for XYZ market/ [＿＿＿＿＿]

[Update]

To delete the discussion items for a particular URL, select the check box next to the URL, and then click **Delete**. To delete all discussion items on your server, click **Delete all discussions**.

✗Delete   ✗Delete all discussions

☑ 8 item (s)   http://localhost/sites/bigproject/Market strategy for XYZ market/default.aspx

☐ 4 item (s)   http://localhost/sites/bigproject/Market strategy for XYZ market/Shared Documents/Market strategy for XYZ market.doc

Figure 14-15:
Deleting
Web
discussions.

Chapter 15

Backup and Restore

In This Chapter

▶ Backing up your SharePoint portal

▶ Developing a backup strategy that suits your company

There are many choices for backing up your SharePoint portal. In fact, you could say there are too many choices. The tool you choose depends on what you are expecting to restore.

There are tools for backing up:

✔ The entire portal

✔ All sites or specific sites in the portal

✔ Just the databases

Although it may be tempting to back up the entire portal and call it a day, this approach makes it difficult if you need to restore a single site or single document within a site. In this chapter, I show you how to perform all three types of backups and discuss when you should use each.

Choosing the Right Backup Tool

No matter how you choose to handle backups, at some point you'll have to do a restore. Although it might be tempting to think of backups as part of a disaster-recovery plan, in reality natural disasters aren't the top reason to do backups and data restoration. (When was the last time your data center caught on fire? Flooded? Got hit by a tornado or a meteor?) Don't get me wrong — backups are great for your peace of mind (especially these days), but that isn't the most common reason for doing them.

Best backup/restoration practices

Backing up mission-critical data is a vital element in every company's risk management and disaster recovery plans. Audit your policies and procedures to see how they measure up to these best practices:

✔ Check backup logs daily and resolve any errors or warnings.

✔ Build redundancy into mission-critical systems.

✔ Store physical backup media off-site, preferably in an off-site vault, NOT at your IT manager's house.

✔ Have the distribution media for your operating system and software applications (such as the original discs) available off-site; also have tape drives (or whatever other hardware is necessary for restoring data) available off-site in the event of disaster.

✔ Test your capability to restore the entire backup and smaller units of the backup.

✔ Have an overall disaster-recovery and risk-management plan.

✔ Schedule backups to minimize downtime, but make sure they have enough time to complete.

✔ Know how long data should be stored in the archive.

✔ Have a library for storing media and make sure media are labeled properly.

✔ Have a media pool, but track reusable media so you can designate them as expired when they reach the end of their service life.

✔ Physically destroy all expired media; don't just throw them away.

✔ Have a monthly or quarterly restore-and-test schedule.

Requests to restore files usually result from

✔ Server failure, either hardware or software

✔ Human error (such as accidental deletion)

✔ Theft or viruses

Each different kind of restoration request requires a different kind of backup. You wouldn't want to restore an entire server just because someone deleted a single file on that server. For that reason, SharePoint has several backup tools that can accommodate any kind of restore that your hardware and end users can throw your way.

For a primer on backup best practices, see the sidebar "Best backup/restoration practices."

Backing it all up

The simplest backup tool in your arsenal is the SharePoint Portal Server Data Backup and Restore application. This tool enables you to back up and restore

- ✔ All your portal and site databases
- ✔ All content indexes and sources

In short, you can back up and restore all of your corporate portal content and all your sites (including personal sites).

How much control you have when you want to restore your backup is called *granularity.* The SharePoint Backup and Restore tool is low granularity because restore operations are an all-or-nothing proposition. It works great when you want to restore your entire portal. For restoring a single site or a document within a site, you need a tool that gives you higher granularity — better control over the restoration.

To back up your entire portal site, follow these steps:

1. **On the Start menu, select All Programs⇨SharePoint Portal Server⇨ SharePoint Portal Server Data Backup and Restore, as shown in Figure 15-1.**

   The Microsoft Office SharePoint Portal Server 2003 Backup and Restore window opens.

2. **Enter or browse to the file path where you want to save your backups.**

3. **At the end of the file path, enter any characters you want placed in front of the backup filename.**

   For example, you may want to enter the date of the backup.

4. **Enter a comment if desired.**

5. **Specify whether to overwrite existing files.**

   Unless you know you want to overwrite a backup, you should probably leave this blank. If you are using the same filename and know that the backup is being copied to tape or other media, then you could overwrite the previous backup.

6. **Select the components to back up.**

   All server components are selected by default. If you want to specify specific portals to be backed up, you may do so. Also, you can specify whether you want both the site databases and the indexes backed up. Both are selected by default.

7. **Click the Backup button to start the backup procedure.**

   See Figure 15-2 for an example of what the screen should look like.

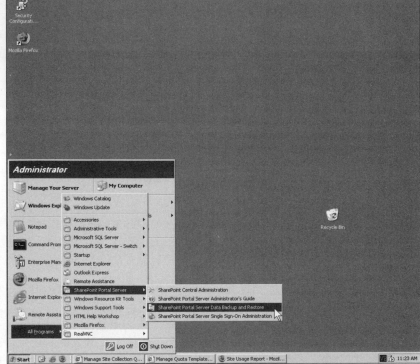

Figure 15-1:
Open the
SharePoint
Portal
Server 2003
Backup and
Restore
window.

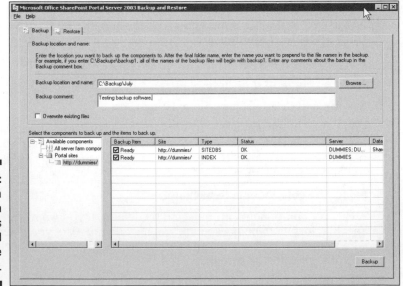

Figure 15-2:
Creating a
backup with
SharePoint's
Backup and
Restore
utility.

After the backup procedure begins, the screen provides a lot of feedback about what's happening. You can watch the jobs get scheduled and executed. You can also see the progress of the jobs, as shown in Figure 15-3.

When a job completes, its status is updated to Succeeded. The tool then moves on to the next job.

When all jobs are complete, the status column shows Succeeded.

To start a new backup job, click the Reset button in the lower-left corner. All the backup options are reset to their defaults, and you can start another backup.

If you look in the file directory where you stored your backup, you should see an XML file and backup files that end with the file extension .SPB. Your backup folder should look similar to Figure 15-4.

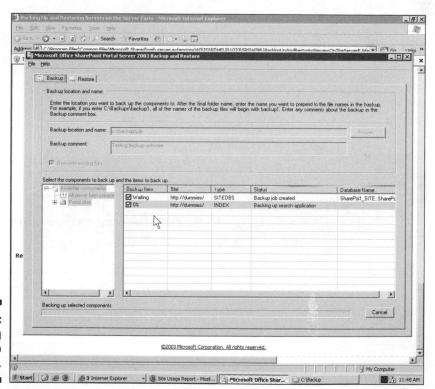

Figure 15-3:
Viewing backup job progress.

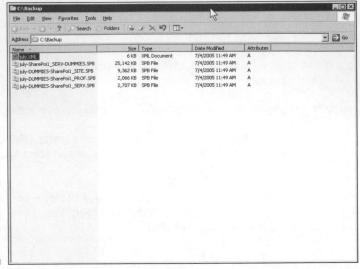

Figure 15-4:
Files in
backup
folder.

The files created in the backup folder are

- ✔ The XML file (a manifest file that details what's backed up)
- ✔ A backup of the sites database
- ✔ A backup of the user profile database
- ✔ A backup of the services database
- ✔ A backup of the portal server index database

Backing up from the command line

Portal Server Data Backup and Restore can be executed from a command line. Table 15-1 shows the command-line options.

Table 15-1 Backup and Restore options from the command line

Command	What It Does
/all	Backs up everything
/teamdbs	Backs up team databases
/ssodb	Backs up single-sign-on databases
/doclib:	Backs up document libraries backwards compatible with SharePoint Portal Server 2001
/portal site:	Backs up the portal at the URL specified

Command	What It Does
/file:	Specifies the path to the backup file and the name to prepend to the filename
/overwrite:	Specifies to overwrite a backup image with the same name

To run a complete backup from the command line, type this command:

```
spsbackup.exe /all /file C:\backup\07052005
```

Replace 07052005 in this example with the value you want to prepend to the backup file. In a default installation, the spsbackup.exe file is located in

```
C:\Program Files\SharePoint Portal Server\Bin
```

To find out more about the databases available for backup, see the sidebar "What to back up."

Restoring a backup

At first blush, restoring a backup seems as simple as backing up the portal. After all, supposedly you'd just open the SharePoint backup software, click Restore, browse to the XML manifest file, click Restore, and presto! Well, smarty-pants, when you do that, your screen looks like Figure 15-5.

What to back up

Most of the time you will back up an entire portal or site collection. As your backup strategy matures, you may choose to back up specific databases within a portal or site collection. Here's a list of the databases and what they store:

✔ PortalSiteName_prof Stores user profile and audience data

✔ PortalSiteName_serv Stores services data such as alerts and searches

✔ PortalSiteName_site Stores content such as lists and libraries

✔ sps_config_db Configuration database that stores server layout information

✔ sso_db Database for single sign-on

Because configuration is unique to an installation, the configuration database should never be restored. Instead, a new configuration database is created when a SharePoint backup is restored.

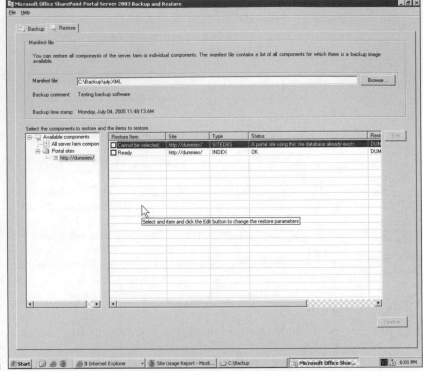

Figure 15-5:
Restoring a
backup,
using the
SharePoint
Backup and
Restore
utility.

Notice that the site database (SITEDBS) can't be selected. Before you can restore the portal, you have to delete it. Ouch! I don't recommend testing this approach the day you plan to demo the portal to the top brass.

Create a test server by installing SharePoint and then restoring your production backup image onto the test site. Voila! Now you have a test portal that looks like your production site!

Backing up specific sites

Besides hardware failures, most of your restore requests will come from end users who have accidentally deleted a file or list. To protect yourself against accidental deletions and other user errors, use the Windows SharePoint Services Administration tool. This is a command line tool that enables you to back up top-level sites and the sites contained within.

Top-level sites are called site collections. A site collection consists of a top-level site and all the sites created within that top-level site.

The Windows SharePoint Services Administration tool is a command-line tool. The tool's filename is `stsadm.exe` and it's installed by default at

```
C:\Program Files\Common Files\Microsoft Shared\Web server extensions\60\BIN
```

Backing up a site

To back up a site, use the `backup` option of `stsadm.exe` like this:

1. **Open a command line in the directory where `stsadm.exe` is saved.**

2. **Execute the command with the `backup` option, like this:**

   ```
   stsadm.exe -o backup
   ```

3. **Enter the URL for the site you want to back up, like this:**

   ```
   -url http://server_name/site
   ```

   The URL for personal sites should follow this format:

   ```
   http://server_name/personal/username
   ```

4. **Enter the filename to which you want to save the backup, like this:**

   ```
   -filename backup.bak
   ```

5. **To overwrite an existing file, specify this command:**

   ```
   -overwrite
   ```

To back up the site `testsite` on the `dummies` portal, the command would look like this:

```
stsadm.exe -o backup -url http://dummies/testsite -filename backup.bak
```

Use the `enumsites` option of the `stsadm.exe` to create a list of all the sites in your portal. Doing so enables you to verify that you are backing up all your sites. The command to enumerate all the sites on the `dummies` portal (for example) looks like this:

```
stsadm.exe -o enumsites -url http://dummies
```

Restoring a site

To restore a site, use the `restore` option of `stsadm.exe` like this:

1. **Open a command line in the directory where `stsadm.exe` is saved.**

2. **Execute the command with the `restore` option, like this:**

   ```
   stsadm.exe -o restore
   ```

3. **Enter the URL for the site you want to restore, like this:**

   ```
   -url http://server_name/site
   ```

4. Enter the filename you want to restore, like this:

```
-filename backup.bak
```

5. To overwrite an existing site, specify this command:

```
-overwrite
```

Use caution if you choose to overwrite; the existing site is completely deleted in the process. Microsoft recommends one of two approaches:

- Restore the site to a new server, and then manually copying the site to the production portal.

- Restore the site to an existing server with a new site name.

  To restore the site `testsite` on the `dummies` portal, for example, the command would look like this:

```
stsadm.exe -o restore -url http://dummies/testsite -filename backup.bak
```

To restore anything smaller than a top-level site (such as a single file, an entire document library, or a subsite), you need only two steps:

1. Restore the site to a test server.

2. Manually copy the item to be restored to the production server.

Additional tools

Additional tools you should consider using are as follows:

- **SQL Server Backup:** Use the backup tools in SQL Server to back up the SharePoint databases.

- **SharePoint Migration Tool:** The SharePoint Migration tool `smigrate.exe` serves to migrate sites from one server to another. It can also be used to back up specific sites and restore them. Configuration settings such as user permissions aren't restored with this tool.

- **SPBackup Utility in the SharePoint Portal Server Resource Kit:** Use the `spbackup.exe` utility to back up site collections that have changed since the previous backup.

While you *can* use any of these tools to make a SharePoint backup, you should not use these tools to restore to your production site. This means you should not rely on any of these tools exclusively, especially SQL Server Backup. Instead, restore to a nonproduction server — and then grab the site, library, list, or file and move it to the production server manually.

Automating backups

If the prospect of daily backups is less than thrilling, relax. Automating back-ups is like automating any administrative (by-definition-tedious) task:

1. **Find the name of the file (called the *executable*) that you double-click to start the software.**

2. **Specify parameters or options for how the software should start.**

3. **Schedule the backup, using a tool like Task Scheduler.**

Any SharePoint backup tool can be scheduled by using the Task Scheduler. Follow these steps to automate and schedule a backup, using the SharePoint Portal Server Backup and Restore tool:

1. **Open the Task Scheduler on your SharePoint portal front-end server (click Start⇨All Programs⇨Accessories⇨System Tools⇨Scheduled Tasks).**

   Figure 15-6 shows the Scheduled Tasks window.

   It's best to schedule this job on the server that it will run against — that is, the one you're backing up. Don't schedule it from someone's worksta-tion and point it at a target server. Keeping all of a server's jobs in one place allows easier administration.

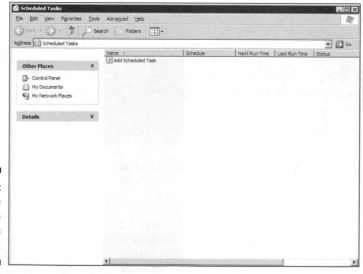

Figure 15-6 :
The
Schedule
Tasks
window.

2. In the Schedule Tasks window, double-click the Add Scheduled Tasks icon.

The Scheduled Task Wizard appears.

3. Click Next to call up a list of applications available for scheduling; click the Browse button instead of selecting an application.

If you browse down this list, you find SharePoint Portal Server Backup and Restore — the same application used to back up the portal manually. Don't use the application name in the list; it's just a link, not the actual application file.

4. Browse to the directory where the `spsbackup.exe` file is saved.

In a default installation, the directory is `C:\Program Files\ SharePoint Portal Server\Bin`. Click the `SPSbackup.exe` file, as shown in Figure 15-7, and click Open.

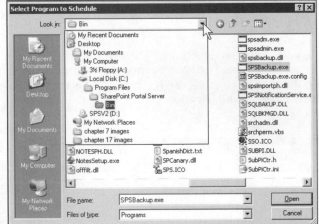

Figure 15-7:
Browse to
the file you
want to
execute.

5. Give the job a name and select how frequently the job should run. Click Next.

6. Select the time of day for the job to run. Enter a start date and click Next.

Typically, the best run time is at night when people aren't using the portal.

7. Enter the username and password that has the authority to run this job.

It's a best practice to set up a special user account for doing backups; don't use the administrator account.

The job is ready to be saved.

8. Place a check mark next to Open Advanced Properties for this task when I click Finish, and then click Finish.

You have scheduled a backup job. But all that job does right now is open the backup software. You still have to tell the software what you want it to back up so it doesn't have to prompt you. So this step brings up a window like the one in Figure 15-8, displaying the advanced properties for your job.

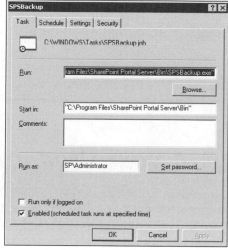

Figure 15-8:
The
Scheduled
Task
Advanced
Properties
window.

To specify advanced properties for your job, follow these steps:

1. Place your cursor in the Run line.

2. Enter the options you would usually specify if you were running the application from the command line, as shown in Figure 15-9.

3. Click OK to save your job.

Run your job from the command line manually a few times to make sure the command does exactly what you want.

Saving your command in Notepad with the file extension .bat creates an executable *batch file* (a file containing commands that run in sequence). You can schedule the batch file just as you would any other application.

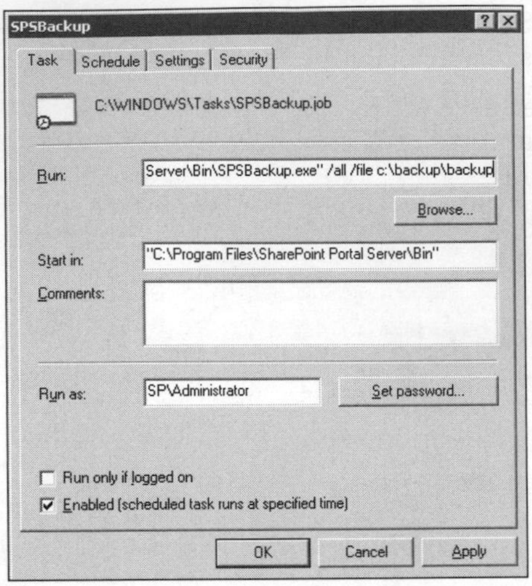

Figure 15-9:
Additional
options for
running
a job.

Fitting Your Backup to Your Organization

This chapter has shown you the building blocks for creating a backup strategy. There is no one-size-fits-all recommendation for doing backups. You should create a plan with the best fit for your organization. To build your plan, follow these steps:

1. **Create backups with each of the tools in this chapter.**

2. **Attempt a restore operation with every backup.**

3. **Decide which tools best suit your organization's needs in terms of**

   - How much data has to be backed up

   - How frequently you need to back up (and restore)

   - How mission-critical your data is

   - How much you've customized your portal

   - How many users are affected

4. **Test, test, test your backups on a regular basis.**

It isn't likely that just one of these tools will provide everything you need. Instead, plan on creating a hybrid solution like this:

✔ Use SharePoint Portal Server Backup and Restore (`spbackup.exe`) once a week. This gives you a full backup of your portal every week.

✔ Use the Windows SharePoint Services Administration tool (`stsadm.exe`) nightly. Backing up your sites every night protects your users in the event of accidental file deletion.

✔ Use the SQL Server backup program once a month.

Of course, all this is a supplement — done in addition to the periodic backups of the server itself that you do using your corporate backup software.

For a sample test plan for restoring SharePoint, you can find a link to Microsoft MVP Joe Schurman's test plan on my Web site, `www.sharepointgrrl.com`.

Part VIII
The Part of Tens

The 5th Wave — By Rich Tennant

"Amy surfs the web a lot, so for protection we installed several filtering programs that allow only approved sites through. Which of those nine sites are you looking at now, Amy?"

In this part . . .

I impart a few more tidbits of wisdom to help you with your SharePoint implementation. I share with you ten ways that SharePoint can add value to your business. To help you avoid common implementation mistakes, I share with you ten ways to screw up SharePoint — and some suggestions for avoiding them.

Chapter 16

Ten Ways SharePoint Adds Business Value

In This Chapter

▶ Saving your business some money

▶ Making a big, happy business family

▶ Solving problems quickly

▶ Keeping your business up to date

*B*efore you decide to implement SharePoint, make sure you have a good reason for doing it. Plenty of projects you can implement for no good reason other than "the boss said so." If you need some better reasons, this chapter offers you ten — specific ways that SharePoint adds value to your business.

Searching Can Cost You

Keep your employees at their desks and working by using SharePoint to provide the reference information your employees need.

Self-Service Saves Money

Sending paper copies is expensive and wasteful. You could send electronic copies via e-mail, but then you'd be taxing your e-mail server and burdening the recipients with the decision of whether (and where) to save the attached file.

Skip all that nonsense and use SharePoint to store and distribute electronic versions of your documents:

- ✔ Use document, image, and form libraries to store electronic versions of your files.
- ✔ Send a hyperlink to the file in e-mail.
- ✔ Create a listing on the portal's home page, announcing any long-anticipated documents such as next year's marketing plan. (I hear it makes for great bathroom reading.)

Bridging Your Islands

Instead of viewing a company in terms of its functional departments (such as Marketing and Accounting), use SharePoint to connect islands and break the chains of your formal reporting structure.

Building Solutions Super-Fast

How well (and how much) your nontechnical staff can use SharePoint to build their own intra- and interdepartmental solutions depends largely on how much access the business users are given to use SharePoint. If you keep SharePoint locked up and don't show your business users its capabilities, then don't expect much ownership from the business community.

When you use SharePoint to build internal Web sites, you don't have to think about all that plumbing — the code you normally write when creating Web sites for internal consumption — and you don't have to worry about security, look-and-feel, or navigation.

Let your business community take ownership of the content while you act as a technical consultant — advising (and evangelizing) the possibilities of SharePoint.

Showing Off the Latest Versions

By using a version-enabled document library, you can ensure that only the latest version of a policy, form, or image is available for consumption.

Sending a Unified Message

Use SharePoint to send a unified message to your employees about your business through the following portal elements:

- **Home page:** Communicate the value of a message, such as the company's vision statement, by placing it right on the portal's home page for everyone to see.

- **Navigation:** Use your portal's navigation features to direct employees to information about products and promotions.

- **Listings:** Use the listings — the links and announcements — on your portal to direct employees' attention to the internal team sites and company news you want them to notice.

- **Audiences:** Target groups of employees, such as supervisors or everyone in customer service, with listings that reinforce a message, such as the value of upselling.

- **Look and feel:** Use the color scheme and branding of your portal to transform your SharePoint portal from an impersonal piece of software to *the* source for internal company news and information.

Creating a Sense of Community

Use SharePoint to keep your employees up-to-date with new-baby and new-hire announcements. You or your employees may even want to use SharePoint to create a carpool or find a lunch buddy.

Keeping Executives in Touch

Use dashboards to provide summary views of the business to executives. SharePoint provides the Presentation Layer, and you can send the data from your data warehouse or transactional systems.

Cutting the Cost of Information Systems

Imagine reducing the number of homegrown departmental solutions that use spreadsheets and Access databases. By replacing these with lists and libraries in SharePoint, you achieve some immediate improvements:

✔ **Ease of administration:** Your business-specific solutions will be more consistent — which makes them easier to administer, support, back up, and restore.

✔ **Accessibility, portability, and reusability:** Where are your company's spreadsheets and Access databases stored? Do you even know how many of these files there are, who uses them, and how frequently they're accessed? With SharePoint, you know the answer to these questions. And, you can use Web services and InfoPath to reuse the data in your SharePoint sites. It's not locked away in a spreadsheet that's only used by one department.

✔ **Increased security:** SharePoint builds upon your existing investment in Active Directory. Even better, your departments can use that model to manage who has access to what — without calling the help desk.

✔ **Capability to eliminate Office clients:** By using lists and libraries in SharePoint, you may not need to have Office applications like Excel installed on all your client machines.

✔ **Simplified planning:** By bringing all this content under one roof and on the radar, your capacity planning is greatly simplified.

✔ **Training aid:** Because SharePoint provides a consistent look and feel, training is easier.

✔ **Application prototyping:** SharePoint is the ideal environment for building prototypes by using lists, libraries, and InfoPath forms to simulate the feasibility of a new application *before* construction starts in earnest. (Chapter 8 offers some pointers for creating prototypes.)

SharePoint Is the Next Big Thing

Gotcha! SharePoint's sheer novelty isn't a good reason to use it. Work through the exercises in Chapter 5 before you decide whether SharePoint is right for your business. If you find that your organization isn't ready for SharePoint, you want to draw that conclusion *before* you implement.

Chapter 17

Ten Ways to Screw Up SharePoint

▶ Anticipating people problems that can keep you up at night

▶ Spotting technical woes that you can avoid

S harePoint costs a lot to implement. It costs in hardware, software, and resources. That's why this chapter tells you ten ways to screw up your SharePoint implementation — "people problems" and technical troubles — and offers some suggestions for avoiding those mistakes.

People Problems

SharePoint is a product that's designed to be used and influenced by a lot of people. If you try to gloss over the people element, SharePoint eats you alive. Avoid these problems and increase your likelihood of success:

✔ **Don't put off setting business goals and outcomes:** Know what you want to achieve *before* you go into implementing SharePoint for your business — and have a way to measure that achievement.

✔ **Don't ignore the business community:** Your business users' needs are what drive your SharePoint implementation. Have representatives from the business community actively involved from day one.

✔ **Don't neglect planning:** Get your plans ready — for installation, implementation, content management, training, and a lot more — *before* you install SharePoint.

✔ **Don't assume that everyone wants to play:** Users may not want to contribute content to the portal. If information equals power in your company, don't expect employees to give it away for free.

✔ **Don't try to do everything in-house:** Assess skills to figure out when and where you need help. And budget for the time and help you need!

✔ **Don't assume IS folks are experts in both information *and* systems:** "Information Services" doesn't mean "all-knowing." You may find someone with a degree in library science at least as valuable as your technical staff. What do your IS folks know about taxonomies, ontologies, and epistemologies? You might even want to throw in a sociologist to explore the role of organizational culture and informal power structures in fouling up your implementation. (If those words make you glaze over, then some help is in order.)

Chapter 5 discusses some of the people and business-value issues associated with implementing SharePoint. Chapters 9 through 13 give examples of different ways you can use SharePoint in your business to add value.

Technical Headaches

There's a whole host of technical problems waiting for you — potentially exacerbated by some human foibles:

✔ **Poking around in the database:** When your overzealous database administrator offers to get into the SharePoint databases to "fix" something, tell him or her (politely but firmly), "No, thank you." SharePoint provides many ways to access data in the database, in addition to the browser user interface.

SharePoint's SQL databases are tuned so they work best when *only* SharePoint accesses them. Accessing the databases directly can throw off that tuning and corrupt data. Never access the SharePoint databases directly by using any Microsoft SQL Server tool, for any reason!

✔ **Using Front Page willy-nilly:** You *can* use Microsoft Front Page 2003 to open and edit your SharePoint sites — but should you? Performance problems may emerge if you edit a SharePoint site in Front Page because of the way SharePoint processes its edited pages.

✔ **Indexing external Web sites:** When you add external Web sites to the site directory, don't add them as sites to search. The entire Web site gets indexed — which means your SharePoint server is stepping through every page of somebody else's Web site, adding links to that content so it can be searched on *your* portal. It isn't pretty.

Chapter 11 talks about indexing external Web sites and offers an alternative approach to searching them.

✔ **Not minding the store:** Make sure that someone who knows SharePoint administers your SharePoint server. Your administrator should know databases and Web servers — specifically, how SharePoint uses them together. SharePoint has its own backup-and-restore tools (Chapter 15), and its own monitoring and configuration tools (Chapter 14).

Index

• C •

• N •

• O •